Country Locator for Volume 6

CAMBODIA, LAOS, AND VIETNAM

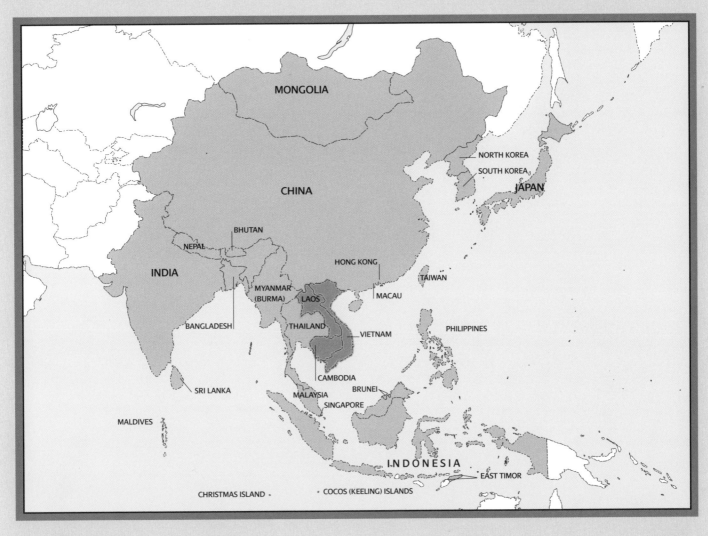

The following countries and political regions are covered in the eleven-volume encyclopedia *World and Its Peoples: Eastern and Southern Asia*. Detailed discussion of the following can be found in the volumes indicated in parentheses.

Bangladesh (3,4)
Bhutan (3,4)
Brunei (9)
Cambodia (6)
China (1,2)
Christmas Island (10)
Cocos (Keeling) Islands (10)

East Timor (10)
Hong Kong (1,2)
India (3,4)
Indonesia (10)
Japan (8)
Laos (6)
Macau (1,2)
Malaysia (9)

Maldives (3,4)
Mongolia (1,2)
Myanmar (Burma) (5)
Nepal (3,4)
North Korea (7)
Philippines (9)
Singapore (9)
South Korea (7)

Sri Lanka (3,4)
Taiwan (1,2)
Thailand (5)
Vietnam (6)

EASTERN and SOUTHERN ASIA

6

CAMBODIA, LAOS, AND VIETNAM

Marshall Cavendish
Reference
New York

SET CONSULTANTS

Anne Blackburn, Department of Asian Studies, Cornell University, Ithaca, New York

Ellen Fuller, Department of Sociology, University of Virginia, Charlottesville

Jeffrey E. Hanes, Center for Asian and Pacific Studies, University of Oregon, Eugene

Suvir Kaul, Department of South Asian Studies, University of Pennsylvania, Philadelphia

Philip Kelly, York Centre for Asian Research, York University, Toronto

Mike Parnwell, Department of East Asian Studies, University of Leeds, England

Ronald Skeldon, Department of Geography, University of Sussex, Brighton, England

VOLUME CONSULTANTS

Grant Evans, Sociology Department, University of Hong Kong

Judy Ledgerwood, Department of Anthropology, Northern Illinois University, DeKalb

Thomas Leinbach, Department of Geography, University of Kentucky, Lexington

Edwin Moise, History Department, Clemson University, South Carolina

WRITERS

Rachel Bean, Church Stretton, England

Mariam Beevi Lam, Department of Comparative Literature and Foreign Languages, University of California, Riverside

Ann Cullen, School of Humanities and Social Sciences, Bond University, Robina, Australia

Joseph Duemer, Department of Humanities and Social Sciences, Clarkson University, Potsdam, New York

Chris Elders, Geology Department, Royal Holloway College, University of London, England

Michelle Felton, School of the Environment, University of Leeds, England

Alexandra Haendel, Monash Asia Institute, Monash University, Clayton, Australia

Kenneth Hall, Department of History, Ball State University, Muncie, Indiana

Anne Hansen, Center for Southeast Asia Studies, University of Wisconsin-Madison, Madison

Henry Heller, Department of History, University of Manitoba, Winnipeg, Canada

Janet Hoskins, Department of Anthropology, University of Southern California, Los Angeles

James Martin, London, England

Martha May, Department of History, Western Connecticut State University, Danbury

Emmanuel K. Mbobi, Department of Geography, Kent State University, Canton, Ohio

Karen Romano-Young, Bethel, Connecticut

R. Anderson Sutton, Center for Southeast Asia Studies, University of Wisconsin-Madison, Madison

Charles J. Wheeler, History Department, National University of Singapore

Patrick Ziltener, Northeast Asia/Pacific Country Officer, Swiss State Secretariat for Economic Affairs, Bern, Switzerland

Marshall Cavendish Corporation
99 White Plains Road
Tarrytown, New York 10591-9001

www.marshallcavendish.us

© 2008 Marshall Cavendish Corporation

Created by **The Brown Reference Group plc**

Library of Congress Cataloging-in-Publication Data

World and its peoples : Eastern and southern Asia.
  p. cm.
  Includes bibliographical references and indexes.
  ISBN 978-0-7614-7631-3 (set) -- ISBN 978-0-7614-7632-0 (v. 1) -- ISBN 978-0-7614-7633-7 (v. 2) -- ISBN 978-0-7614-7635-1 (v.3) -- ISBN 978-0-7614-7637-5 (v. 4) -- ISBN 978-0-7614-7638-2 (v. 5) -- ISBN 978-0-7614-7639-9 (v. 6) -- ISBN 978-0-7614-7640-5 (v. 7) -- ISBN 978-0-7614-7641-2 (v. 8) -- ISBN 978-0-7614-7642-9 (v. 9) -- ISBN 978-0-7614-7643-6 (v. 10) -- ISBN 978-0-7614-7645-0 (v. 11)
  1. East Asia. 2. Southeast Asia. 3. South Asia.

  DS504.5.W67 2007
  950--dc22

                                            2007060865

Printed in China

12 11 10 09 08 07 1 2 3 4 5

PHOTOGRAPHIC CREDITS
Front Cover: Corbis: Vittoriano Rastelli (main image); **PhotoDisc:** Tim Hall (right and left).
Ardea: Masahiro Lijima 740; **Corbis:** Ivan Alvarado 818, Bettmann 762, Christophe Boisvieux 836, Free Agents Limited 829, Christophe Loviny 770/771, Wally McNamee 837, Tim Page 797, Caroline Penn 805, Steve Rayme 843; **Eye Ubiquitous/Hutchison:** 730/731, 733, 793, 808, 847, Bennett Dean 855, Khanh Do 831, Rene Giudicelli 810, Jeremy Horner 851, Sarah Longden 781, Anna Mockford 803, Sarah Murray 773, 835, 846, Tim Page 728, 764, 775, 782, 823, 842, 844, Paul Seheult 745, 785, Sarah Seheult 832, Liba Taylor 801; **David Noble:** 724; **NHPA:** Mark Bowler 739; **Photodisc:** Tim Hall 721, 783; **Photolibrary.com:** Cavalli Angelo 757; **Robert Hunt Library:** 749, 750, 752, 763, 792, 819, 821; **Still Pictures:** Peter Schickert 758; **Superstock:** Age Fotostock 833, Prisma 726, 788, Lome Resnick 737; **Sylvia Cordaiy Photo Library:** Richard Ellis 777, 778, Gable 743, 766, 776, Claire Stout 768, Cees Van Leeuwen 850, Nick Vereker 729, 849; **Topham:** 794, 804, 807, 809, Bandphotof/uppa.co.uk 760, Lou Dematteis/The Image Works 853, Margot Granitas/The Image Works 839, Deborah Harse/The Image Works 857, Hubertus Kanus 742, 747, 786, 845, Bill Lai/The Image Works 202, Roger-Viollet 774, Sean Sprague/The Image Works 755, 779, Leslie Hugh Stone/The Image Works 816, The Image Works 802; **TravelInk:** Grazyna Bonat 838, 848, Martyn Evans 790, 806, Patrick Ford 735, 854, Charlie Marsden 800, Jeremy Richards 780; **Patrick Ziltener:** 798, 799.

For **MARSHALL CAVENDISH**
Publisher: Paul Bernabeo
Project Editor: Stephanie Driver
Production Manager: Alan Tsai

For **THE BROWN REFERENCE GROUP**
Project Editor: Clive Carpenter
Deputy Editors: Felicity Crowe, Paul Thompson, Aruna Vasudevan
Design: Focus Publishing
Cartography: Encompass Graphics Ltd
Picture Research: Clare Newman
Art Editor: Lynne Ross
Senior Managing Editor: Tim Cooke
Indexer: Kay Ollerenshaw

CONTENTS

Geography and Climate

The three southeast Asian nations of Cambodia, Laos, and Vietnam form a compact territorial block, sometimes known as Indochina, that includes a considerable diversity of landscape. Demographically and economically, Vietnam, which occupies the eastern seaboard of Indochina, dominates its two poorer neighbors. The region is characterized by central and northwestern mountains and hills and by two major river basins: the Red River Valley in the northeast and the Mekong River basin in the west, center, and south.

MEKONG RIVER

The Mekong River is 2,702 miles (4,350 km) long, making it the longest river in southeastern Asia and the twelfth-longest waterway in the world. The river and its tributaries drain Laos, most of Cambodia, and southern Vietnam, as well as parts of China, Myanmar (Burma), and Thailand, altogether an area twice the size of the state of California. Along much of its length, the Mekong River is an important navigable waterway. However, through navigation is impossible because of the obstacles formed by the Khone Falls and the Khemmarat Rapids in southern Laos. In southern Vietnam, the river reaches the ocean in a broad delta that is formed by many distributaries.

The river's flow varies dramatically with the seasons, and from August or September through October or November, the large volume of floodwater on the Mekong River reverses the direction of flow on the lower Mekong's major tributary, the Sab River. The lower Mekong River has a mean annual flow of around 500,000 cubic feet (14,200 cubic m), and the waterway carries large quantities of sediments, particularly in southern Laos upstream from the Khone Falls.

The Red River flows through a broad valley in northern Vietnam.

THE PLAIN OF JARS

The Plain of Jars, which is part of the Xiangkhoang Plateau in northern Laos, is named for hundreds of carved stone jars, the tallest of which are over 10 feet (3 m) tall, that dot its surface. The jars date from the period between the first and seventh centuries CE and were made by a people about whom little is known. The plain is a relatively flat limestone and sandstone upland, some 3,000 feet to 3,600 feet (900 to 1,000 m) above sea level. It is cut by narrow valleys, including the gorge of the Ngum River.

RED RIVER

The Red River (Song Hong in Vietnamese) rises in southwestern China and flows 750 miles (1,200 km) to the ocean. For part of its course through northern Vietnam, the Red River runs in a narrow gorge before widening into a delta along the Gulf of Tonkin. The delta is a major agricultural region that supports a large farming population. Two major tributaries join the Red River: the Clear River (Song Lo) on the left bank and the Black River (Song Da) on the right bank. Because of great seasonal variations in rainfall in the river basin, the Red River is characterized by an uneven flow of water through the year.

KHONE FALLS

In terms of volume of water, the Khone Falls on the Mekong River in southern Laos are the world's second largest. Only the Buyoma Falls on the Congo River in Africa have more water. The Khone Falls form a series of cataracts (rapids) rather than a single obstacle, but they effectively obstruct the navigation of the river. The falls are a double series of cataracts where the waterway crosses a hard bed of basalt. Despite the huge volume of water in the river, the falls have little height, tumbling only 45 feet (14 m) into a pool. Many rocky outcrops and small islands dot the waterway, and a small port has been established on the largest island in the river to unload and portage barge cargoes around the falls.

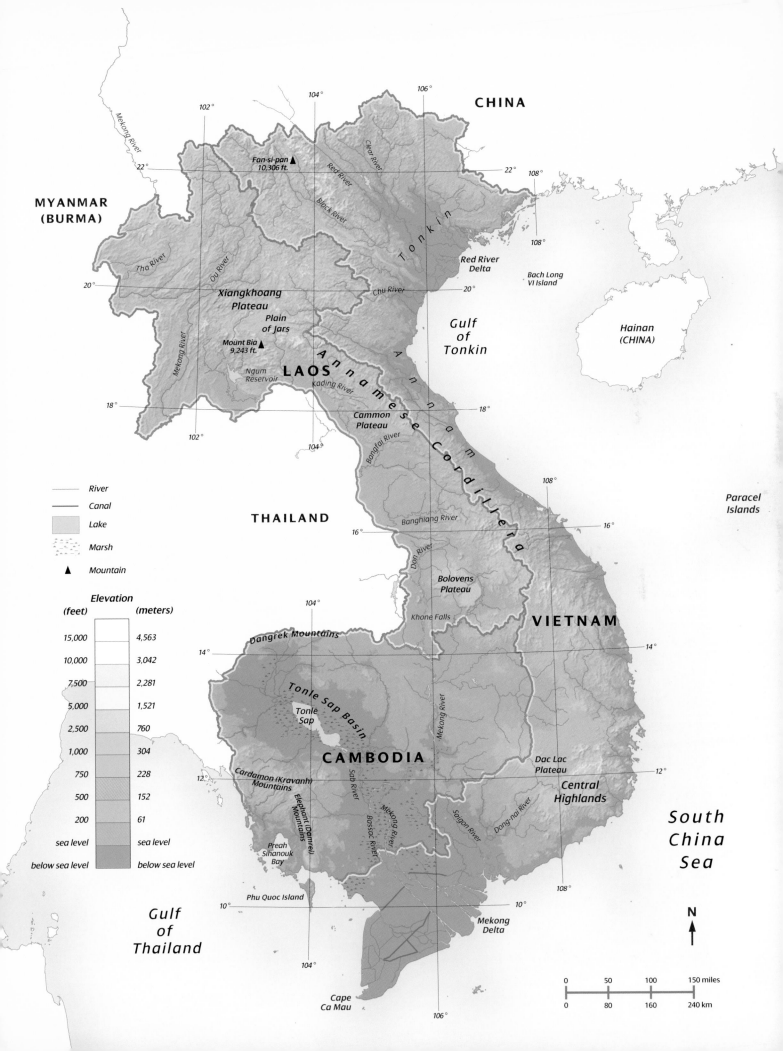

CHINA

MYANMAR
(BURMA)

Mekong River

Tha River

Ou River

Fan-si-pan ▲
10,306 ft.

Red River

Clear River

Black River

22°

108°

108°

Red River Delta

Xiangkhoang
Plateau

Plain
of Jars

Chu River

20°

Bach Long VI Island

Gulf
of
Tonkin

Hainan
(CHINA)

Mount Bia ▲
9,243 ft.

Mekong River

LAOS

Kading River

Ngum Reservoir

Annamese

Annamese Cordillera

18°

Cammon
Plateau

Bangfai River

THAILAND

Banghiang River

108°

16°

Don River

Bolovens
Plateau

VIETNAM

Paracel
Islands

Khone Falls

Dangrek Mountains

14°

Tonle Sap Basin

Tonle
Sap

Mekong River

CAMBODIA

Cardamon (Kravanh)
Mountains

Dac Lac
Plateau

12°

Central
Highlands

Elephant (Damrei)
Mountains

Sab River

Mekong River

Bassac River

Saigon River

Dong-nai River

108°

South
China
Sea

Preah
Sihanouk
Bay

10°

Phu Quoc Island

Mekong
Delta

Gulf
of
Thailand

N

Cape
Ca Mau

River
Canal
Lake
Marsh
▲ Mountain

Elevation

(feet)	(meters)
15,000	4,563
10,000	3,042
7,500	2,281
5,000	1,521
2,500	760
1,000	304
750	228
500	152
200	61
sea level	sea level
below sea level	below sea level

0	50	100	150 miles
0	80	160	240 km

Tonkin

102°

104°

106°

22°

20°

18°

16°

14°

12°

10°

102°

104°

106°

104°

104°

The Land of Cambodia, Laos, and Vietnam

Cambodia, Laos, and Vietnam together form a peninsula that historically was under the influence, culturally and otherwise, of both India and China. For this reason, the region became known as Indochina. The three nations, which lie entirely within the tropics, are made up of heavily populated alluvial deltas and more sparsely inhabited mountainous regions.

Indochina can be divided into a small number of major physical regions. In the south, the delta of the Mekong River forms a broad, low-lying region that is mainly in Vietnam but also includes part of neighboring Cambodia. Upstream, the Mekong Lowlands along with the Tonle Sap Basin form the greater part of Cambodia. The rest of Cambodia—the west and north—contains the Cambodian Uplands. Most of landlocked Laos is either hill country or mountainous, and the nation's few lowlands are along the eastern bank of the Mekong River. The various hills, plateaus, and ranges of Laos are often known collectively as the Laotian Uplands. Northwestern Vietnam is a mountainous region that is a continuation of the Laotian Uplands. Much of northern Vietnam lies within the valley and delta of the Red River and its tributaries. Between the Red River Delta in the north and the Mekong Delta in the south is an upland region known as the Annamese Cordillera, and between the Annamese Cordillera and the sea is a long, relatively narrow coastal plain.

Foggy woodlands and marshes cover parts of the highlands of the Laotian Uplands. Communication between peoples living both within and outside this sparsely populated remote region is very difficult.

THE MEKONG LOWLANDS AND TONLE SAP BASIN

Cambodia is a compact country, much of which is lowland. The Mekong and Tonle Sap lowlands account for around 75 percent of the total area of Cambodia. The two dominant physical features in the region are the Mekong River, which flows through central and eastern Cambodia from north to south, and Tonle Sap lake.

The flow of the Mekong River varies by season. Rainfall brought by the monsoon winds rapidly increases the river's flow to a maximum in August and September, when the Mekong floods to such an extent that its course cannot carry the increased volume of water. Excess water is forced up the course of the Mekong's major tributary, the Sab River, which flows from Tonle Sap. As a result, the direction of the flow of the Sab is reversed, and floodwater is carried toward Tonle Sap. Because of flooding, the lake more than doubles its area. In the fall, the water level on the Mekong drops, and the river's channels can handle the volume of water once more. The flow of the Sab River then reverts to its normal direction. In the following drier season, the Tonle Sap slowly drains, exposing a wide extent of muddy plain around the lake.

Most of the major rivers in Cambodia drain toward the Tonle Sap Basin or the Mekong River. The only notable exceptions are west of the divide created by the Damrei (or Elephant) and Kravanh (or Cardamom) mountains, where rivers flow toward the Gulf of Thailand. The Mekong River in Cambodia flows southward from the Lao border through a region where the river is marked by extensive rapids. Downstream, the Mekong elbows west for about 30 miles (50 km) and then turns southwest toward Phnom Penh, the national capital of Cambodia. From Kompong Cham to Phnom Penh, the gradient of the river slopes very gently, and the river usually floods and breaks its banks between June and November. Four major waterways meet at Phnom Penh at a point called Chattomuckh (literally, "four faces"). Phnom Penh, the only large city and industrial center in Cambodia, was repopulated after 1979 following the effects of forced evacuation and a genocidal regime. By 1998, the city and its environs had a population of nearly 1.1 million inhabitants. Immediately downstream from Phnom Penh, the river divides into two roughly parallel channels, the Mekong River proper and the Bassac River, which flow independently through the Mekong Delta.

The Tonle Sap Basin and the Mekong Lowlands form a rolling plain with an elevation less than 300 feet (100 m) above sea level. Much of the Cambodian lowland is still forested, but the extent of the tropical forest is diminishing as a result of the shifting agriculture practiced by its inhabitants.

THE CAMBODIAN UPLANDS

The plains of the Mekong and the Tonle Sap lowlands become more dissected (divided into hills and ridges) toward the west as elevation increases. The lowlands end at the barrier formed by

RIVERS OF CAMBODIA, LAOS, AND VIETNAM		
River	Length in miles	Length in km
Mekong*	2,702	4,350
Red River* (or Song Hong)	750	1,200
Black River* (or Song Da)	503	805
Bangfai	241	386
Ou	236	380
Da Rang	188	300

* Not all the course of these waterways flows through the region.

the Cambodian Uplands. These mountains, which run parallel to the coast, form two ranges: the Kravanh (Cardamom) Mountains, which run 100 miles (160 km) from northwest to southeast in the west, and the Damrei (Elephant) Mountains, which run from north to south in the east.

The Kravanh range receives heavy rainfall from the monsoon rains and is densely forested. The peaks of the Kravanh Mountains rise to elevations of more than 4,500 feet (1,500 m) above sea level, and the eastern part of the Kravanh Mountains contains the highest point in Cambodia, Phnom Aural, with an elevation of 5,940 feet (1,810 m).

The other mountain range of western Cambodia, the Damrei (Elephant) Mountains, forms a lower extension of the Kravanh Mountains. The Damrei Mountains, which stretch toward the sea, rise to between 1,500 feet (450 m) and 3,000 feet (900 m) high.

West of the Kravanh and Damrei ranges is a narrow coastal plain along the Gulf of Thailand. The short Cambodian coastline includes Preah Sihanouk Bay, on the shore of which lies Cambodia's principal seaport, Preah Sihanouk (formerly known as Kompong Som and Sihanoukville).

There are two smaller areas of upland in Cambodia. In the east, along the border with Vietnam, is a restricted hill region that merges with the highlands of central Vietnam, the Annamese Cordillera. Another small highland area lies along Cambodia's northern boundary with Thailand, where it forms the northern rim of the Tonle Sap Basin. In the east, the upland rim is known as the Dangrek Mountains.

Westward, the rim becomes an escarpment with an average elevation of about 1,500 feet (450 m). The highest points of the south-facing escarpment rise to above 2,100 feet (650 m). The escarpment marks the southern edge of the extensive Khorat Plateau, which occupies most of eastern Thailand. The escarpment, which is a watershed that marks the national boundary between Cambodia and Thailand, impedes transportation links between the two countries. However, there are several passes, including the O Smach Pass, which is followed by the main highway and railroad link between Cambodia and Thailand.

◀ *The Mekong River forms much of the border between Thailand (left) and Laos (right). Deposition of silt carried by the river forms many islands in the waterway.*

THE MEKONG DELTA

The extensive Mekong Delta begins downstream from Phnom Penh, where the river divides to flow across the Cambodian Plain. A large gently sloping fan of material laid down by the Mekong River is crossed by many distributaries of the river, each one flowing between levees (embankments built on either side of the river by accumulated deposits of silt). Brackish back marshes that are connected to one of the delta waterways in times of flood are a characteristic feature.

Although some of the delta lies in Cambodia, most of the Mekong Delta is in Vietnam. The delta has a total area of about 16,000 square miles (40,000 sq. km) and forms the region formerly known as Cochinchina. The Vietnamese delta has three major sections. The upper section, upstream from Chau Phu (formerly known as Chau Doc), has strong natural levees, behind which are low, wide depressions. The middle section has some well-drained areas, but much of the region is poorly drained and seasonally inundated. In the lower section, formed by the river mouths, sediment carried down from the upper river is deposited, in places forming large silt islands. The lower section is less prone to flooding. South of the largest southern distributary, a flat, low-lying peninsula that is forested and swampy stretches to Cape Mau, the most southerly point of mainland Vietnam.

Immediately north of the Mekong Delta, a series of low terraces rise above the level of the delta. The terraces are the alluvial plains of the Saigon and Dong-nai rivers. The largest urban area in Vietnam, Ho Chi Minh City (formerly Saigon) stretches along the Saigon River. The city, which was capital of the former South Vietnam until 1976, had a population of 3,924,000 people in the metropolitan area in 1989 (the most recent published Vietnamese census), but unofficial estimates suggest a figure in excess of 5 million. The Saigon River is one of a number of waterways that flow south from the southern end of the largest area of uplands in Vietnam, the Annamese Cordillera.

THE ANNAMESE CORDILLERA

The mountainous region known as the Annamese Cordillera (or Nui Truong Son) extends 700 miles (1,130 km) from north to south through central Vietnam along the border with Laos. The largest physical region in Vietnam, the Annamese Cordillera dominates the interior of the country. The uplands run parallel to the coast in central Vietnam, with several peaks rising to heights of more than 6,000 feet (1,800 m). The uplands form a watershed: the shorter rivers that flow eastward from the divide run toward the South China Sea, while the longer rivers to the west of the divide flow into the Mekong River.

The southern portion of the Annamese Cordillera is divided into several plateaus, each of which forms a subregion. Around the cities of Pleiku and Kon Tum, the northern subregion, the Kon Tum Plateau, is heavily eroded. The plateau rises to around 2,500 feet (760 m). However, farther south, the Dac Lac Plateau, near the city of Buon Ma Thuot, has experienced very little erosion. Still farther south, the Di Linh Plateau, located near the city of Da Lat, rises about 4,900 feet (1,500 m) above sea level.

VIETNAMESE COASTAL PLAIN

A narrow coastal plain lies between the Annamese Cordillera and the South China Sea. The plain is narrowest in the region between Hué, the former royal capital of Vietnam, and Da Nang, the nation's fourth-largest city. As a result, both cities gained

The coastal plain near Da Lat in south-central Vietnam supports thriving agriculture. The plain is relatively narrow and is confined in the west by the foothills of the Annamese Cordillera (in the distance).

strategic importance on a natural routeway. Farther north, the plains widen around Quang Tri. In places, however, spurs of the Annamese Cordillera reach the coast in rocky headlands. The central region of Vietnam that contains both the Annamese Cordillera and the coastal plain is historically known as Annam.

THE RED RIVER VALLEY AND DELTA

Northern Vietnam is centered around the valley of the Red River and its major tributaries, the Song Lo (Clear River) and the Song Da (Black River). The Red River Valley is relatively wide, but for part of its upper course within Vietnam, the waterway flows through a narrow gorge. Toward the sea, distributaries spread out into a delta where Haiphong, the port for Vietnam's national capital Hanoi, is situated. Off the northeastern coast are many small islands, most of which are the remnants of a heavily eroded limestone plateau. With their steep sides and heavily eroded surfaces, the limestone islands of Vietnam are a classic example of the features that are formed when limestone is eroded. In Halong Bay, there are 1,969 small limestone islands, nearly 990 of which are named.

The Red River Valley and the delta are fertile and support a large farming population; they also have important mineral deposits. The region, which is historically known as Tonkin, is home to a large concentration of population centered on Hanoi. The city has a population of around 3 million in the metropolitan area. The landscape of Tonkin is varied: some areas have low limestone plateaus; other areas have low hills. Much of the region is alluvial plains. The highest ground in the Red River Valley lies between the Red River and the Clear River.

THE LAOTIAN UPLANDS AND NORTHWESTERN VIETNAM

West and southwest of the Red River Valley is an extensive series of plateaus extends across northwestern Vietnam into Laos, where it covers the greater part of the north and center of the country. In Vietnam, the upland region includes several distinct plateaus that are separated by deeply eroded valleys. The region contains the highest peak in Vietnam, Fan Si Pan, which is 10,306 feet (3,141 m) above sea level.

In northern Laos, toward the borders with China and Myanmar (Burma), the highlands are folded jagged mountain ranges that reach heights of about 9,000 feet (2,750 m). The landscape is heavily dissected, and the uplands, through which are cut deep river gorges, have steep sides. Until the twentieth century, most of the northern uplands were covered by forest, but the forest cover has diminished due to felling for shifting cultivation. The region is inhospitable and communication is difficult because of natural obstacles. The Mekong River enters

northern Laos from China and forms the border between Laos and its western neighbors, Myanmar and Thailand, for much of its course, except in the region of the former Lao royal capital, Louangphrabang.

The Annamese Cordillera forms much of eastern Laos along the border region with Vietnam, and a series of three principal plateaus and various lower hill ranges lies between the mountains and the restricted lowlands along the Mekong River. In the northeast, the Xiangkhoang Plateau, including the Plain of Jars, is a rolling grassland, which is an important hub of routes in a region where mountains, gorges, and steep plateau sides otherwise form an obstacle to transportation links.

Fishers ply the waterways between the mangrove swamps that line the distributaries of the Mekong Delta in southern Vietnam.

In central Laos, a heavily eroded limestone plateau lies between the Annamese Cordillera and the Mekong Valley. There are many caves and in places waterways disappear into deeply eroded clefts to run underground. Elsewhere, isolated pillars of limestone—all that is left of a former plateau—form a lunar landscape. This type of eroded limestone landscape is known as karst scenery.

In the far south, the Bolovens Plateau, east of the city of Pakxé, is wooded. The plateau is relatively well-watered and has fertile soils that support a farming population. South of the Bolovens Plateau, the land falls toward the Cambodian border and the eastern section of the Mekong Lowlands.

THE LAOTIAN LOWLANDS

The lowlands of Laos are restricted mainly to a few small districts along the Mekong River in the west of the country. The Mekong River flows through a broad valley that widens into a lowland basin around Vientiane, the national capital of Laos. Another lowland adjoins the central city of Savannakhet, and a larger southern lowland beside the Mekong River lies to the south of the city of Pakxé. The greater part of the population of Laos lives in these three areas and other lowlands along the Mekong River.

E. MBOBI

Geology of Cambodia, Laos, and Vietnam

Knowledge of the local geology across the Indochina region is uneven. Large parts of the region are mountainous and covered by dense forest. Consequently, wide areas are sparsely populated and inaccessible. Vietnam is the most extensively studied of the three countries, but large areas exist, particularly in Laos, where knowledge of the geology remains superficial.

The lithosphere, the outer layer of Earth's crust, is made of tectonic plates that move across the partially molten layer beneath. The three nations of Indochina—Cambodia, Laos, and Vietnam—are surrounded by active plate boundaries, yet within these boundaries the region does not experience pressures or distortions that cause earthquakes and create land forms.

Cambodia, Laos, and Vietnam lie at the heart of Sundaland, an ancient continental mass that forms the core of southeastern Asia. Tectonically, it is a relatively quiet region, despite being at the edge of several tectonic plates that are moving. To the southwest, the Indian Ocean crust is sliding under the plate that contains Sumatra and the Andaman Islands along a deep section of the ocean called the Sunda Trench. This process is known as subduction. Toward the east, the Philippines Sea Plate is being subducted under the plate to the north. Indonesia and the Philippines bear the full brunt of this tectonic vise and experience frequent earthquakes and volcanic activity as a result.

Cambodia, Laos, and Vietnam lie away from the zones of subduction, but they do not escape earthquakes entirely. Indochina is cut by large faults that run southward from Tibet and the Himalaya mountain range. These faults are strike-slip faults—faults in which any movement is along the strike (the horizontal direction of the fault). The faults were formed when the Indian Plate collided with the huge Eurasian Plate to the north and squeezed parts of southeast Asia out toward the east in the process.

MAJOR FAULTS OF INDOCHINA

The two main faults that dominate the area are the Red River Fault zone, which forms the long, straight northwest-southeast trending valley that is occupied by the Red River in the north of Vietnam, and similarly trending faults that form the Tonle Sap Basin in central Cambodia. Both faults are of considerable length. The Red River Fault extends several thousand miles through southern China to join the Ailao Shan Fault in Tibet, while the Tonle Sap Basin is a possible continuation of the Mae Ping Fault, which originates in southern Myanmar (Burma) and crosses the central plains of Thailand to reach Cambodia.

Both faults have long histories of strike-slip movement, the horizontal sliding of slivers of the Earth's crust past one another. Most of this activity occurred during the Cenozoic era (the most recent 65 million years of the Earth's history) and was a result of segments of the Sundaland crust being pushed out sideways as India moved north and collided with Eurasia. The clear expression of the Red River Fault (and other northwest-southeast and northeast-southwest trending faults in land forms in northern Laos and Vietnam) shows that the faults continue to be active, although earthquake activity along them is at relatively low levels. Where different strands of the fault begin to diverge, subsidence occurs between them to create lowland features such as the Tonle Sap Basin.

THE ROCKS OF THE REGION

The area between the major faults at either end of Indochina is occupied by a wide range of rock formations encompassing a large proportion of Earth's history. However, many of the formations are highly deformed, making it difficult to be sure of their precise age. Geologists have suggested that strongly deformed rocks are very old. Some rock formations in northern Vietnam have been ascribed to the Archean age (some 2.5 billion years ago) and the Ediacaran period (before 545 million years ago) on this basis. However, extensively deformed rocks that are much younger have been described in other areas in the region, and scientists cannot be sure of the exact ages of the north Vietnamese rocks until further research is carried out.

Within the region, there are sediments that contain fossils as old as the Cambrian period (between 545 million and 495 million years ago), and all the major more recent periods of geological time are also represented. Sediments have been deposited in a variety of environments, and they share characteristics with sediments of similar age elsewhere in southeast Asia. For example, limestones laid down in the Permian period (between 290 and 248 million years ago) are geological evidence of an extensive sea across the region in Permian times.

Northern Laos and Vietnam are dominated by limestone laid down in the Carboniferous period (from 354 million years ago to 290 million years ago) and the Permian period. In places the

In Halong Bay along the coast of northern Vietnam, many small limestone islands rise out of the sea. In recent geological time, a rise in sea level rapidly eroded away the sides of layers of limestone that were laid down between 340 and 240 million years ago and created hundreds of islands.

limestone layers are up to 3,300 feet (1,000 m) thick. The wet climate of the region led to rapid erosion and the formation of extensive cave systems. Along the coast of Vietnam, a rise in sea level in recent geological times has led to the rapid erosion of a low limestone plateau, which is represented by hundreds of small steep-sided islands. Northern Vietnam is a classic example of karst landscape, the characteristic scenery of a limestone region, including gorges, caves, and underground streams.

Deformation has resulted in folding and faulting of the sediments and has also resulted in metamorphism (changes to rock types because of higher temperatures and pressures). Further evidence of a violent past comes from the association of some sediments in both the Permian period and the Jurassic period (between 205 and 142 million years ago) with volcanic rocks and the intrusion of granites into the metamorphosed

sediments. The deformation and igneous activity are probably the result of the progressive collision of small continental fragments and island arcs with Sundaland, a history of accretion that allowed the Eurasian continental mass to grow until the first stages of development of the present-day tectonic regime in the Cenozoic era. A variety of mineral deposits are associated with these deformed rocks and their associated igneous intrusions.

RECENT DEPOSITS

Cenozoic sediments are lightly deformed, and their deposition is confined to areas that subsided along the strike-slip faults that developed during the period. The sediments are associated with small onshore coal deposits in Vietnam but contain more significant oil deposits offshore. In the Neogene period (the last 24 million years), eruptions and lava flows in eastern Cambodia and southern Vietnam formed considerable areas of rock basalt.

C. ELDERS

733

Climate of Cambodia, Laos, and Vietnam

The tropical climate of Cambodia, Laos, and Vietnam (the region historically known as Indochina) is characterized by two major phenomena: monsoons and typhoons. Monsoons are seasonal reversals of prevailing winds caused by temperature differences between land and sea. Typhoons are destructive hurricane winds of 74 miles per hour (119 kph) or more that occur mainly in the coastal regions.

Monsoons are relatively predictable because the temperature differences that cause them are regular and seasonal. Indochina is generally warm with rainy southwesterly monsoon winds from May through September, and dry with northeasterly monsoon winds from October through April. Hurricane-force typhoons are, however, more unpredictable. Although the typhoon season in Southeast Asia is from June through the fall, individual typhoons may occur at any time during the season.

Cambodia, Laos, and Vietnam can be divided into three broad climatic zones: coastal areas, highlands, and delta plains. The coastal areas are subject to tropical storms and typhoons, as well as monsoon rains. The highlands are dominated by monsoon rains that can cause frequent flash floods and by local droughts. The climate of the flat, low-lying delta plains is characterized by monsoon rains and flooding. Northern Indochina—the Red River Valley in Vietnam and the uplands of northern Laos—is distinctly cooler during the northeasterly monsoon, when cooler air is brought in from China.

THE EAST ASIAN MONSOONS

In summer, intense heating gives rise to an area of low air pressure over the Asian landmass. The deep low-pressure area, or depression, attracts air toward it from the Indian Ocean. Southeasterly winds from the southern Indian Ocean are deflected to become southwesterly when they pass north of the equator, blowing toward the depression. These moist winds flow into southern Asia toward Indochina and the northwest Pacific region of Asia. They bring monsoon rains, heavy cloud cover, and high humidity to Cambodia, Laos, and Vietnam from May through September.

In winter, solar radiation (heat from the sun) is weaker in the Northern Hemisphere. This allows the Asian landmass to cool rapidly, causing a cold high-pressure system to develop over Siberia. Air flows from areas of high air pressure to areas of low air pressure. As a result, cold air flows southeastward across Asia toward the coast of China, where the wind direction changes and veers southwest toward Indochina. The interaction of these northeasterly winds with low-pressure depressions near the equator results in strong storms over the South China Sea and contributes to early winter rainfall along the coast of Vietnam.

Heavy monsoon rains cause frequent flooding in low-lying river delta regions. The flooding of the Mekong Delta in July through September of 2000 caused widespread devastation, including landslides. Nearly five hundred people were killed, and 5 million people were seriously affected, mostly in Vietnam, although Cambodia and Laos were also affected.

The effect of flooding in Indochina is intensified by deforestation in the hilly regions. With the tree cover gone, erosion of the land by heavy rainfall and floods is greater. Widespread, severe floods occur several times per decade. Although devastating, the floods increase the fertility of the land downstream by depositing nutrient-rich sediments that allow intensive rice cultivation in the lowlands.

Weak or intermittent monsoon winds frequently cause drought. Localized droughts tend to affect the highland regions, but large-scale drought also affects river-fed agriculture on the deltas, particularly those of the Mekong River and Red River, when the river flow is dramatically reduced. Drought in the 1998 to 1999 season—the worst in 50 years—left more than 1.5 million people in Vietnam facing starvation after their staple crop, rice, and the main cash crop, coffee, both failed. Widespread severe drought occurs approximately once every ten years.

TYPHOONS AND TROPICAL STORMS

Tropical storms form over the warm waters of the northwest Pacific Ocean and the South China Sea. These tropical storms with winds of over 74 miles per hour (119 kph) are called typhoons (in the Caribbean Sea and the North Atlantic Ocean, they are known as hurricanes). The typhoon season is from June through November, when the sea is warmest. During the typhoon season, an average of four typhoons make landfall (move inland) over Vietnam. However, although typhoons easily pass over flat land, they die out once they meet the obstacle of significant uplands. The wind strength also rapidly weakens over land. For this reason, typhoons rarely reach Cambodia and Laos. The strong winds of a typhoon at sea can cause devastating storm surges onshore. Typhoon Linda in 1997, with winds reaching 81 miles per hour (130 kph), caused storm surges and flooding that devastated large areas of rice plantation and killed four thousand people in southern Vietnam.

EL NIÑO-SOUTHERN OSCILLATION

El Niño-Southern Oscillation (ENSO) events are warmings (El Niño) or coolings (La Niña) of part of the Pacific Ocean in winter, which cause significant changes in wind patterns and precipitation on a global scale. Both events affect the weather of Indochina. Warm (El Niño) events tend to affect the intensity of monsoon rainfall in the region and also influence the paths of storms reaching Cambodia and Vietnam.

THE CLIMATE OF VIETNAM

Vietnam frequently experiences extreme climate events: floods, drought, tropical storms, and up to four typhoons each year. The southwesterly monsoon rains occur from May through September. From the early fall, the northeasterly monsoon brings significant cloud cover but little rain until April.

Vietnam has three main climatic regions: coastal regions, highlands, and delta plains. The coastal regions and sea-facing highlands of Vietnam are characterized by strong tropical storms and typhoons from the South China Sea. The maximum rainfall occurs between September and January, and humidity is high throughout the year. Da Nang, in southern Vietnam, is typical, with monthly rainfall reaching 20 inches (50 cm) during September and October and average daytime temperatures ranging from 75°F (24°C) in January to 93°F (34°C) in July. *Crachin* is the local word used to describe the persistent drizzly rain and cloudy skies during the rainy season from May through September.

After the monsoon rains, the Mekong River swells with excess water that flows up the Sab River, a tributary of the Mekong, to flood much of central Cambodia. The Tonle Sap lake more than doubles in size, and many villages, such as the one above, gain a shore for a season.

The Vietnamese highlands, known as the Annamese Cordillera, cover the central part and far northwest of the country, where the highest peaks above 8,000 feet (2,450 m) occasionally receive snow or frost. The mountainous regions are prone to flash floods and drought during the rainy monsoon season.

The delta plains of the Red River in the north and the Mekong River in the south are flat and low-lying, with intensive rice cultivation and a large population that is vulnerable to monsoon flooding. Ho Chi Minh City (formerly Saigon) in the south has average maximum temperatures over 86°F (30°C) and minimum temperatures around 73°F (23°C) all year. Humidity is high or extremely high, with some cloud cover all year giving around five hours of clear sunshine each day. The rain falls mostly from May through October, peaking in September. The northern Red River Delta area has a slightly shorter rainy season and a distinctly cooler and cloudier dry season, with minimum temperatures dropping to around 57°F (14°C) between December and February.

THE CLIMATE OF CAMBODIA

In Cambodia, southwesterly monsoon winds dominate from April through October; then weaker, drier northeasterlies prevail from November to March. Cambodia is generally warmer, has less rain and cloud cover, and experiences fewer typhoons and severe storms than Vietnam. However, southwesterly monsoon floods can cause devastation, and severe widespread droughts occur every decade in the winter and spring.

Cambodia has extensive inland and coastal lowland regions and a small upland area in the southwest. The coastal regions receive the highest rainfall, up to 200 inches (500 cm) annually, peaking in October. Occasional tropical cyclones add to the total. Phnom Penh, the Cambodian national capital, has a typical regional lowland climate with high daytime temperatures above

86°F (30°C), high humidity, and an average annual rainfall of around 55 inches (140 cm), with a maximum in September and October. Temperatures drop to 63°F (17°C) in January and peak in the dry season at 100°F (38°C) in April, with an average nine hours of sunshine daily. Lowland river plains in Cambodia are subject to flooding from both upstream rains and local heavy rains.

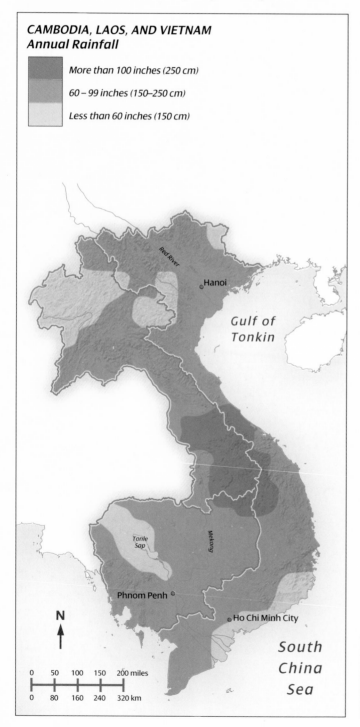

CAMBODIA, LAOS, AND VIETNAM
Annual Rainfall

- More than 100 inches (250 cm)
- 60 – 99 inches (150–250 cm)
- Less than 60 inches (150 cm)

CLIMATE

PHNOM PENH, CAMBODIA
11°55'N 104°80'W Height above sea level: 32 feet (10 m)

	J	F	M	A	M	J	J	A	S	O	N	D
Mean maximum												
(°F)	90	91	95	95	93	93	91	91	90	88	86	86
(°C)	32	33	35	35	34	34	33	33	32	31	30	30
Mean minimum												
(°F)	72	73	75	77	77	77	77	77	75	75	73	72
(°C)	22	23	24	25	25	25	25	25	24	24	23	22
Precipitation												
(in.)	1.0	0.5	2.3	4.0	4.4	7.0	7.7	6.8	9.8	12.6	5.3	3.1
(cm)	2.5	1.2	5.8	10.1	11.2	17.7	19.6	17.2	24.9	31.9	13.5	8.0

HANOI, VIETNAM
21°01'N 105°52'E Height above sea level: 35 feet (11 m)

	J	F	M	A	M	J	J	A	S	O	N	D
Mean maximum												
(°F)	66	68	73	81	90	91	91	90	88	84	77	72
(°C)	19	20	23	27	32	33	33	32	31	29	25	22
Mean minimum												
(°F)	57	59	64	70	75	79	79	79	77	72	66	59
(°C)	14	15	18	21	24	26	26	26	25	22	19	15
Precipitation												
(in.)	0.7	1.0	1.7	3.5	7.4	9.4	11.3	12.5	10.4	5.2	1.7	0.9
(cm)	1.9	2.6	4.4	9.0	18.9	24.0	28.8	31.8	26.5	13.1	4.3	2.3

HO CHI MINH CITY, VIETNAM
10°46'N 106°43'E Height above sea level: 20 feet (6 m)

	J	F	M	A	M	J	J	A	S	O	N	D
Mean maximum												
(°F)	90	91	93	95	93	90	90	90	88	88	88	88
(°C)	32	33	34	35	34	32	32	32	31	31	31	31
Mean minimum												
(°F)	70	73	75	79	77	77	75	75	75	75	73	70
(°C)	21	23	24	26	25	25	24	24	24	24	23	21
Precipitation												
(in.)	0.6	0.1	0.4	2.0	8.9	12.3	11.6	10.6	12.9	10.5	4.6	1.9
(cm)	1.4	0.2	1.1	5.0	21.8	31.2	29.4	27.0	32.7	26.7	11.7	4.8

THE CLIMATE OF LAOS

Laos is dominated by the wet humid southwest monsoon from May through October, with a two- to three-week break in the rains in June and July. The dry, cooler northeast monsoon that blows from November through April is similar to that experienced in northern Vietnam but with less cloud cover. Because Laos has no coastline, it rarely suffers from typhoons, but the nation may experience up to three tropical cyclones per year, when heavy rains can bring floods. Annual rainfall in Laos varies from 55 inches (140 cm) to 138 inches (350 cm).

Laos has two main climatic zones: the highlands and the Mekong plains. Mountainous regions cover much of the country, reaching a highest point of 9,248 feet (2,819 m). Lao agriculture relies on rain rather than irrigation, and variable rains frequently cause flash floods. Forest fires are also a particular problem and are exacerbated by droughts. Lowland areas, such as the district around Vientiane, receive up to 12 inches (30 cm) of rainfall per month, with daytime temperatures around 86°F (30°C) and extremely high humidity in the rainy season. The daytime temperature drops to 57°F (14°C) in January during the dry season.

HEALTH EFFECTS

The majority of climate-related health risks are caused by the effects of floods, when diseases such as cholera, typhoid, and diarrhea occur due to lack of sanitation and clean drinking water. Children and elderly people are particularly at risk. Flood and storm damage to housing, transportation, communication, and agriculture also cause health problems and hazards. The warm wet season allows mosquitoes to breed, beginning a malarial cycle. As a result, malaria is present over much of the Indochina lowlands. Symptoms of heat stress during extremely hot and humid conditions can also be a hazard.

CLIMATE CHANGE

Global climate change is expected to bring an increase in annual temperature in the region of about 4.5°F (2.5°C) by 2070. Because warmer temperatures cause more evaporation of water, droughts will be more likely where rainfall is low. Changes in the monsoon rains are also likely, with an increase over northern and central Vietnam in the wet season and a decrease during the dry season. River flow in the dry season is likely to be significantly reduced, making irrigation difficult. The predicted sea-level rise would cause increased flooding and erosion of lowland coastal regions.

Since the 1970s, typhoons have tended to form over the South China Sea, closer to the Indochina region, rather than over the Pacific Ocean as they did previously. This is possibly due to increasing sea temperatures in the South China Sea. More typhoons are expected to move onto land in the future. Mangrove forests along the coast have been shown to reduce the impact of storms and surges, and they also act as wind breaks. However, mangrove deforestation for charcoal production is reducing this protection, and sea-level rises would also damage the forests.

M. FELTON

A combination of high temperatures and heavy rainfall provides water for irrigation that allows Vietnam to grow three crops of rice a year.

Flora and Fauna of Cambodia, Laos, and Vietnam

The dominant biome throughout Cambodia, Laos, and Vietnam is rain forest, although the forest is far from homogenous, ranging from moist evergreen forests with dense canopies to semi-arid deciduous woodlands. The dominant vegetation is determined by the altitude and rainfall, with drier regions sheltered from the monsoon rains by high plateaus.

Some parts of Indochina (the historic name for Cambodia, Laos, and Vietnam) contain pristine forest that is rich in plant and animal life. Areas of the northern Truong Son Mountains, part of the Annamese Cordillera (the principal north-south mountain range that runs through western Vietnam and eastern Laos), are still largely untouched by human activity. However, much of the region has suffered severe deforestation. There are many different floral and faunal regions within Cambodia, Laos, and Vietnam but, at its simplest, the region can be divided into lowland forests, upland forests, swamp forests (including coastal mangrove swamps), and river deltas.

LOWLAND FORESTS

Dry evergreen forest extends in a swathe through northern Cambodia, southern Laos, and southern Vietnam. Dipterocarps (giant trees up to 130 ft. or 40 m high, with distinctive "cauliflower" tops) are the dominant forest trees. Often called tropical hardwoods, they grow straight without any lower branches. Other common trees include dongtchem, sompong, and figs. Bamboo grasses are common in patches of open ground, and palms grow along streams and around water holes. The region contains a rich fauna, including Asian elephants and tigers. Other mammals of the region include wild cattle, such as bantengs and gaurs, a tiny relict population of Javan rhinoceroses, and carnivores such as sun bears, leopards, and clouded leopards.

Most of the rest of Cambodia, and much of the Mekong Valley into Vietnam, is cloaked by dry deciduous forest, made up of trees that drop their leaves during the long dry season. Only six species of the world's dipterocarps are deciduous, and they form the dominant vegetation through this region. The forests are prone to fire during the driest months, and trees have thick bark that can withstand such blazes. A range of large herbivores once grazed in the woodlands, but hunting has eliminated or severely diminished most of them. Javan and Sumatran rhinoceroses, kouprey (a rare forest ox that grazes in clearings by night but retreats to dense forest by day), and wild water buffalo are all probably gone from the area, while Schomburgk's deer, once a native of the Mekong Valley, is now considered globally extinct.

Just a small fraction of the lowland dry forest of southern Vietnam remains. The drier lowland forest is arid due to the rain-shadow of the southern Annamese Cordillera, and it is one of the most denuded habitats in Asia. Scrubby hill-forests with patches of *Baeckea* shrub in the valleys give way to dunes near the coast. The dunes support a unique range of plants, including at least two dipterocarps that grow nowhere else. More than 90 percent of this region has been cleared, in part for logging. The small pockets of forest that remain contain populations of endangered species, such as Germain's peacock-pheasants, the douc langur (an endangered species of monkey), and red-cheeked gibbons.

The lowland wet forest of northern Vietnam is as badly affected as its dry counterpart in the south of the country. The remaining small pockets of woodland contain diverse floral assemblages. The upper canopy is dominated by madhuca trees, while fan palms are common at lower levels. Endangered animals in this diminishing habitat include white-cheeked gibbons, François's leaf monkeys, and Owston's civets, while the Vietnam leaf-nosed bat is found nowhere else.

HIGHLAND FORESTS

The vegetation changes markedly in the wetter highland areas. Broad-leaved forests grow on the humid uplands that stretch from the Annamese Cordillera through northern Laos. The dominant flora includes elaeocarps (a genus of trees and shrubs with glossy leaves), oaks, laurels, and podocarps (a type of conifer, some of which are relatively small). Due to its isolation from similar areas, this forest is rich in endemic trees (species unique to the area). Such diversity extends to the fauna, too, with a range of endemic mammals, including the saola or Vu Quang ox, a forest-dwelling ox discovered in the 1990s; the giant muntjac, a deer species also discovered in the 1990s; and birds such as Vietnamese firebacks and white-winged ducks.

The forests of the southern Annamese Cordillera extend from Central Vietnam to the Bolovens Plateau in Laos and west to northern Cambodia. This region contains stands of pines at

▶ *The forests of Vietnam are home to many species of small monkeys, including the endangered red-shanked Douc monkey.*

Mammalian Discoveries

Before the 1990s, biologists assumed that few if any large mammals were still to be discovered. However, in 1992, biologists in the Vu Quang nature reserve, which is in the northern Truong Son forest straddling Vietnam and Laos, received some long, straight horns from local hunters. They came from a strange and undescribed bovid (the group of mammals that includes cows and antelopes), which the scientists named *Pseudoryx nghetinhensis*, or the Vu Quang ox. Local people know it as the saola. The discovery of any new mammal species is unusual. That something as large as the saola, now known to weigh around 220 pounds (100 kg) and standing almost 3 feet (90 cm) high at the shoulder, could remain unknown until 1992 was sensational, and its discovery is considered one of the zoological highlights of the last century. Although never seen by scientists in the wild, biologists have observed captive animals and now know a little about their biology and behavior.

The discovery of the saola led to a flurry of unparalleled zoological finds in Vu Quang and other remote northern forests. Four other large mammals have been discovered to date, including Truong Son and giant muntjac deer, Annam striped rabbit, Tainguen civet, and the rediscovery of a species thought extinct, the Vietnamese warty hog. Through the 1990s, ten previously unknown mammals were discovered in the forests of Vietnam, including the kting voar (a goatlike species), the Laotian black muntjac, and the giant cream loris, a primate that is active at night. Discoveries continue to be made in the area. Perhaps the most remarkable was announced in May 2005. Biologists chanced upon the body of a foot- (30 cm) long rodent with long whiskers and a thick, hairy tail, which was on sale in a Laos food market. Known by local people as a *kha-nyou*, this species is so different from all other rodents that it has been placed in an entirely new family.

The Vu Quang ox, or saola, was discovered in the forests of Vietnam in the 1990s. It is characterized by long horns and a face that has a bulging appearance.

higher altitudes; the highest uplands are drenched with mist, encouraging the growth of lush moss forests, within which conifers, oaks, and members of the *Theaceae* (the camellia family) and *Ericaceae* (the heather family) are among the dominant plants. The fauna is rich, with species such as tigers, elephants, the dhole (an endangered Asiatic wild dog), clouded leopards, and pig-tailed macaques. The goatlike serow lives on the steeper slopes.

Wet forests also occur to the north of the dry-forest zone, including the Louangphrabang montane forest in the highlands of northern Laos. The Louangphrabang forest is relatively undisturbed, with many large mammals, including tigers, gaurs, elephants, and both sun and Asian black bears. The forest is particularly rich in bird life, with almost 550 species. With heavy rainfall during monsoon months but a long dry season, the montane woodlands contain a range of habitats from hardwood forests of laurel and oak through mixed conifer and hardwood regions. The montane forest grades into the wetter subtropical forest, which extends from Laos through northern Myanmar (Burma). Oaks and magnolias dominate in this region.

SWAMP FORESTS

It is not just the wet and dry forests of Vietnam that have suffered devastating habitat and biodiversity loss. The Tonle Sap freshwater swamp forests in central Cambodia, for example, consist of a shrubland of short trees surrounding a stunted forest, encircling a permanently flooded peat forest rich with reeds and sedges. The peat forest grades into the Tonle Sap, the largest lake in Southeast Asia. The freshwater swamp forest floods for six to eight months of the year, at which time the trees shed their leaves. Many trees produce fruit at this time, and fish swimming through the flooded forest may be important seed-dispersers for these trees. Mammals of the swamp forest are threatened, including the Thamin deer (a graceful deer that is one of the most endangered deer species in the world), Indochinese hog deer, and bantengs. The reed beds are an important habitat for waterbirds, including rarities such as the giant ibis and Sarus crane, one of the tallest crane species.

With its regular floods, the Tonle Sap forests provide an ideal habitat for rice cultivation. The original habitat has now almost completely gone, and much of the rest has been colonized by giant mimosa, an introduced species that outcompetes native plants. Other swamp forests along the Mekong River and its tributaries are similarly affected by development and agriculture.

RIVER DELTAS

There are two great rivers in the region: the Red River, which flows to the Gulf of Tonkin southeast of Hanoi, and the Mekong River, which flows through southern Laos and central Cambodia to form a wide delta in southern Vietnam. The rivers of Indochina support a great deal of aquatic life, and the waters nourish plant and animal life in the floodplains and valleys. During the rainy season, the floodplains provide rich breeding grounds for fish.

The reaches of the Mekong in Laos are dotted with sand-bars and rocky islands, with bush running along the banks. This habitat contains a rich bird community, including river lapwings and Jerdon's bushchats, while the rare small pratincole nests on the sandbars. Sandbars may also provide basking spots for Siamese crocodiles.

The Mekong is home to a wide variety of fish, including carp, murrels, and gouramis. Catfish are particularly diverse; the endangered giant catfish, which lives in the lower reaches of the river, can reach up to 660 pounds (300 kg). The fish support small populations of mammals, such as black finless porpoises, Irawaddy dolphins, smooth-coated otters, and fishing cats, as well as many waterbirds.

The seasonally flooded grasslands and forests along the river are also important for birds such as white-winged ducks, masked finfoots, and green peafowls. Slender-billed and white-rumped vultures, which have suffered catastrophic population crashes since the 1990s, still soar overhead.

As the Mekong broadens into its delta, the surrounding vegetation is dominated by extensive mangrove forest, behind which lie banks of flooded *Melaleuca* woodland (called paperbark swamp). Mammals such as tapir and crab-eating macaque live in the forests. Vast colonies of cormorants, ibis, and egrets breed there, as do smaller numbers of wetland species such as purple swamp-hens, jacanas, and pratincoles, and eight species of kingfishers. The mangroves also provide an important habitat for some of the region's rarest waterbirds, such as spot-billed pelicans and Storm's storks. The mangrove swamps are also home to populations of some threatened reptiles, such as the false gharial, a species of crocodile, and estuarine crocodiles. Both the Mekong and Red River deltas are important for a range of migratory birds. Xuan Thuy in the Red River Delta, for example, provides a wintering ground for several globally threatened species, including spoon-billed sandpipers and black-faced spoonbills. Mangroves occur along the Vietnamese coast between the two great deltas, but they are rarer along the coast of Cambodia, where the shore is rockier and there are no major estuaries.

BIODIVERSITY

The diversity of plant and animal life in Indochina is great. There are at least 120,000 insect species in Vietnam alone and 826 bird species—more than in the entire contiguous United States, despite Vietnam's small area, less than half that of Texas. Biologists frequently discover new species in the forests. Indochina is a region of endemic species; some groups have diversified spectacularly, such as the freshwater turtles. Many endemic birds live only within one specific habitat. In Vietnam, for example, Edward's pheasant lives in the southern wet forests, grey-crowned crocias on the Da Lat Plateau, and orange-necked partridge in the

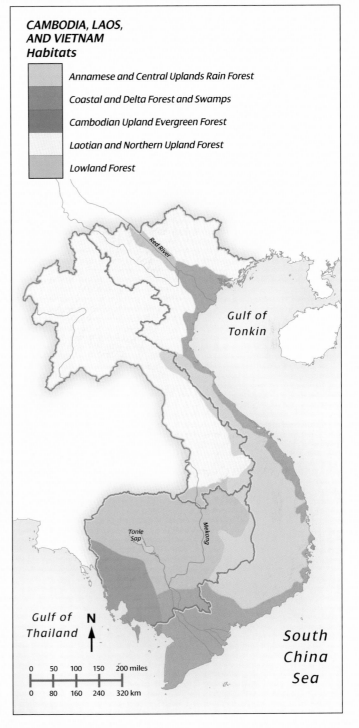

CAMBODIA, LAOS, AND VIETNAM Habitats

Annamese and Central Uplands Rain Forest

Coastal and Delta Forest and Swamps

Cambodian Upland Evergreen Forest

Laotian and Northern Upland Forest

Lowland Forest

southern dry forest. More unusually, a number of endemic genera and even a few endemic families exist. The region is rich in animal diversity, with at least 70 endemic species. Some endemic species, however, may have declined to extinction, such as the kouprey. The region is home to a range of endemic primates, several of which are critically endangered, including Cat Ba langur, Tonkin snub-nosed monkey, and Delacour's leaf monkey, which lives only in the Pu Luong limestone region of northern Vietnam.

J. MARTIN

History and Movement of Peoples

Early Vietnam and the Khmer Empire

The first kingdoms in Indochina (the region now occupied by Cambodia, Laos, and Vietnam) were based more on international trade than on agriculture. In time, the rich agricultural base of the Mekong River Valley in the Cambodian lowlands and the Red River Valley in northern Vietnam came to support more powerful states.

The Vietnamese in the Red River Valley centered on a settlement near the present site of Hanoi on the northern edge of the Red River Delta. To the south were the kingdoms the Chinese called Linyi, in central Vietnam, and Funan, in southern Vietnam and Cambodia. Chinese records show all three kingdoms well established by the third century CE, but Funan was the most prosperous of them.

THE CHINESE INVASION

Vietnam was conquered by a southern Chinese ruler in the third century BCE, and again by the Chinese Han dynasty in the second century BCE. Early Chinese political interest in Vietnam was a consequence of the Han rulers' desire to secure southern trade routes and to gain access to luxury goods from the south, including pearls, incense, drugs, elephant tusks, rhinoceros horn, tortoiseshell, coral, parrots, kingfishers, peacocks, and other rare treasures to satisfy the demands of the Chinese aristocracy. Under Chinese rule, Vietnam's Lac elite was allowed to rule in traditional ways, although the social system was modified to suit Chinese patterns. The Chinese found some Lac practices inconsistent with Chinese traditions, notably their disregard for a Chinese-style patriarchal system and their preference for bilateral kinship patterns (where the child is equally related to its mother's and father's kin).

In 39 CE, Trung Trac and Trung Nhi (both died 42 or 43 CE), daughters of a Lac lord, led an uprising against the Han and drove Han authority out of northern Vietnam and parts of southern China. The Han general Ma Yuan (14 BCE–49 CE) captured and beheaded the Trung Sisters in 42 or 43 CE. The rebellion was the final attempt of the pre-Han Vietnamese ruling class to resist Chinese authority, and subsequently Han authority over Vietnam became more direct.

In the subsequent Han-Vietnamese culture, status derived from wealth and the private ownership of land. Great families lived in fortresslike compounds and supported a private community of "guests" that included scholars, technical experts, spies, assassins, and private armies. When the Han dynasty in China fell in the third century CE, the Han-Vietnamese elite took greater interest in seaborne trade as a secondary source of income. Commerce in luxury goods was a major preoccupation of local administrators.

The coast in general became an international emporium during this period, notably in the kingdoms of Linyi and Funan but also in a Vietnamese port in the vicinity of modern Hanoi. By the fourth century CE, the rulers of Funan and Linyi proclaimed themselves kings in the Indian Hindu tradition, while the Vietnamese north, in common with post-Han Chinese society, found the Buddhist tradition appealing in this era of dynastic transition.

Large stone burial containers dot the surface of the Plain of Jars in northern Laos. They were made between 2,000 years ago and the sixth century CE by a people of whom little is known.

FUNAN

At the beginning of the first century CE, ports on what are now the southern Vietnamese coast, in Cambodia, Thailand, and on the Malay Peninsula were under the authority of a Hindu state the Chinese called Funan (Funan left no written records and the local name for the kingdom is unknown). These ports had developed to service the growing numbers of merchants traveling the sea route from India to China and had facilities, including buildings for storing goods and hostelries for merchants who stayed there until the next season's monsoon winds allowed their return voyage. A water management system that drained portions of the adjacent upper Mekong Delta allowed Funan's farmers to produce multiple rice harvests annually, supplying sufficient surplus to easily feed foreign merchants resident in Funan's ports and to provision their ships.

By the fourth century CE, significant changes were taking place in international trade routes that had a profound impact on Funan. In the second half of the fourth century CE, China no longer had access to the central Asian caravan routes and was forced to turn its attention to the maritime route. Southeast Asian trade centers beyond the Malay Peninsula responded to Chinese initiatives. The Funan Mekong Delta domain declined as

Galleries of reliefs, such as this carving of Khmer soldiers, line the walls of Angkor Wat. The temple was constructed by Khmer King Suryavarman II in the middle of the twelfth century CE.

the centers of the Cham civilization on the Vietnam coast north of the Mekong Delta, as well as the Khmer civilization in Cambodia and eastern Thailand, became the new focal points for civilization in the Indochina region.

CHAMPA

The Chams developed a Hindu-Buddhist river-based civilization south of their Vietnamese neighbors, who were centered in the Red River Valley. Champa, the Cham state, incorporated the earlier Linyi and Funan ports and their populations. Farther west, the Khmers built a great agrarian civilization that eventually centered on Angkor.

Both these successor civilizations traced their lineage to Funan and rooted their evolving states on the Indianized patterns of statecraft initially developed by Funan's rulers. By the eighth century CE, the Hindu-Buddhist Champa state had evolved based on wet-rice economy and participation in

The Age of Disunity

From 1428 through 1788, members of the Le dynasty ruled Vietnam, although only nominally for much of that period. Regionally based family rivalries continued throughout the history of the Le dynasty, and regular revolts and territorial divisions occurred within the Le kingdom of Dai Viet ("Great Viet").

The Le rulers promoted Confucian (rather than Buddhist) education, greater reliance on a universal legal code, and in the 1440s implemented Dai Viet's first Chinese-style examinations, whose successful candidates entered a bureaucracy based on merit. One of the most important impacts of the so-called "Neo-Confucian revolution" of the Le era was the separation of the educated classes from the Vietnamese peasantry. The Le law code tried to regulate every daily activity. At its heart was the insistence on codified family relations, which included fixed mourning procedures, marriage rites, and male inheritance.

REVOLTS AND DIVISIONS

In 1471, the Le rulers annexed most of the once-powerful central kingdom of Champa. From 1511 through 1521, thousands of alienated Vietnamese aristocrats, military, and impoverished peasants joined a series of popular rebellions that succeeded in destroying the power of the dynasty and in dividing Le territory into smaller units. A modified version of the Le political system survived the turmoil, and the dynasty continued, although weakened, after 1527.

Early Laos

The first Lao state, Lan Xang, was formed by King Fa Ngum (1316–1374) toward the middle of the fourteenth century and by 1371 included most of modern Laos and well as northern and eastern Thailand. A period of relative peace ended under King Photisarath (reigned 1520–1548), who became involved in wars against the Burmese and Thais to the west. As a result, his kingdom gained territory and enemies. In the reign of Photisarath's son, Setthathirat (reigned 1548–1571), the Burmese invaded twice, and the Lao king moved his capital from Louangphrabang to Vientiane. When Setthathirat died, the Burmese invaded, taking Vientiane. The Lao state declined until 1637, when King Suliyavongsa (reigned 1637–1694) reestablishehd a strong Lao kingdom. However, a dynastic dispute after his death divided Lan Xang into three separate kingdoms (1707–1713): Louangphrabang in the north, Vientiane in the center, and Champasak in the south. The small states were at the mercy of their stronger neighbors, the Thais and Vietnamese. The Laotians remained divided, and in the early nineteenth century, Vientiane and Champasak were annexed by the Thais.

Regionalism fractured the Le state, and monarchs of the Mac dynasty ruled from Thang Long (modern Hanoi) until the Le restoration of 1592, when the allied forces of the Trinh and Nguyen military lords (*chua*), respectively from the Red River Delta and the south, finally captured Thang Long and expelled the Mac rulers. However, unity was short-lived, as the victors soon split Dai Viet along regional lines. The Trinh lords retained authority over Thang Long and the north, while the Nguyen and their supporters formed a rival court, based in the former Cham territories of central and southern Vietnam. For almost two hundred years, the Vietnamese-speaking lands remained split between the Trinh and the Nguyen, whose heads ruled as hereditary princes. The head of the Le dynasty remained as a figurehead after 1600 until 1788. Intermittent warfare between the Trinh north and Nguyen south finally ended in 1672, when the seventh Trinh campaign against the south failed to conquer the breakaway region.

THE ARRIVAL OF EUROPEANS

During the early seventeenth century, especially after the arrival of Jesuit Catholic priests expelled from Japan, Roman Catholicism gained a following at the Trinh court, and it spread particularly among women and the rural population, who found Christianity appealing owing to their perceptions of the failure of the Neo-Confucian society. Christianity was especially appealing as it promised its followers miracles and, in contrast to Jesuit practice elsewhere, Jesuit priests recruited Vietnamese clergy. Vietnamese priests were provided with rigorous local seminary training, which included elementary medical instruction. The priests were then sent out to proselytize (convert) throughout the countryside.

Competition between two Roman Catholic orders, the Jesuits and the (French) Society for Foreign Missions (often called the Société), resulted in the Pope's intervention in 1738, ruling that the Jesuits would have dominion in the Trinh regions while the Société would have authority in the Nguyen south. The presence of the French Société encouraged the initiatives of French commercial firms in the region, whose Nguyen rulers were interested in foreign trade and in securing military technology (particularly guns) that the French commercial companies offered. As a result, French influence grew in southern Vietnam. In the same era, many Vietnamese were also attracted to devotional Buddhism, which offered an alternative to Christian doctrine.

THE TRINH AND NGUYEN COURTS

In the face of the religious challenges from Christians and Buddhists, Neo-Confucianism was threatened, although it retained the following of the Trinh court in the north and the aristocracy. In 1663, as a rebuttal to these religious challenges, the Trinh court (on behalf of the figurehead Le emperor) issued a collection of 47 ethical suggestions, rather than state laws, designed to spread Confucian values through society. The Trinh court directed local officials to proclaim the rules to the ordinary people in the villages. The rules reinforced the official "three

At the beginning of the nineteenth century, the Nguyen emperor Gia Long (1762–1820) moved his capital to the central city of Hué. Successive emperors ordered the construction of temples, palaces, and pavilions, such as the Reading Pavilion, within the imperial city.

bonds"(the *tam cuong*): the loyalty of state officials to the Le emperor, the loyalty of children to their parents, and that of wives to their husbands.

In the eighteenth and the early nineteenth centuries, intellectual and aesthetic ferment and increased literacy supported the flowering of an extensive lay literature in the Vietnamese script, *chu nom*, rather than in classical Chinese. This literature popularized Vietnam's own history, and patriotically highlighted the repeated successes of the Vietnamese against Chinese invaders.

The Nguyen rulers in the south, in contrast to the Trinh in the north, derived greater revenues from maritime trade than from the land. As a result, they supported the development of skilled naval forces, as well as military forces to guard ports, both proficient in the use of Western guns. Nguyen rulers claimed to be the only loyal subjects of the deposed Le dynasty, and they committed themselves, at least in word, to free northern Vietnam from the Trinh "usurpers."

Nguyen rulers invited Chinese Buddhist monks to reform local practices and attracted Chinese emigrants to their court to benefit from their administrative expertise. Nguyen administrators retained the Sino-Vietnamese calendar and language, and in the 1700s they began to fund Confucian state schools. Between 1691 and 1740, the Nguyen expanded civil-service examinations and rewarded successful candidates with senior posts.

In the seventeenth century, cultural boundaries tended to harden, and Chinese-style ideas about the "civilized" and "barbarians" were more clearly defined in Nguyen society. The concern over Vietnamese and non-Vietnamese ethnic differences in the south resulted from Nguyen attempts to discourage pre-existing Indian traditions among the Cham, Khmer, and upland tribes that had previously been subject to Champa's authority. The lingering Cham kingdom was finally abolished in 1697, and its territories were resettled by Vietnamese refugees.

REUNIFICATION

From 1771 through 1786, both the Nguyen and Trinh court networks collapsed. The Tayson rebellions of 1771 through 1802 (named for the Tay Son region where the peasants' revolt began) broke the Nguyen-Trinh stalemate. The rebels advocated a return to moral government, as exemplified in ancient laws, and a more equitable distribution of resources. The conflict suddenly rendered internal boundaries within the entire Vietnamese-speaking region exceptionally fluid. Eventual Nguyen victory over the Tayson rebels stemmed in large measure from their success in tapping the military technology and strategies of their French and Thai allies, and also from temporary military intervention by their Chinese neighbors. By 1802, after their defeat of the last of the Tayson rebels, the Nguyen claimed authority over all Vietnam, and the nation was reunited.

K. HALL

French Indochina

French Indochina, the French colonial empire in southeastern Asia, included modern-day Vietnam, Laos, and Cambodia. Indochina was officially created in 1887 and dissolved in 1945, but the first French invasion of Vietnam in 1859 marked the start of French rule, and the final Vietnamese defeat of the French in 1954 marked its end.

French presence in southeast Asia predated the formal creation of French Indochina by more than two centuries. Roman Catholic missionaries first became established in the region in the seventeenth century, and French priests were prominent among them. Later, ambitious empire builders in France used this missionary legacy as one of their justifications for colonial conquest of the region.

THE FIRST COLONIES

Conflict between the Vietnamese authorities and French missionaries in Vietnam in the early 1800s led to calls in France for intervention. French commercial interests were also strong in the region, and the impetus for a colonial presence grew. In 1858, French troops captured the city of Saigon (modern Ho Chi Minh City), and in 1862, southern Vietnam became the French colony of Cochinchina. By 1867, France controlled the southern regions of Vietnam.

Once in control of the lower Mekong River, the French hoped to control a waterway route to China and turned their attentions to Cambodia and Laos. In 1863, the French coerced Cambodia's king to declare his country a French protectorate; they compelled the Lao monarchs to do the same thirty years later. By 1883, the French had transformed northern and central Vietnam into two protectorates, Tonkin (the Red River Valley region around Hanoi) in the north and Annam in the center.

THE UNION OF INDOCHINA

The Union of Indochina was established in 1887, with its capital in Hanoi. Indochina included the three different Vietnamese territories (Tonkin, Annam, and Cochinchina) and Cambodia. In 1893, the French added Laos, which eventually comprised the kingdom of Louangphrabang (a French protectorate from 1893), the principality of Champasak (a protectorate from 1904), and two colonies, Vientiane (annexed in 1887) and Xiangkhoang (added in 1893). Technically, Cambodia, Annam, Champasak, and Louangphrabang were sovereign states and retained their own monarchs, governments, and laws. Cochinchina was legally a part of France and operated solely under French law.

All the territories were placed under the control of a French governor-general in Hanoi, who ruled through a system of French residents, or representatives, placed at all levels of government, with the power of veto over local administrators. This system effectively overrode the small amount of power the protectorates had on paper and ensured that the French were the real rulers of Indochina.

FRENCH COLONIALISM

The French justified their conquest in three ways. Pointing to the growing colonial empire of Great Britain, France's main political rival, many argued that France should vigorously compete and that national interest justified colonial conquest. Others were motivated by the economic ideas of the day and theorized that French economic and political power depended on capturing natural resources to supply its rapidly growing industry and, at the same time, subjugating a population of consumers for its products. Still others, embracing new political philosophies that saw the world composed of a hierarchy of competing nations, civilizations, or races (an idea that would later be called Social Darwinism), argued that empire was the highest form of state and civilization. Moreover, they felt, as an "enlightened civilization," France was duty-bound to conquer "less civilized" societies in order to raise them to its high cultural standards. This idea eventually became policy in French colonies, under the name *mission civilisatrice*, or "civilizing mission." These French ideals of prestige, power, and progress carried with them profound implications for the peoples and territories of French Indochina.

The promotion of French language and education instilled the ideals of "Mother France," such as liberty, equality, and brotherhood, in the colonies' young elites. However, at the same time, the law reinforced the power of a few thousand French over Indochina's millions, which limited the options of young educated Indochinese. The principle of making Indochina profitable for France drove a policy that produced a modern infrastructure and expanded commerce but placed harsh demands on rural villages and the urban poor.

As contradictions between the ideals expressed by French rulers and the reality of colonial experiences grew, increasing numbers of Indochinese became sympathetic to radical calls to end French rule. This sentiment grew acute in Tonkin, Annam, and Cochinchina, where the Vietnamese spearheaded the independence struggle. Taxes imposed by the French, particularly those on salt and alcohol, were resented.

French officers capture the Annamese ruler Ham Nghi (reigned 1884–1885) in 1885. In 1883, his predecessor had signed a treaty with the French that had recognized a French protectorate over Annam, but Ham Nghi organized resistance against French rule.

RESISTANCE TO FRENCH RULE

Ironically, the ideals of the French played one of the greatest roles in shaping the resistance that would result in the demise of the French Indochinese empire. Early anticolonial endeavors had proved fruitless owing to lack of organization and guiding ideals. However, by the 1920s a new generation of French-educated intellectuals, immersed in the history and literature of the French Enlightenment and French Revolution, began to develop their own conceptions of self-determination and national identity.

GROWING NATIONALIST MOVEMENTS

The road to independence took a fateful turn when a young Vietnamese in Paris, later known as Ho Chi Minh (born Nguyen Sinh Cung; 1890–1969), encountered the ideas of German philosopher Karl Marx (1818–1883) and Russian revolutionary Vladimir Lenin (1870–1924) and embraced communism as the best solution to defeating the French and modernizing Indochinese societies. However, Ho's later success in achieving both independence and Communist rule for Vietnam was hardly assured at the time. Ho was a member of one of a number of radical pro-independence groups that formed in Vietnam during the 1920s (and later in Cambodia and Laos) and initially Ho's group was not the largest or the most influential. Demand for independence grew in Vietnam during the 1920s and 1930s, but the Vietnamese nationalists were unable to recruit sufficient numbers of people or to organize effective strategies to avoid the attention of the French secret police. This led to continual setbacks. The most serious competitor to Ho, Nguyen Thai Hoc (1904–1930), had formed a viable political party, the Vietnamese Nationalist Party (VNQDD), modeled on republican ideals. Following an unsuccessful uprising by the VNQDD at Yen Bay, Hoc and the rest of the leadership were executed, and the party never regained its strength.

In 1930, Ho helped form the Indochinese Communist Party (PCI), and the party enjoyed a brief period of popularity. After a hastily planned uprising by the PCI in 1930 and 1931 in Annam's Nghe Tinh region, many of the party leadership were executed or jailed and hundreds of supporters were killed. Throughout the 1930s, reformers and nationalist revolutionaries attempted to change the situation in Indochina, but their efforts brought little success and many setbacks.

THE JAPANESE INVASION

World War II (1939–1945) changed the balance of power in Indochina, creating opportunities for pro-independence movements. In early 1940, Japan demanded that the French allow its army free movement within Indochina to aid their invasion of China and Southeast Asia. At first the French colonial authorities resisted the demand, but when France fell to Germany in May 1940, they relented, and Japanese troops occupied Indochina.

Although the French colonial authorities in Indochina technically remained in power during the occupation until the final months of the war, they lost their aura of invincibility. Encouraged by the Japanese, patriotic sentiment for independence from France grew in the region. New nationalist parties emerged in Cambodia, Laos, and Vietnam, and French power in the nations of Indochina was doomed.

C. WHEELER

The Struggle for Independence

After the surrender of the Japanese forces occupying Indochina in 1945, the French quickly restored their rule in Cambodia, Laos, and the southern part of Vietnam. However, the local governments in those countries had been encouraged by the Japanese to declare independence from France in the closing months of the World War II (1939–1945), and it was clear that nationalist feelings were growing in the region.

The Viet Minh (short for Viet Nam Doc Lap Dong Minh, literally the "League for the Independence of Vietnam," a coalition of Communists and nationalists opposed to the presence of both Japan and France in Vietnam) was formed in August 1941 by Ho Chi Minh (1890–1969), a longtime Communist revolutionary. Ho gathered together a disparate group of Communist cells and other Vietnamese nationalists for the purpose of opposing the Japanese occupation of Vietnam during the war and also laying the groundwork for Vietnamese independence. The organization grew by developing a secret nationwide network of small groups or cells; it also received help from the Office of Strategic Services (the U.S. predecessor of the CIA) in exchange for rescuing downed U.S. pilots in Indochina.

FRENCH POWER WANES

The desire for independence grew among the peoples of Indochina whose anger against the French intensified as they watched their rulers capitulate to Japanese aggressors. The Japanese occupied the different French possessions in Indochina but allowed the French colonial administration to remain in place until final months of the war in 1945. In Cambodia, the Japanese encouraged King Sihanouk (born 1922) to declare independence, but following the defeat of the Japanese, the French regained control of Cambodia in October 1945.

Bicycle units of Japanese forces enter Saigon in 1941.

In Laos, the king of Louangphrabang, Sisavang Vong (1885–1959), renounced French protection, but he also opposed Japanese rule. Two rival Lao nationalist groups emerged. An anti-Japanese movement was led in the north by Sisavang Vong and in the south by Boun Oum (1912–1980), the former prince of Champassak. In Vientiane and central Laos, the radical anti-French Lao Issara movement seized power. When French forces regained control over Laos in 1946, the leaders of the Lao Issara movement fled to Thailand. At the same time, a unified Laos was formed from three formerly separate Lao territories: the northern kingdom of Louangphrabang, the colony of Vientiane in the center, and Champassak in the south. France granted Laos internal self-government, with Sisavang Vong as king. While some members of Lao Issara accepted the compromise, many continued the campaign for complete independence. Cambodia also gained limited independence in 1949. In both Laos and Cambodia, a return to the former colonial status was not possible, however, because France was otherwise involved in a bitter war against the Viet Minh Communists in Vietnam.

THE VIET MINH

Whereas Laos and Cambodia gained autonomy without an armed struggle, the situation in Vietnam was different. Vietnamese frustration was compounded by perceived French indifference to their suffering during the great famine of 1944 and 1945, when one to two million Vietnamese starved to death as the result of rice hoarding by the occupying Japanese forces. This also promoted anti-Japanese sentiment in Vietnam, where some people had initially welcomed the forces of Japan as liberators. In contrast, the popularity of the Viet Minh grew when local guerrilla forces seized granaries and opened them to the public. When news came in 1945 that the United States had dropped two atomic bombs on Japan, hastening the defeat of the Japanese, the Viet Minh wasted no time in seizing the opportunity to fill a political vacuum left by Japan's collapse.

Upon the Japanese surrender, the Viet Minh launched the "August Revolution," seizing control of the government and declaring the Democratic Republic of Vietnam in Hanoi on September 2, 1945. Although early Allied negotiations supported some form of Vietnamese independence, the British forces arriving in Saigon (modern Ho Chi Minh City) to handle the Japanese surrender defied Allied intentions and organized the return of French forces. Immediately after French troops reached Saigon, violence broke out between the Viet Minh and French supporters. In northern Vietnam, Chinese forces occupied the region after Japan's surrender as part of the peace agreement.

The Chinese withdrew in 1946, and French troops began to reoccupy the north. Tense negotiations between the French and the Viet Minh lasted throughout 1945 and 1946, and Ho Chi Minh journeyed to France to negotiate independence. France was only willing to grant autonomy, and the talks broke down. War became inevitable when French naval ships bombarded the northern port of Haiphong in November 1946, killing thousands

of civilians. Viet Minh leaders who had been stationed in Hanoi retreated from the cities, establishing bases in the countryside. The Viet Minh then declared a national war of liberation.

The First War for Vietnam (1946–1954) marked the start of a violent struggle over what political form an independent Vietnamese state would take. For supporters of the Viet Minh, the war was a revolution for independence. For the Viet Minh's Communist leaders, however, it was also a revolution to transform Vietnam into a socialist society. For French leaders, it was a war to stop independence. French colonists and many members of the Vietnamese elite supported the restoration of French rule. However, many Vietnamese who hoped for independence were distrustful of their colonial rulers but also wary of what a Communist state might mean. Some Vietnamese reluctantly supported France, because they feared a potential Communist dictatorship; others joined the Viet Minh, believing that any form of independent government was acceptable.

THE COLONIAL WAR

When the war began, it looked as though the French could win an easy victory. Although the Viet Minh enjoyed widespread popularity, which would win it many recruits, its army was small, ill-trained, and poorly equipped. The Viet Minh also received little foreign support. However, the French people were still recovering from the effects of World War II, reconstructing their own country after war damage, and there was little enthusiasm for another war, even one far away. Moreover, five years of foreign occupation by the Germans had made many French sympathetic to the independence movements in French colonies.

The Communist movement was growing in France itself, and French president Charles de Gaulle (1890–1970) used the Communist threat in France to his advantage when he warned the U.S. government that France could become Communist if the Viet Minh won in Vietnam. De Gaulle's warning redefined the war in Vietnam from one of colonial reconquest to a battle in the global Cold War between the Soviet Union and its satellites and the anti-Communist world led by the United States. As a result, France secured U.S. diplomatic and financial support, and the United States was left footing most of the bill for the war.

Involving the Cold War superpowers changed the nature of the war. U.S. intervention in the war spurred Communist China and the Soviet Union to intervene on the side of the Viet Minh. Forced to abandon the appearance of purely colonial aspirations in exchange for U.S. support, on June 14, 1949, France announced an independent State of Vietnam, but it was to have limited sovereignty (like Laos and Cambodia). The state was effectively restricted to those areas of Vietnam controlled by French forces. Its chief of state was Bao Dai (1913–1997), who had abdicated as emperor of Annam in 1945, but he proved no match for his Communist counterpart, Ho Chi Minh, and had little support. France retained control, and its reluctance to relinquish any real power undermined the already ambivalent support for the French among the Vietnamese.

Peoples of Cambodia, Laos, and Vietnam

Indochina is home to three main peoples: the Khmer (or Cambodians), the Lao, and the Vietnamese. However, only Cambodia has a relatively homogeneous population. The Lao are divided into three main populations, and Vietnam is ethnically complex.

The populations of Cambodia, Laos, and Vietnam contain many ethnic minorities, including Thais, ethnic Chinese, Cham, Muong, Nung, Burmese, Yao, Hmong, and other groups. Some of these peoples inhabit traditional homelands. Others, such as the Chinese, are migrants into the region.

THE KHMER

The Khmer, or Cambodian, people form the overwhelming majority of the population of Cambodia. Ethnic Khmer account for 90 percent of the population of Cambodia, and 95 percent of

Cambodia's people speak Khmer as a first language. The Khmer also form a minority in parts of Laos and in the Mekong Delta of Vietnam. The Khmers' historic homeland is the lowlands surrounding the Mekong River and Tonle Sap lake. They moved there in the third century BCE from what is now northeastern Thailand. The Khmer were strongly influenced by Indian culture and religion, but contact with these influences was through Hindu communities on the island of Java rather than with India. Later waves of Thai immigrants (from the tenth century CE through the fifteenth century) and Vietnamese migrants (since the seventeenth century) also had an effect upon Khmer culture and ethnicity. The Khmer speak a language of the Mon-Khmer group that also includes Vietnamese, Muong, and Mon.

THE VIETNAMESE

Vietnam is a patchwork of different languages and ethnicities, of which the Vietnamese are by far the largest: 87 percent of the people of Vietnam are Vietnamese by language and ethnicity. One thousand years of Chinese rule introduced many Chinese influences into Vietnamese culture and language, one of the Mon-Khmer group of languages. Ethnic Vietnamese are concentrated in the Red River lowlands in the north and the Mekong Delta region in the south, as well as along the coast. The hill country inland is home to a number of ethnic minorities.

THE LAO

The Lao are not a single people, ethnically or linguistically. There are three

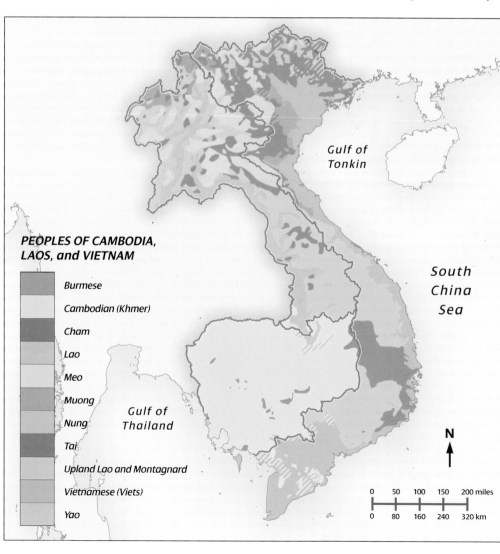

PEOPLES OF CAMBODIA, LAOS, and VIETNAM

- Burmese
- Cambodian (Khmer)
- Cham
- Lao
- Meo
- Muong
- Nung
- Tai
- Upland Lao and Montagnard
- Vietnamese (Viets)
- Yao

Gulf of Tonkin

South China Sea

Gulf of Thailand

N

0 50 100 150 200 miles
0 80 160 240 320 km

main Lao groups: the Lao Loum, the Lao Theung, and the Lao Soung. The Lao Loum are also known as the Lowland or Valley Lao. They account for 68 percent of the people of Laos and live along the banks of the Mekong River and its tributaries and in the cities of Laos. The Lao Loum are the traditional ruling elite of Laos. Their language is closely related to the Thai language.

The Lao Theung are Mon-Khmer people who are scattered throughout Laos, although they are mainly concentrated in the uplands (they are also known as the Upland Lao). They speak a variety of languages and dialects, variously estimated at between 20 and 30, and account for 22 percent of the population of Laos. The Lao Soung peoples, including the Hmong or Meo people and the Yao (or Man), are believed to have come from China. They live in the remote mountainous parts of Laos and are also known as Mountain Lao.

THE CHAM

The ancestors of the Cham ruled a strong kingdom (Champa) in central Vietnam in the first millennium CE and the first half of the second millennium CE. In modern times, the Cham are a minority in the southern part of Vietnam's coastal plain, in the Mekong Delta region, and in Cambodia. Most of the Western Cham in Cambodia are Muslims and speak Khmer. The Eastern Cham in Vietnam follow a number of different religions. Some are Hindus—medieval Champa was much influenced by Indian culture, which was received through Java and the Khmer Empire. Some Eastern Cham still speak their own language. Both communities are well integrated into modern Cambodia and Vietnam, but some distinct cultural elements remain. The Cham were traditionally matrilineal, descent and kinship being passed down through the female line. The traditional Cham script is based on Sanskrit from the Indian subcontinent.

PEOPLES OF THE VIETNAMESE UPLANDS

The French colonial authorities who ruled Vietnam before 1954 collectively referred to the different peoples of the interior hill country as Montagnards, literally "highlanders." The many different peoples, none of whom form a large population group, are variously related to the Cham, to Malays, Khmers, or to the peoples of the East Indies (modern Indonesia). The Chru, Jarai, and Rhade peoples are related to Malays and other peoples to the south; the Bru, Cua, Hre, Katu, Mang, Mnong, Pacoh, and related groups are part of the Mon-Khmer group. The Chinese who ruled Vietnam for a millennium had little influence on the Montagnards, who still retain a fierce independence and a determination to preserve their distinct cultures. The languages of the Montagnards were written in the Roman script by the French and none is widespread.

Each of the highland peoples are few in number, but they form distinct communities in remote areas. The largest groups include the Meo or Hmong, the Muong, the Nung, and the

A Hmong mother takes her family into the fields while she works.

groups known as the Tai tribes. The Hmong or Meo account for about 0.8 percent or some 600,000 of the population of Vietnam. The Muong, who number between 700,000 and 800,000, live mainly in central Vietnam and are culturally and ethnically close to the Thais. The Nung, who number about 600,000, were widely dispersed, but after the partition of Vietnam in 1954, the Nung concentrated into the Central Highlands.

OTHER MINORITIES

Burmese people live in small scattered pockets in the western part of Laos. Thais form minorities in Cambodia and Laos. There are Chinese communities in all the major cities of the region, where they have traditionally been traders. The Chinese minority fled Cambodia from 1975 through 1979 (when the country was ruled by the extreme left-wing Khmer Rouge regime), but they have since returned in smaller numbers. The Yao, who are an important minority in southwestern China, also live in Vietnam and Laos. The Yao are mainly Buddhists.

C. CARPENTER

Cambodia

In the six decades in which Cambodia has regained independence after French colonial rule, the nation has suffered many upheavals. In the 1960s, Cambodia could not prevent involvement in the war in neighboring Vietnam, and in 1970 the monarchy was overthrown by a pro-U.S. military junta. In 1975, the military government was in turn overthrown by the Communist Khmer Rouge movement, which forcibly dismantled the economy, evacuated the cities, and massacred at least one million Cambodians (and possibly twice that number). Cambodia's traditional rival, Vietnam, invaded in 1979, dislodging the Khmer Rouge, but civil war broke out. In 1991, the warring factions agreed to a peace plan that included elections supervised by the United Nations (UN). Multiparty elections were held in 1993, and the monarchy was restored.

GEOGRAPHY

Location	Southeast Asia, along the Gulf of Thailand between Thailand and Vietnam
Climate	Tropical climate with little seasonal variation in temperature; wet monsoon season from May through November; dry season from December through April
Area	69,898 sq. miles (181,035 sq. km)
Coastline	277 miles (443 km)
Highest point	Phnum Aural 5,940 feet (1,810 m)
Lowest point	Gulf of Thailand 0 feet (0 m)
Terrain	Low flat plains in the east, center, and southeast; mountains in the southwest and north
Natural resources	Oil, natural gas, gemstones, timber
Land use	
Arable land	20.4 percent
Permanent crops	0.6 percent
Other	79.0 percent
Major rivers	Mekong, Sab
Major lake	Tonle Sap
Natural hazards	Flooding, drought

METROPOLITAN AREAS, 1998 POPULATIONS

Urban population	18 percent
Phnom Penh	1,078,000
Phnom Penh City	999,000
Battambang	124,000
Sisophon	85,000
Siem Reap	84,000
Preah Sihanouk (formerly Kompong Som)	67,000
Kompong Cham	45,000
Suong	45,000
Poipet	43,000
Kampong Chhang	42,000
Kampong Spoe	41,000
Kampot	36,000

Source: Cambodian census, 1998

FLAG

The national flag of Cambodia has three horizontal bands: blue at the top, red in the center, and blue at the bottom. There is a white emblem in outline at the center of the red band representing the great temple of Angkor Wat. The pedestal of the temple represents the structure of the universe; the temple itself represents the Buddhist religion; and the top of the temple represents the monarchy. The flag, the national flag of Cambodia from independence until 1970, was reinstated upon the restoration of the monarchy in 1993.

NEIGHBORS AND LENGTH OF BORDERS

Laos	338 miles (541 km)
Thailand	502 miles (803 km)
Vietnam	768 miles (1,228 km)

POPULATION

Population	13,807,000 (2005 official estimate)
Population density	198 per sq. mile (76 per sq. km)
Population growth	1.8 percent a year
Birthrate	26.9 births per 1,000 of the population
Death rate	9.1 deaths per 1,000 of the population
Population under age 15	35.6 percent
Population over age 65	3.4 percent
Sex ratio	95 males for 100 females
Fertility rate	3.4 children per woman
Infant mortality rate	68.6 deaths per 1,000 live births
Life expectancy at birth	
Total population	59.3 years
Female	61.3 years
Male	57.4 years

A woman sells vegetables at a market in the town of Siem Reap near Angkor in the Tonle Sap Basin.

ECONOMY

Currency	Riel (KHR)
Exchange rate (2006)	$1 = KHR 4,125
Gross domestic product (2005)	$30.7 billion
GDP per capita (2005)	$2,200
Unemployment rate (2000)	3 percent
Population under poverty line (2004)	40 percent
Exports	$2.4 billion (2004 CIA estimate)
Imports	$3.5 billion (2004 CIA estimate)

GOVERNMENT

Official country name	Kingdom of Cambodia
Conventional short form	Cambodia
Former names	Khmer Republic, Kampuchea
Nationality	
noun	Cambodian (or Khmer)
adjective	Cambodian (or Khmer)
Official language	Khmer
Capital city	Phnom Penh
Type of government	Constitutional monarchy
Voting rights	18 years and over, universal
National anthem	"Nokoreach"
	(Heaven protects our King)
National day	Independence Day, November 9, 1953

Elephants and handlers wait for tourist passengers at Angkor Wat.

TRANSPORTATION

Railroads	374 miles (602 km)
Highways	7,659 miles (12,323 km)
Paved roads	1,241 miles (1,996 km)
Unpaved roads	6,418 miles (10,327 km)
Navigable waterways	1,492 miles (2,400 km)
Airports	
International airports	1
Paved runways	6

POPULATION PROFILE, 2000 ESTIMATES

Ethnic groups	
Khmer	90 percent
Vietnamese	5 percent
Chinese	1 percent
Others	4 percent
Religions	
Theravada Buddhist	95 percent
Christians, others, and nonreligious	5 percent
Languages	
Khmer	95 percent
Vietnamese, Chinese, and other minorities	5 percent
Adult literacy	73.6 percent

CHRONOLOGY

1st century CE	Cambodia is part of the Hindu Funan kingdom that also covers parts of what are now Vietnam and Thailand.
802 CE	King Jayavarman II (reigned 802–834) successfully merges Buddhist and Hindu traditions to unite Khmer territories and establish the Khmer Empire.
889–900	King Yasovarman I (reigned 889–900) establishes his capital in Angkor in the center of present-day Cambodia.
12th century	Cambodia's most famous buildings, the Hindu temple Angkor Wat and the Hindu-Buddhist temple Angkor Thom, are built at Angkor.
1431	Forces from the Thai kingdom of Ayutthaya overcome the Khmer Empire. Much of Cambodia comes under Thai control. The Khmer king abandons Angkor and makes Phnom Penh his capital.
16th century	Khmer dynasties and Thai leaders struggle for control of Cambodia.
1863	Cambodia becomes a French protectorate. Cambodian monarchs continue to reign, but real power rests with the French.
1941	France appoints Prince Norodom Sihanouk (born 1922) as king of Cambodia. Japan occupies Cambodia during World War II (1939–1945) but leaves the French administration in place.
1945	Japan takes over the government of Cambodia. Encouraged by the Japanese, King Sihanouk declares independence.
1949	Cambodia gains autonomy as an "associated state" of France.
1953	Cambodia gains its independence from France with King Sihanouk as chief of state.
1955	King Sihanouk abdicates to become head of the government.
1967	A revolt by the extreme Khmer Rouge Communist movement begins.
1970	In a right-wing military coup, General Lon Nol (1913–1985) deposes Sihanouk and proclaims Cambodia a republic.
1975–1979	The Khmer Rouge seize power and, under Pol Pot (1925–1998), attempt to establish a classless rural society. The cities are evacuated and the people are forced into peasant labor. More than one million Cambodians (possibly many more) are murdered.
1979	Vietnam invades Cambodia and the Khmer Rouge flee. A Vietnamese-sponsored Communist republic is established.
1979–early 1990s	Civil war is fought between forces of the Vietnamese-backed government and the Khmer Rouge.
1991	A cease-fire is arranged, to be monitored by United Nations (UN) forces. The UN establishes a transitional authority to prepare elections.
1993	Multiparty elections are held. The monarchy is restored, with Sihanouk as king.
2004	King Sihanouk abdicates and is succeeded by his son Norodom Sihamoni (born 1953).

GOVERNMENT

Three decades of civil war and dictatorship in Cambodia ended in 1991, when a United Nations (UN)–sponsored peace plan was arranged. Multiparty elections were held and the constitutional monarchy, which had been overthrown in 1970, was restored.

The centuries-old Cambodian monarchy enjoys great respect among Cambodians. While the sovereign is, in theory, a constitutional monarch, King Norodom Sihanouk (born 1922; reigned 1941–1955 and 1993–2004) frequently intervened in the political process, and in 1955 he abdicated in order to lead the government himself. During his second reign, Norodom Sihanouk often made his views known through the media. In 2004, the king abdicated and was succeeded by his youngest son, Norodom Sihamoni (born 1953).

Succession to the Cambodian throne is not hereditary. A nine-member Throne Council chooses a member of the royal house as king or queen within seven days of a vacancy. The new monarch must be at least 30 years of age. The council comprises the prime minister, the president, and both deputy presidents of the lower house of the legislature, the president and both vice presidents of the upper house of the legislature, and Cambodia's two leading Buddhist religious officials.

Hun Sen, premier of Cambodia since 1985, was once a member of the Khmer Rouge.

POLITICAL PARTIES

The dominant (former Communist) Cambodian People's Party (Kanakpak Pracheachon Kampuchea, or KPK) has been accused of abuses of power, including threats, violence, and other acts of intimidation against the opposition. The KPK has been led since 1985 by Hun Sen (born 1952), a former Communist Party official who defected to Vietnam in the late 1970s. Hun Sen returned to Cambodia in 1979, when Vietnamese forces intervened to depose the extreme Communist Khmer Rouge regime.

Until 2003, the main opposition party was the conservative royalist United Front for an Independent, Neutral, and Free Cambodia (FUNCINPEC), which is led by Prince Norodom Ranariddh (born 1944), the eldest surviving son of King Norodom Sihanouk. The other main political party in Cambodia is the reformist Sam Rainsy Party (PSR), a populist movement that is named for its founder, a leading dissident. Since the restoration of a multiparty system, the government is usually a coalition of the KPK and FUNCINPEC, with the latter as junior members of the administration. No single party is large enough to form a majority in the legislature. The PSR is the effective opposition. Four smaller parties contest elections but are not represented in the legislature.

THE NATIONAL ASSEMBLY AND THE GOVERNMENT

The National Assembly (the Radhsphea ney Preah Recheanachakr Kampuchea) has 123 members, who are elected for a five-year term by universal adult suffrage under a system of proportional representation. The voting age is 18 years. In the 2003 election, the KPK won 69 seats, while the PSR won 28 seats and FUNCINPEC 26. Due to intimidation of voters, international observers judged that the election was not free and fair.

The upper house of the legislature, the Senate, has 61 members who serve for five years. Two members are appointed by the monarch and two by the National Assembly. The remaining 57 members are elected by those political parties represented in the lower house and are then appointed by the monarch.

Following legislative elections, the National Assembly elects a chairperson, who selects the leader of the largest political party in the assembly as prime minister. When the prime minister is able to form an administration, he or she is appointed to office by the monarch. The prime minister chooses a cabinet and submits their names to the monarch for approval.

LOCAL GOVERNMENT

Cambodia is divided in 20 provinces (*khaitt*), including Phnom Penh (the national capital), and four autonomous municipalities (known as *krong*), which have provincial status. The provinces are divided into municipalities, which have elected councils. The country's principal local officials are appointed.

C. CARPENTER

MODERN HISTORY

The Independent Cambodian Kingdom

In 1941, during World War II (1939–1945), Cambodia was occupied by Japanese forces that allowed the French colonial administration to continue to function. In the same year, the French named Prince Norodom Sihanouk (born 1922), as king, following the death of his granfather, Monivong (reigned 1927–1941). Sihanouk was to dominate Cambodian political life for much of the following six decades.

In March 1945, in the final months of World War II, Japan removed the French administration in Cambodia and encouraged the young king, Sihanouk, to declare independence. However, following the defeat of Japan in October 1945, French forces regained control of Cambodia. A return to colonial status was not possible, because the French were involved in a bitter war in Vietnam against the Viet Minh Communists. Consequently in 1949, Cambodia gained limited independence.

The newly autonomous Cambodian nation was sharply divided among different political factions, including supporters of independence, Communists, and royalists. In 1952, Sihanouk took personal control of the government.

INDEPENDENCE

In 1953, France was forced to grant Cambodia complete sovereignty. The nation's independence and neutrality were confirmed in the Geneva Accords (1954) following the defeat of the French army at Dien Bien Phu in Vietnam by the Viet Minh. Although King Sihanouk was popular, he became increasingly autocratic and unwilling to share power with politicians. In 1955, Sihanouk renounced the throne in favor of his father and established his own political party, known as Sangkum Reastr Niyum (People's Socialist Community), which subsequently won 83 percent of the seats in the national assembly.

Through the 1950s and 1960s, Sihanouk established a more or less benevolent dictatorship while suppressing the liberal democratic and Communist opposition. Respect for the monarchy and the rural Buddhist priesthood dominated the consciousness of the overwhelmingly peasant population of the country. Rural Khmers initially benefited from major improvements in health and education introduced by Sihanouk.

Sihanouk became a prominent figure on the international stage as a leader of the Nonaligned Movement (those nations that were not allied with either the Communist bloc or the West). He portrayed his kingdom as a kind of tropical paradise. However, the reality in the countryside from the 1950s onward was one of steady economic deterioration and rising social tension. The population rapidly rose from 2.5 million in 1945 to 7.2 million by 1970. Land shortage, declining agricultural productivity, growing inequality, and indebtedness plagued the peasant majority. Meanwhile, a largely urban middle class composed of French, Chinese, and Vietnamese merchants dominated economic life. The social divide between the rural population and the citizens of the national capital, Phnom Penh, deepened. Cambodia's economic problems intensified in the 1960s as imported manufactured goods and luxuries created a growing balance of payments problem. Sihanouk's attempt to control this problem in 1965 by instituting state control of the export-import trade alienated much of the urban population.

THE VIETNAM WAR

Cambodia's problems grew because of war in neighboring South Vietnam, where Communist insurgents from North Vietnam and local Communists (the Viet Cong) attempted to overthrow the pro-Western South Vietnamese government in Saigon (modern Ho Chi Minh City). The increasing Communist insurgency against the Saigon government in the early 1960s led to the growing intrusion of North Vietnamese and Viet Cong forces into Cambodia, where the Vietnamese Communists established supply bases in eastern districts. In the face of foreign intrusion into Cambodia, Sihanouk at first maintained neutrality. He stopped accepting U.S. military assistance in 1963, and in 1965 he broke off diplomatic relations with the United States, accusing the U.S. government of trying to overthrow him. Convinced of an ultimate Communist victory in Vietnam, he maintained good relations with the North Vietnamese authorities in Hanoi and the Communist Chinese government in Beijing. He allowed the Viet Cong and North Vietnamese troops to operate from bases in Cambodia close to the border with South Vietnam.

Sihanouk ignored the North Vietnamese development of the Ho Chi Minh Trail, a supply route through Cambodia to bring military personnel and equipment from North Vietnam to South Vietnam. He also permitted Communist forces to use the port of Sihanoukville (later called Kompong Som and now known as Preah Sihanouk) to supply their bases in eastern Cambodia. Sihanouk also looked the other way when on March 18, 1969, the United States began bombing the Vietnamese Communist bases and the Ho Chi Minh Trail in Cambodia. In later years, the bombing would spread more widely across Cambodia, and it was believed eventually to have killed several hundred thousand people. Also in 1969, U.S. and South Vietnamese forces made cross-border raids against the Communist encampments.

Norodom Sihanouk held office as king of Cambodia (1941–1955), prime minister ten times, chief of state in all but name (1960–1970), chief of state (1991–1993), and king (1993–2004).

GROWING INSTABILITY

Sihanouk had become the effective Cambodian chief of state again (but not king) after the death of his father in 1960, although his mother, Queen Kusumana (1904–1975), was symbolic chief of state. However, his grip on power became increasingly tenuous. His decision to impose state controls on foreign trade in 1965 alienated the urban middle class. The middle class and the military were further disturbed by Sihanouk's break in diplomatic relations with the United States in the same year, while his close ties with the North Vietnamese and Chinese regimes alarmed them. In an attempt to appease these elements, Sihanouk appointed a right-wing, pro-American general, Lon Nol (1913–1985), as prime minister.

Although Sihanouk cultivated good relations with the North Vietnamese and Chinese Communists, he otherwise kept internal Communist opposition in check through repressive measures. Prime Minister Lon Nol's authoritarian rule inflamed a growing Communist-led insurrection in the countryside, where the rural population suffered growing poverty. The revolt centered around Battambang, Cambodia's second largest city. Communists known as the Khmer Rouge were active in the area from the late 1950s but to little effect.

INSURRECTION

In late 1966, Lon Nol's government decided to build a sugar refinery near the northwestern town of Samlaut. Little compensation was offered to the peasants whose lands were affected by the development. At the same time, the Cambodian army vigorously enforced the collection of taxes from peasants in the region. In response, the soldiers were attacked and a military armory was ransacked in a Communist-led insurrection that soon embraced the whole area. Lon Nol ordered massive army and police repression that killed ten thousand peasants.

As a result of the government's reaction to the uprising, Sihanouk dismissed Lon Nol. However, by mid-1967, the rebellion had spread through six western provinces, and by the end of the year, the Khmer Rouge was said to have a force of 2,000 regulars and thousands of auxiliary peasant militia at their disposition. By 1970, the size of the Khmer Rouge regular army had doubled and 50,000 peasants had joined their part-time forces. Faced with growing insurgency, Sihanouk was forced to move toward the right. In 1969, he denounced the presence of North Vietnamese troops and (South Vietnamese) National Liberation Front forces (the Viet Cong) on Cambodian soil. In May 1969, he denied the Communists access to the port of Sihanoukville, and in June he restored diplomatic relations with the United States. These moves were insufficient from the perspective of pro-U.S. elements in the military and the commercial and political elites. Sihanouk's cousin and longtime rival Prince Sirik Matak (1914–1975) led the opposition to Sihanouk's socialist and neutralist policies.

As early as May 1969, the disgraced former premier Lon Nol began to organize a coup against Sihanouk. Lon Nol established contacts with Cambodian mercenary forces who were fighting for the South Vietnamese government. Sihanouk went to France for medical reasons in January 1970, and in March 1970, while he was in the Soviet Union, seeking assistance, the army under Lon Nol seized power. The United States immediately airlifted several thousand Khmer mercenary troops from Saigon into Phnom Penh to support Lon Nol. President Richard Nixon (in office 1969–1974) publicly welcomed the overthrow of Sihanouk.

H. HELLER

Wars, Genocide, and Invasions

For nearly three decades, Cambodia's leader King Sihanouk (born 1922) had attempted a precarious path between different political factions in Cambodia. In March 1970, when the right-wing former premier Lon Nol (1913–1985) ousted Sihanouk, two decades of civil war began.

Communist insurgents in Cambodia immediately responded to the seizure of power by pro-American Lon Nol. The Cambodian Communists (the Khmer Rouge) and North Vietnamese troops marched on Phnom Penh, the national capital, from the jungles of eastern Cambodia. The fall of the Cambodian capital to the Communists would mean that the country could become a base for aggression by the North Vietnamese against South Vietnam. The United States and its ally South Vietnam rallied to support Lon Nol, while North Vietnam, Communist insurgents in neighboring Laos, and the exiled Prince Sihanouk fought to topple him.

CIVIL WAR

Lon Nol renamed his country the Khmer Republic, and the new regime was initially popular in Phnom Penh. The overthrow of Sihanouk was greeted with enthusiasm by the majority of the city's population. Tens of thousands of young men rushed to join the Cambodian army to throw back the Vietnamese invaders. The United States then invaded eastern Cambodia at the end of April to support Lon Nol's government and to root out North Vietnamese military bases. Exiled in China, Sihanouk announced the formation of a national movement of liberation in league with the Khmer Rouge, the so-called National United Front of Kampuchea (FUNK). He called for the overthrow of Lon Nol's government and for victory by the Communists in neighboring Laos and Vietnam.

The invasion of Cambodia by the United States relieved the immediate pressure on Lon Nol and gave the Cambodian army time to build up strength. In the nine months following the 1970 coup, Lon Nol became totally dependent on the United States, both economically and militarily. From 1970 through 1975, the United States provided a total of $1.6 billion in aid to try to keep the regime afloat. Many Cambodian army officers took advantage of the massive flows of U.S. assistance to line their own pockets. The Cambodian army was largely made up of inexperienced recruits who were no match for the Khmer Rouge and North Vietnamese troops. Two Cambodian government offensives, in July 1970 and August 1971, were routed with heavy losses. In the aftermath, Lon Nol abandoned any attempt at confronting the enemy offensively and focused instead on keeping control of the capital and the main provincial cities.

In rural areas, news of the overthrow of Sihanouk and continued U.S. bombing swelled FUNK's ranks with increasingly militant peasant recruits. By 1972, FUNK had 140,000 regular and irregular armed troops and controlled 85 percent of Cambodia. Sihanouk's control of FUNK waned, and effective power passed into the hands of the highly organized Khmer Rouge cadres (cells of indoctrinated revolutionaries).

Sihanouk's influence over events in Cambodia was eclipsed by mid-1974. While Phnom Penh filled with hundreds of thousands of refugees from the countryside, the government of the Khmer Republic was increasingly hard pressed to feed the urban population by keeping open a supply corridor to the coast. In January 1973, FUNK launched a major offensive. Only a massive escalation of U.S. bombing kept the Communists at bay. During 1974, the Communists' grip on Phnom Penh tightened, and a U.S. airlift became critical. On January 1, 1975, the Khmer Rouge launched a final offensive. On April 1, Lon Nol fled Cambodia, followed by the U.S. diplomatic mission 12 days later. On April 17, the Khmer Rouge occupied Phnom Penh.

Mass graves throughout Cambodia testify to the genocide practiced against their compatriots by the Khmer Rouge (1975–1979).

THE KHMER ROUGE

Upon taking Phnom Penh, whose population was swollen to three million by refugees, the Khmer Rouge ordered its immediate evacuation. Among the reasons given by the Khmer Rouge for the evacuation were fear of further U.S. bombing and severe health and food supply problems. The true reason for the evacuation was a desire to control the population, many of whom had opposed the Khmer Rouge and its extreme ideology.

According to the doctrines of party leaders Pol Pot (formerly Saloth Sar; 1925–1998) and Son Sen (1930–1997), the unequal relation between city and countryside could only be rectified by abandoning the cities. Phnom Penh and other cities were forcibly evacuated within a few days of the cessation of hostilities. The year 1975 is often referred to as Year Zero, the start of one of the most violent social experiments in history. City dwellers were driven into rural collective farms, where they were compelled to plant rice and dig canals. Soldiers, merchants, and civil servants were executed, and at least one million people (possibly double that number) lost their lives. Imbued with rural resentment against city dwellers and indoctrinated into the primitive agrarian Communist notions of the Khmer Rouge, young soldiers from the poor peasant population carried out these policies with considerable cruelty. Major population transfers involving hundreds of thousands of people were ordered in 1975 and also in 1978, officially for security reasons.

The borders of Cambodia were closed, and the Khmer Republic was renamed Democratic Kampuchea. Sihanouk, who had returned from exile in China, was proclaimed chief of state again, but without power. The government was wracked by dissent between different radical and Communist factions. By early 1976, Sihanouk was sidelined, and in April 1976, he was deposed and imprisoned.

Throughout the existence of Democratic Kampuchea, the Khmer Rouge leadership struggled against Stalinist, Maoist, and other factions within the party, and in 1977 and 1978 carried out systematic purges and brutal repression to eliminate them. Anyone perceived as a potential threat, including people with more than a basic education, was killed. Estimates vary, but up to one-fifth of the population may have perished during the Khmer Rouge era as a result of mass killing and maltreatment. The sites of mass murder became known as the "Killing Fields," and the mass slaughter by the Khmer Rouge of their compatriots is usually referred to as genocide.

Among those who perished were many members of the moderate leadership of the Khmer People's Party, who had gone into exile in Hanoi during the 1950s to escape Sihanouk's repression. The party had advocated ties with the Vietnamese and an accommodation with Sihanouk in the 1960s and early 1970s because of his close links with North Vietnam and Communist China. The Khmer People's Party had opposed the Khmer Rouge, whose leadership was in the hands of Pol Pot by 1962. The Khmer Rouge had advocated armed struggle against Sihanouk even to the point of offending North Vietnam and the rest of the Communist bloc.

Supporters of the reformist Sam Rainsy Party hold banners that show the candle, the symbol of the party, in the 2003 election.

RELATIONS WITH VIETNAM

The Khmer Rouge came to view the Vietnamese as sacrificing the interests of the Cambodian revolution for the sake of their own interests. A turning point in relations had come in 1973 with the conclusion of the Paris Peace Accords between the United States and North Vietnam to end the war in Vietnam. Because the North Vietnamese did not consult the Cambodians, the Khmer Rouge felt betrayed. Internationally, Pol Pot's regime closely allied itself with China, in part because the Vietnamese had established cordial relations with the Soviet Union, China's Communist rival. Border clashes broke out between Cambodian and Vietnamese forces in 1976 and escalated in 1977. Vietnam occupied part of Cambodian territory in September 1977, and in December of the same year, the Cambodian army mobilized for war. Vietnamese troops withdrew in January 1978, and the Khmer Rouge heralded the retreat as a victory. An assertive anti-Vietnamese nationalism became a hallmark of Khmer Rouge ideology.

Under the Khmer Rouge, many Cambodians in eastern border areas were punished for suspected complicity with the Vietnamese. In forced evacuations in 1978, up to 50,000 people died and some 150,000 fled into Vietnam. On December 3, 1978, state radio in Hanoi announced the creation of the Khmer National United Front for National Salvation. Led by Heng Samrin (born 1931) and other pro-Vietnamese Communists, the front was a disparate coalition that included non- and anti-Communists. The emergence of the anti–Khmer Rouge front in exile set the stage for a full-scale invasion of Cambodia by 120,000 Vietnamese troops. Khmer Rouge forces were no match for the onslaught, and in early January 1979, Pol Pot's regime fell. The Khmer Rouge leaders who did not surrender fled into Thailand or the forests of northwestern Cambodia. The extent of the mass murders carried out under the Khmer Rouge became evident, and political prisoners, including Sihanouk, were released.

HENG SAMRIN

Heng Samrin, installed as chief of state by a Vietnamese army of occupation, proclaimed the People's Republic of Cambodia. However, the new government had difficulty gaining international recognition. China maintained financial and other support for the dispossessed Khmer Rouge, while the United Nations (UN) continued to recognize the Khmer Rouge regime as the legitimate government of Cambodia. The United States supported to this policy based on its ongoing hostility to Communist Vietnam and the Vietnamese occupation of Cambodia. The remnants of the Khmer Rouge, as well other opposition groups, harassed the new regime from bases in Thailand.

Over the next decade, a slow restoration of economic and social life took place. In 1989, Vietnam withdrew its forces from Cambodia. Heng Samrin announced a cautious move toward private enterprise, and the unpopular rural collectives were dissolved. On May 1, 1989, the name of the country was changed to the State of Cambodia, and political and economic ties with Thailand were restored.

TOWARD RECONSTRUCTION

In 1991, a peace treaty was signed between the government and the opposition, excluding the Khmer Rouge. A supreme national council, including four different political movements, formed under the presidency of Prince Sihanouk, who had again returned from exile, to govern until elections in 1993. A multinational UN body (the United Nations Transitional Authority in Cambodia; UNTAC), with more than 20,000 military and civilian personnel, was established to oversee the process, keep order, resettle refugees, guarantee human rights, and promote the reconstruction of Cambodia.

In the elections, the (conservative royalist) United Front for an Independent, Neutral, and Free Cambodia (FUNCINPEC), led by Prince Norodom Ranariddh (born 1944), a son of Prince Sihanouk, won 58 seats. The former Communist Party led, by Hun Sen (born 1952), obtained 51 seats. The two leaders initially shared the post of prime minister. On September 24, 1993, Cambodia became a kingdom again, and Sihanouk resumed the throne he had abdicated in 1955.

Charged with planning a coup in collusion with the Khmer Rouge, Prince Ranariddh was ousted by military officers loyal to Hun Sen in 1997, but King Sihanouk pardoned his son, who participated in the election of 1998. The 1998 legislative election was won by Hun Sen's party, the Cambodian People's Party (Kanakpak Pracheachon Kampuchea, known in Cambodia as the KPK). The dominant KPK, which has been accused of abuses of power, won an overwhelming victory in local elections in 2002 thanks to its effective organizational and patronage networks. However, the Cambodian national government is usually a coalition because no single party is large enough to enjoy a majority in the assembly.

An internal power struggle within the remnants of the Khmer Rouge led to its collapse. Some leaders defected, and in 1997 Pol Pot was detained, tried, and sentenced to life imprisonment. He died in 1998. Many members of the Khmer Rouge managed to reintegrate themselves into public life, but the issue of bringing to justice those responsible for Khmer Rouge atrocities did not disappear. In 2001, the Cambodian assembly established a tribunal to prosecute those guilty of crimes in the Khmer Rouge era.

Foreign investment, especially from Thailand, brought economic growth to Cambodia. In the twenty-first century, the political landscape also changed. The fortunes of FUNCINPEC waned, and a reformist populist movement, the Sam Rainsy Party, became the second largest party. King Sihanouk, the dominant figure in Khmer life for six decades, abdicated for health reasons in 2004 and was succeeded by his youngest son, Norodom Sihamoni (born 1953).

H. HELLER

CULTURAL EXPRESSION

Literature

The vast majority of the Cambodian population speak Khmer: official figures place the percentage as high as 95 percent. The ancient Khmer culture has been influenced by contact with other Asian civilizations and, in turn, had a profound influence on neighboring peoples.

From the ninth century CE through the fifteenth century, the Khmer Empire encompassed large regions of present-day Vietnam and Thailand. In subsequent centuries, these countries came to exercise influence over Cambodia. In the mid-1860s, France established a colonial protectorate over Cambodia, introducing a new cultural influence. The most devastating threat to traditional Khmer culture came when the extreme left-wing Khmer Rouge seized power in 1975. Intending to sever all links with the country's past and create a classless peasant society, the regime closed schools and cultural and religious institutions, and persecuted artists, writers, and intellectuals.

Sanskrit, seen in these inscriptions, was the written language of the early Khmer Empire.

THE KHMER LITERARY TRADITION

Khmer, the national language of Cambodia, belongs to the Mon-Khmer family of languages. Written examples survive from the seventh century CE, and carved stone inscriptions at Angkor show that as Khmer civilization flourished from the ninth century, its language evolved into what is today called "Old Khmer." Khmer became standardized in the nineteenth century and that is the form of the language spoken today. Khmer also borrows from the classical Indian languages of Sanskrit and Pali and from Thai.

Cambodia's literary tradition was mainly oral. For centuries, most literary works were passed down by professional story-tellers and older family members. A few stories were written on palm leaf manuscripts, but only in the twentieth century, after the French introduced printing technology, did traditional Khmer stories begin to be recorded in written form on a large scale Many Cambodian myths and legends are based on the great epics of Hindu India, such as the *Mahabharata* and the *Ramayana*. The

Reamker, the Khmer version of the *Ramayana*, dates from the sixteenth century and is at the center of the Cambodian literary tradition. A substantial body of Buddhist literature was created in temples from the sixteenth century, and in wider Khmer society the *Jataka*—some 547 stories relating to the life of the Buddha—became hugely popular. Other traditional literary forms include *reuang preng* (folk tales) and *chbap*, moral proverbs in verse form.

MODERN LITERATURE

Under the influence of the French colonists, Cambodian novels began to appear in the 1930s, and by the early 1970s about 50 new titles were published every year. However, the Khmer Rouge regime brought an end to literary production with the destruction of a huge number of books and manuscripts and, with its widespread slaughter, the deaths of many people who had kept the storytelling tradition alive.

Much Cambodian literature produced in the 1990s and the early years of the twenty-first century has been written by Khmers living abroad. The writing mainly deals with the Khmer Rouge years. A notable example is Haing S. Ngor (1940–1996), a physician and later an Academy Award–winning actor for his role in the 1984 movie *The Killing Fields*, who described life under the Khmer Rouge in *Haing Ngor: A Cambodian Odyssey* (1988). Journalist Dith Pran (born 1942), whose story is told in *The Killing Fields*, compiled *Children of Cambodia's Killing Fields* (1997), a collection of accounts of survivors of the Khmer Rouge genocide. A patriarch of Cambodian Buddhism, Maha Ghosananda (born 1929) has written many spiritual works, including *Step by Step: Meditations on Wisdom and Compassion* (1992).

R. BEAN

Art and Architecture

The culture of ancient and classical Cambodia was influenced extensively by that of India. It is not known when relations with India commenced, but it was probably during the first millennium BCE, through trade routes that linked China via southeastern Asia with India and then as far west as the Mediterranean Sea.

Physical evidence for the Indian religions Brahmanism and Buddhism, in the form of inscriptions, sculpture, and temples, can be found in Cambodia dating from around the mid-third century CE, when these religions had already firmly established themselves in the region.

Other influences on Khmer culture came from within southeastern Asia, mainly the island of Java (now part of Indonesia) and the kingdom of Champa (in present-day central and southern Vietnam). Javanese influence is visible in decorative elements, most notably the *kala-makara* (two mythical beings) combination found in door lintels. This characteristic decoration originated in Javanese temples. Cham influence is evident in brick work.

KHMER TEMPLES

Temples from the Khmer Empire, which ruled much of the region from the ninth through the fourteenth centuries, are the most characteristic buildings of Cambodian architecture. The temples of Angkor, designated a UNESCO World Heritage Site in 1992, are the best-known buildings in Cambodia, and their designs remain influential on Cambodian architecture in modern times.

In addition to the concentration of remains from the Khmer Empire in the Angkor plain of central northern Cambodia, temples are found all over Cambodia, in the south of present-day Laos, and in northeastern Thailand. Most of the early Khmer Hindu sacred complexes were dedicated to the god Shiva (the deity of destruction and of regeneration), with fewer honoring Vishnu (the Hindu preserver god). There were also some sanctuaries dedicated to the deities of Mahayana Buddhism (the school of Buddhism that was paramount in Cambodia).

The main building materials used in Khmer temples were laterite, sandstone, and brick. Laterite, found as a soft soil that hardens irreversibly when exposed to air, was used for foundations, enclosure walls, stepped pyramids, and, in early temples, even for whole buildings. Sandstone, a sedimentary rock, is a very soft stone and can be carved almost like wood or ivory. It was used for the decorative elements in early temples, such as doors, lintels, columns, and figures. From the early eleventh century onward, sandstone became the preferred building material for entire temple complexes. Brick was a readily available material and could be produced in large quantities locally. The binding element was a strong vegetable glue, making the brick buildings the most structurally sound, since sandstone and laterite blocks were merely stacked without using cement or proper jointing techniques.

The lack of cement and jointing—as well as the effects of invasive undergrowth over the centuries—are the main reasons for the deterioration of most early Khmer buildings. Usually, the brick and laterite parts of the temples were covered in plaster and stucco (a fine plaster used in decoration, often on exterior walls), which probably was painted, although no pigmentation remains to prove this.

EARLY TEMPLES

Early Khmer temples were brick towers built on platforms. They had a square, rectangular chamber that housed either an image or a lingam, the symbolic phallic representation of Shiva. At the sixth century Hindu temple at Sambor Prei Kuk, a huge complex in central Cambodia, the central chamber is unusually octagonal. The exterior of the temple chambers was elaborately decorated with stucco molded onto the brick work. Other decoration included sandstone elements, such as door frames, windows, and sometimes lintels. The decorative program did not change much over time, despite a change of the main building material to sandstone. Next to the doors, guardian figures were set in blind arches (arches that are filled at one end). Elaborately carved lintels were inserted above the doors, one real door facing east and false ones in the other three directions. These false doors were purely decorative and had no structural purpose. The decorative motifs usually incorporated the guardian deity of the respective direction the lintel was facing, surrounded by garlands, foliage, and miniature figures. Next to the doors were elaborately carved columns. This pattern was repeated in the false stories of the superstructure, of which there were usually four.

Over time, the complexity of the layouts of Khmer temple compounds steadily increased. Designs evolved from single tower structures to sites with many buildings. The secondary buildings were used for practical purposes, for instance the preparation of offerings, dance and music performances, or the recital and study of sacred texts.

The functions of these sites were manifold. Fundamentally, they were places of worship, visited by the nobility, priests, and commoners alike. They would have been bustling centers of the community, with people coming from all over the kingdom to worship at the central temples. In addition, they were centers of learning, with students living within the enclosure walls. They were also the centers of administration: economically, the Khmer Empire was organized through a temple network that was coordinated from the central temples at Angkor, the capital.

THE LAYOUT OF TEMPLES

Temples such as those constructed at Angkor were built as representations of the macrocosm (the universe). Although Indian treatises contain many descriptions of the universe, they all share fundamental elements. Mount Meru, the cosmic mountain and the axis of the world, is at the center of the horizontal dimension, with its central peak surrounded by four buttress mountains. Concentrically around Mount Meru were seven mountain ranges and oceans, surrounded at the edge by the iron mountains. Vertically, Mount Meru links the realms of the gods above to the world of humans in the center to the netherworlds below. This cosmology was directly re-created in the temples of Angkor. The central shrines in the temples at Angkor represent the peaks of Meru and were built on top of a stepped pyramid that symbolized the slopes of Meru. In earlier temples, enclosure walls surround the pyramid; in later temples, continuous galleries surround the central structure. The walls or galleries represent the concentric mountain ranges.

Inseparably linked to the symbolic layout of the temples were the extensive water management structures in the central district of Angkor, including the *baray*s (large rectangular tanks), temple and city moats, and canals. The stretches of water signify the oceans and lakes surrounding Mount Meru. However, the water features were not merely symbolic. They also served very practical purposes, such as flood control, water drainage, and small-scale irrigation. The overall orientation of the temples is usually toward the east, the rising sun, and the direction of Shiva, to whom most of the temple complexes were dedicated. There are some exceptions, however, the most significant being Angkor Wat, where the temples are dedicated to Vishnu, whose direction is the west.

The symbolism of the layout would have been apparent to Khmer worshippers. By approaching the central sanctuary, the devotee transcended the world of humans and entered into the realm of the divine on the journey both around the temple (the *pradakshina*) and up toward the gods.

BUDDHIST ARCHITECTURE

The decline of the Khmer Empire during the fourteenth and fifteenth centuries brought about the move of the capital southward, briefly to Oudong and later to Phnom Penh, the present Cambodian national capital. Phnom Penh was founded in the late fourteenth century at a time when the Cambodians were adopting Buddhism. The change of religion necessitated

A Cambodian sculptor carves a statue from stone. During the rule of the Khmer Rouge (1975–1979), such artistic expression would have been banned in favor of politically biased forms of art. In recent years, traditional forms of art have been encouraged.

fundamentally different places of worship. Instead of sanctuary towers surrounded by subsidiary shrines housing icons for individual worship, the new temples comprised communal halls for the laity (*vihan*) and the monks (*bot*), together with living quarters for the monks. These buildings were constructed from wood, with elaborately carved door and window eaves, which in some *wat*s (pagodas or temples) were painted or even gilded.

The interior is sometimes dark, with wall paintings depicting scenes of the life of the Buddha, seated Buddhas, or scenes of the lives of Bodhisattvas (Buddhas-to-be). Usually, the halls faced east, with images of the Buddha—one large main image surrounded by numerous smaller ones—seated in front of the western wall. The style of the buildings was generally very similar to the *wat*s in Siam (modern Thailand), which had become one of the main political powers in mainland southeastern Asia by the fifteenth century. The Thais were a strong influence on the arts and architecture of the Khmers.

An example of the Buddhist architecture of Cambodia is the Silver Pagoda in Phnom Penh. Its name derives from the floor of the *vihan*, which is comprised of 5,000 silver slabs. The building is surrounded by a number of stupas that house the ashes of monks and members of Cambodia's royal family. A stupa is a dome-shaped Buddhist monument, derived from a burial mound and intended to house relics of the Buddha. Within *wat*s, small stupas are constructed to enshrine the ashes of prominent monks or members of the lay community. The compound of the Silver Pagoda, adjacent to the Royal Palace, is enclosed by galleries whose inward facing walls depict scenes of the *Reamker*, the Khmer version of the Indian *Ramayana*, one of the two great epics of Indian culture.

DOMESTIC ARCHITECTURE

Nothing remains of the settlements that surrounded the sacred early Khmer temple compounds. Vernacular architecture, even the palace of the king, was constructed from perishable material, such as bamboo, wood, and palm leaves. Stone was deemed worthy only for the dwellings of the gods, who were as permanent as the temple buildings constructed to house their images. The only remaining evidence for the once large settlements adjoining the temples are pottery shards, house mounds, and the water tanks that were shared by several families.

Houses built during the period of the Khmer Empire were very similar to current architecture. Homes were built on stilts, with storage space beneath to house animals or to store household items, such as looms. Walls would have been constructed from wood, bamboo mats, or woven palm leaves, and the roof from palm leaves or tiles. The interior of houses belonging to ordinary people would have consisted of one large room, shared by all family members, with the stove either in a corner or underneath the house. Additional buildings in a domestic compound included the rice granary, which was made of clay, and, if it was the home of a wealthy family, a second building linked by open-air platforms.

Cambodia's rich vernacular architecture developed over centuries but little is documented. In recent times, many of the traditional methods, building materials, and styles of ornamentation have been replaced by Thai- and Vietnamese-influenced modern structures that are more generic in style.

COLONIAL ARCHITECTURE

Phnom Penh was confirmed as the capital of Cambodia in 1865, when King Norodom (reigned 1860–1904) moved his court there. In 1863, Cambodia became a French protectorate, and from that date French architects and planners influenced the appearance of Phnom Penh and the other main cities, such as Battambang in the northwest of the country. The downtown areas of Cambodian cities were characterized by French colonial buildings, and, in the case of Phnom Penh, by a plan of wide tree-lined boulevards and canals.

Phnom Penh had grown along the banks of the three rivers, the Sab, Mekong, and Bassac rivers, close to their confluence. The mid-nineteenth century city was little more than one long single road parallel to the waterfront. Under the French, the city grew, and perpendicular roads and canals were constructed, enabling a rapid expansion of the city. Phnom Penh was informally subdivided into "villages," or ethnic areas, for instance the Chinese district near the New Market and the Khmer areas around the new Royal Palace, which was completed in 1870. The Khmer royal palace was for the first time constructed from stone; it incorporated many traditional architectural features, for example, the roof shape and the allocation of different ceremonial and other functions to separate buildings.

MODERN ARCHITECTURE

In the post-independence period of the 1960s, Phnom Penh developed into a truly cosmopolitan city. One of its main planners was Vann Molyvann (born 1926), a Cambodian architect educated in France, who designed numerous projects, both public and private. His work ranges from the national sports complex (the so-called Olympic Stadium) and the national theater (the Preah Sura-marit Theater) to the Independence Monument, inaugurated in 1958 to celebrate independence from France. The plan of the Olympic Stadium, with its surrounding moats, was modeled on Angkor Wat. Vann Molyvann also designed a range of houses known as the "One Hundred Houses" spread throughout Phnom Penh and in Sihanouk City, a large urban area of apartment buildings near the Bassac River.

The mass evacuation of Phnom Penh during the Khmer Rouge era (1975–1979), the subsequent invasion by Vietnamese forces in 1979, and the following decade of civil war prevented the natural evolution of most cities in Cambodia, particularly Phnom Penh. Buildings fell to ruins or were later used by squatter communities. Since the mid-1990s, with the influx of tourist and international revenues, old buildings are being restored. Projects, such as a new shopping mall in Phnom Penh, tend to be concrete, steel, and glass structures, devoid of Khmer architectural characteristics. In the first years of the twenty-first century, development in Phnom Penh was rapid but with little cohesive overall planning.

DECORATIVE ARTS AND FINE ART

The Khmers are extremely gifted carvers in both wood and stone, a legacy that dates from at least the construction of the temples at Angkor. In modern times, artisans create copies of the classical sculpture of Angkor for the tourist market. Weaving also plays a significant cultural role. Textiles have functional, social, and religious significance. For instance, the *bidan*, a cloth that portrays Buddhist scenes, is part of many rituals and is traditionally draped over the altar in a Buddhist *wat* (temple). In the early years of the twentieth century, the French revived Cambodia's waning tradition of metalworking. Silver work, in particular, was popular, and artisans made intricate silver boxes that were used to contain a herbal stimulant called betel.

During the years of Khmer Rouge rule in the late 1970s, many artists were killed, and Communist political themes dominated Khmer art. Cambodia experienced a renaissance in both painting and sculpture in the 1990s. However, modern themes are much influenced by the Khmer Rouge period or by Angkor (themes that reflect the heritage of Angkor are common, partly because of the large public and tourist demand). In the twenty-first century, Khmer artists began to break free from earlier thematic restraints and made an attempt to express sociopolitical commentary and criticism through art.

A. HAENDEL

Angkor Wat

Angkor Wat is the largest and most magnificent of the one hundred temples that survive from the ancient city of Angkor. It was constructed at the peak of Khmer power to glorify King Suryavarman II (reigned 1112–1150) and Vishnu, the Hindu god with whom he identified. It is regarded as the pinnacle of Khmer architecture.

Angkor Wat is located in what was the southeastern corner of Angkor and occupies an enormous site of nearly 494 acres (200 hectares). A huge rectangular reservoir surrounds the temple, which rises up through a series of three rectangular terraces to the central shrine and tower. This arrangement reflects the traditional Khmer idea of the temple mountain, in which the temple represents Mount Meru, the home of the gods in Hinduism. Angkor Wat was largely built from sandstone blocks, with hard laterite rock, which has a high iron content, being used for some of the hidden structural elements and for the outer walls. It is not known what agent bound the stone blocks together, but some type of natural resin is usually suggested.

Uniquely for Khmer temples, Angkor Wat faces west. Because west is symbolically the direction of death, the orientation once led scholars to conclude that Angkor Wat was primarily a tomb. However, Vishnu is frequently associated with the west, and most authorities now consider that Angkor Wat was intended to serve as both a temple and a mausoleum for King Suryavarman.

Some researchers have suggested that the architect, or architects, of Angkor Wat encoded calendrical information in the design. This interpretation proposes that the alignment of the site and the arrangement of the decoration record cycles of the sun and moon. Other researchers suggest that the layout of Angkor Wat represents astronomical phenomena, in particular the constellation Draco, but this interpretation is not widely believed.

Angkor Wat is the largest, and best known, temple in a city of temples that is often claimed to be the largest religious site in the world. Originally, the eleventh-century Baphuon Temple was the central temple. Although different Khmer kings built temples in the complex, one of the most extensive building programs at Angkor was under Suryavarman II in the twelfth century. The Hindu architecture of Angkor Wat greatly influenced later building styles and conventions over the three hundred years during which most of the Angkor complex was built.

Jayarvarman II (reigned 1181–1220) also greatly embellished the site during a building program that included the reconstruction of the massive Bayon Temple, which features 3,936 feet (1,200 m) of bas-relief (sculpture in which the carving is slightly raised from the surrounding surface and is not undercut). Jayarvarman also built the large Ta Prohm temple complex, which is enclosed by a moat. Regarded by some scholars as the most beautiful temple at Angkor, Ta Prohm has not been restored and, unlike Angkor Wat, is still surrounded by jungle and is seldom visited by tourists. Jayarvarman also added the large Preah Khan temple, which is well preserved, as well as several other temples.

The Angkor Wat temple complex has five towers that symbolize the peaks of a mountain. The wide moat in the foreground represents the oceans surrounding the edge of the world.

The entire city of Angkor was huge because different monarchs and other members of the Khmer royal family desired great buildings intended to be the center of their own cults, through which they could be assured of immortality. Temples were constructed on a vast scale to reflect the prestige of their royal founders. Khmer rulers organized enormous resources of labor and material to carry out their construction programs, but although their object was to gain prestige for themselves, their dynasty, and their

capital city, these building programs diverted labor and resources from other projects, and Khmer subjects were overtaxed to make the work possible.

Like the other temples in the complex, Angkor Wat was built as a Hindu place of worship but was converted to Buddhist worship in the fourteenth and fifteenth centuries. In 1431, the Thais attacked Angkor, looting the city. In 1432, Angkor was abandoned, and the temples gradually deteriorated, owing to lack of use. Among the Angkor temples, Angkor Wat is unusual in that it was never completely abandoned. Although neglected, Angkor Wat continued to be used for Buddhist worship,

if only intermittently. Angkor's survival was also helped by the great moat surrounding the site, which partly deterred the encroachment of the jungle.

When French colonists first arrived in Cambodia in the 1860s, they were puzzled and impressed by the ruins of Angkor Wat and, as their knowledge of the region increased, by the many other temples at Angkor. The French characterized Angkor as a mysterious lost city, and initially, French explorers and scholars did not believe that the Khmers had built the complex themselves. They thought that Angkor Wat had been constructed by another people who had at one time conquered the Khmers.

Music and Performing Arts

Cambodia is bordered by Vietnam, Thailand, and Laos, and the culture, language, arts, and beliefs of the Khmer, the majority population, are related to those of neighboring countries. However, the arts of the Khmer, including music and the performing arts, are distinct in many ways.

From 1975 through 1979, Cambodia experienced great suffering under the extreme left-wing Khmer Rouge regime. It is estimated that during this period 90 percent of all performing artists in Cambodia were killed. Since 1979, the arts have again been nurtured, and young musicians and dancers are trained formally in schools and in the Royal University of Fine Arts in Phnom Penh, the national capital.

Through its long history, Cambodian culture has incorporated influences from its immediate neighbors. The arts of China and particularly India have also strongly influenced Khmer culture, but despite the effect of neighboring cultures, Cambodia has developed unique musical styles that have, in turn, influenced the arts of its neighbors, particularly Thailand.

TRADITIONAL INSTRUMENTS

The Khmer distinguish three broad categories of instruments: percussion instruments (*kroeung damm*), wind instruments (*kroeung phlomm*), and stringed instruments (*kroeung khse*). Percussion instruments include small and large hand cymbals (known as *chhing* and *chhap*), bamboo or wooden clappers (*krapp*), xylophones (*roneat ek* and *roneat thung*), metal keyed instruments (*roneat dek* and *roneat thong*), gong-chimes in circular frames (*korng vung tauch* and *korng vung thomm*), single gongs (*korng mong*), and various drums. The drums, often in sets, include those played with stick beaters (*skor*), as well as a small, two-headed barrel drum (the *sampho*), and frame and goblet drums. Wind instruments include fipple flutes (straight flutes that have a whistle mouthpiece and finger holes) known as *khloy*, quadruple-reed oboes (called *sralai*), and mouth organs (*ken*). Stringed instruments include various sizes of two- and three-stringed fiddles (*tror*), a plucked lute (*chapey*), plucked zither (known as the *krapeu* or *takhe*), and the hammered dulcimer (*khimm*), which was introduced from China.

ENSEMBLES

Cambodians usually distinguish between court music, which was cultivated at the royal court and now in schools; and folk music, which is practiced among villagers. The main court ensemble, and the loudest with both stringed and percussion instruments, is the *pinn peat*, which dates back at least to the twelfth century CE and the period of the Khmer Empire court at Angkor. In modern times, the *pinn peat* consists of vocalists accompanied by one or two xylophones (*roneat*), one or two oboes (*sralai*), one or two *korng*, a pair of *chhing*, *sampho*, and sometimes a pair of large *skor thomm*. The *sralai* and *roneat* play independent variations of a single melody. This use of different "voices" is known as a heterophonic variation. The *chhing* punctuate the phrases, alternating between closed (*chap*) and open (*ching*) sounds, and the *sampho* directs the tempo and flow of the performance. In addition to playing for religious ceremonies, the *pinn peat* often accompanies other performing arts: masked dance-dramas (known as *lkhaon khaol*) and several varieties of leather shadow puppet plays (called *sbek*).

The softer sound of the *mohori* ensemble is a great contrast to the *pinn peat*. A *mohori* ensemble comprises the *roneat*, *khloy*, one or more fiddles (*tror*), *khimm*, three-stringed zither (*krapeu*), *chhing*, and a pair of small drums (*thaun* and *rumanea*). The *mohori* ensemble is usually joined by one or more singers, who sing in alternation with the full ensemble. The music repertory includes narrative songs, love songs, and other light, secular pieces.

FOLK AND POPULAR MUSIC

Folk music utilizes many of the same instruments as the court ensembles. Performers of folk music may accompany weddings (*kar*), funerals (*korng skor*), and ceremonies of spirit-worship (*arakk*). Several forms of folk theater also involve musical accompaniment. Popular traditional folk theater called *lkhaon yike* presents *Jataka* tales (stories of the Buddha's life) in dance and song. The music and staging of the *lkhaon basakk* tradition show a strong influence from Chinese culture. Small instrumental ensembles also traditionally accompany boxing in Cambodia. Improvised *ayai* (repartee singing with a female and male singer performing alternately), long narrative songs called *chrieng chapey*, and folk dances are also usually accompanied by small instrumental groups.

In modern times, the Khmer also enjoy popular music that combines Western instruments, harmonies, and rhythms with Khmer elements. Modern Cambodian popular music, which is influenced by popular music from Thailand, is heard on the radio and is available in recorded form.

R. A. SUTTON

Classical Dance

Three main forms of dance are popular in Cambodia: classical court dance, folk dance, and modern Western dance. Court dance dates back to the Khmer Empire and is at least one thousand years old. It is characterized by the elaborate costumes worn by the dancers, the elegance of the sinuous movements of the dance, and the hand gestures (known as *kbach*) made by the dancers. Traditionally, dancers were trained from age six at the royal palace and the monarch was the patron of classical dance.

The elegant hand gestures that a Khmer dancer learns are largely drawn from nature. They include the *kbach chung aul* (a pointing gesture that represents a bud), the *kbach cheap* (a flower), and the *kbach koung* (a fruit). The *kbach sung luc* is a backward hand gesture that represents a leaf.

The classical repertoire comprises dramas, romances, and epics that are drawn from the Indian subcontinent, including epics that relate the stories of the Hindu gods. In the twelfth century CE, some dance dramas that relate the life of the Buddha were added to the repertoire. However, classical dance is made up largely of portrayals of episodes from the *Reamker*, the Cambodian version of the Hindu epic the *Ramayana*. The *Ramayana* is a two-thousand year old epic of 48,000 lines that describes the adventures of Rama, an incarnation of the Hindu god Vishnu. It is a moral tale that describes the trials and tribulations of Rama. Although the *Reamker* is based on the original

Hindu epic, it contains many elements that are unique to Cambodian culture. However, not all court dances are drawn from the *Reamker*. Some court dances, such as the Apsara, a dance performed by women, are modern. The Apsara, inspired by the reliefs of dancers on the ruined temple walls of Angkor Wat, was developed in the 1950s by Princess Norodom Bopha Devi (born 1943).

The ancient art of Khmer classical dancing was interrupted by the Khmer Rouge dictatorship (from 1970 to 1975). However, the tradition was kept alive by survivors in refugee camps, mainly in Thailand. Royal patronage continues into modern times because King Norodom Sihamoni (who has reigned since 2004) was trained as a dancer and was for many years a noted choreographer.

Popular dance has two main forms: all-male ensembles known as *lakhon khol*, which perform traditional dramas, and shadow theater (*sbaek thom*). Both styles concentrate on the performance of episodes from the *Reamker*. A seven-night dance performance marks the New Year in some village communities. Some folk dances mimic everyday activities, such as fishing and hunting, and reinforce traditional gender roles.

Students learn classical dance at the Royal University of Fine Arts in Phnom Penh. The Apsara dance is one of the elements of Khmer classical dance.

Festivals and Ceremonies

During a turbulent history in the second half of the twentieth century, Cambodia had several different systems of government and many different public holidays. Since the restoration of the monarchy in 1993, the principal public holidays celebrate traditional festivals and events connected with the monarch.

The main public holiday in Cambodia is Independence Day, November 1. Independence Day marks the formal restoration of national sovereignty to Cambodia in 1953 following French colonial rule. The holiday is celebrated by public events, parades, and ceremonies, particularly in Phnom Penh, the national capital. Public ceremonies generally involve many thousands of troops, police, students, and workers. While speeches and messages in the media mark the national day, the occasion is not generally a time for family celebrations.

RELIGIOUS AND TRADITIONAL HOLIDAYS

The most colorful festival is the Water Festival, a public holiday that is celebrated in the fall. More than one million people flock to the banks of the Sab and Mekong rivers to enjoy boat races. Several hundred boats race in pairs on the rivers and the day ends with elaborate water floats and firework displays. Water Festival celebrations eclipse all other public holidays in Cambodia. The festival marks the change in the direction of the flow of the Sab River as the waterway reverts to its normal downstream flow after several months during which water flows upstream, forced northward by floods on the Mekong River. The holiday is a public thanksgiving to the rivers for their water and fish and for sustaining agriculture.

Dak Ben, the last day of Pchum Ben (the festival of the dead), is a culmination of a 15-day period to honor the dead and to appease the spirits of ancestors. The festival, which is marked according to the lunar calendar, varies from one year to the next in the Western calendar and is celebrated in the fall. On Dak Ben, people journey to the local Buddhist temple to offer food and other gifts to the resident monks. Traditional dishes include sticky rice with beans and pork fat and banana cakes. During Pchum Ben, rice is placed near the temple well to appease the spirits of the ancestors. People pray at the temple or at home, lighting incense and candles to illuminate the way for the spirits.

The birthday of the Buddha is a public holiday in May. Meak Bochea Day (normally in February) is celebrated at the full moon to commemorate a historic spontaneous gathering of monks to hear the word of the Buddha. The plowing ceremony, also in May, marks the beginning of the rice planting season. In a field next to the royal palace, the king leads a plow that is pulled by cattle. The cattle are presented with offerings on silver plates, and the animals' choice is believed to predict events.

Pairs of boats race against each other on the Mekong River during Cambodia's popular Water Festival. Each boat represents a different community, usually a village.

ROYAL HOLIDAYS

Cambodia's royal holidays reflect public respect shown to King Norodom Sihanouk (born 1922; reigned 1941–1955 and 1993–2004) and his son and successor King Norodom Sihamoni (born 1953). The birthday of Norodom Sihamoni in May is a two- or three-day public holiday. Other public holidays are October 31, the birthday Norodom Sihanouk, and June 18, the birthday of Queen Norodom Minineath Sihanouk (born 1936). The coronation day of Norodom Sihamoni (October 29) is a holiday.

INTERNATIONAL AND OTHER HOLIDAYS

Cambodians mark New Year's Day on January 1 according to the Western calendar, but Cambodian New Year (Bonn Chaul Chhnam) in the spring is marked on the lunar calendar. Bonn Chaul Chhnam, which lasts at least three days. is the most important holiday of the year. A great family celebration, people return from the cities to their home villages to meet with their relatives. People celebrate the anniversary by cleaning their homes for a fresh start for the new year, by making offerings at a Buddhist temple, and by playing traditional games.

Other public holidays include January 7 (the anniversary of the fall of Khmer Rouge in 1979), March 8 (Women's Day), May 1 (International Labor Day), June 1 (Children's Day), September 24 (Constitution Day), and December 10 (Human Rights Day).

K. ROMANO-YOUNG

Food and Drink

Cambodia's extensive Khmer Empire, which flourished from the eleventh through the sixteenth centuries, developed on the back of a rice-based economy. The heart of the empire was around the rich inland fishing grounds of the Mekong River, the Sab River, and Tonle Sap lake. Rice and fish are still the staples of Cambodian cooking.

From the 1970s, Cambodia entered a period of extreme political instability and civil war. Hundreds of thousands of Cambodians perished in genocide that was instigated by the Khmer Rouge regime (1975–1979), and many thousands starved. Survival took the place of cuisine, and after the Khmer Rouge and a successor Vietnamese-sponsored regime fell, large numbers of Cambodians relied upon international agencies to feed them. Since the United Nations (UN) peace accord of 1991, the nation has struggled to rebuild its agriculture, which is based on growing rice, raising livestock, and growing corn and sugarcane. From the 1990s, people were able to eat more as greater quantities of food and varieties of ingredients became available.

FISH DISHES

Freshwater fish are a major part of the Cambodian diet. Sea fish are also eaten, but not in such great numbers, although shrimp and crabs are especially popular. Khmer specialties include seafood fritters, grilled fish rolled in a spinach or lettuce leaf, and *amok*, a dish of fish cooked in coconut milk. Fish dishes are frequently flavored with lime, lemongrass, lemon thyme, mint, cilantro, galangal (a pungent member of the ginger family), garlic, pepper, salt, soy sauce, and the fish sauce *dik trey*. Cambodia's cooking shares many traits with the cuisines of neighboring China, Vietnam, and Thailand, but the influence of France, the former colonial power, is evident in a tradition of making good bread.

CAMBODIAN MEALS

Different families have different customs at mealtimes: some eat with their fingers, while others use a spoon or chopsticks. Breakfast is a soup of pork or fish and rice, or noodles with pork or beef, or sweet beef soup, served with bread, coffee, or lemon tea.

A Khmer lunch or dinner usually includes soup (*samla*), such as spiced pork-ball soup full of cellophane noodles (*misuor*) or a selection of pork, fish sauce, and eggs. Rice noodles (*kuy deav*) are popular street foods and can easily be picked up on the way home. Rice is steamed lightly. Skewers of meat or fish, spring rolls, and rice come with dips of *dik trey*. Beef may be marinated in chili, lime, garlic, and galangal.

Certain dishes are often served to tourists. *Cambogee* beef consists of thin slices of beef soaked in a marinade of mashed jalapeños, lemongrass, lime leaves, garlic, galangal, and oyster sauce, and cooked on a skewer over hot coals. *Sapek*, another dish cooked on a skewer over hot coals, is made of small pieces of pork tenderloin alternated with rounds of Chinese sausage and strips of pork fat.

The most common beverages are water and tea. Palm wine is popular, and wealthier Cambodians also drink a rice-based spirit called *choum* and locally made brandy. With meals, tourists are usually offered beer or seltzer water.

Desserts include jackfruit pudding and sticky sweet rice cakes. Foods for holidays and festivals include a noodle soup called *samlaw misuor* and *num ansom*, a cake that is shaped like a cylinder, which is made for Pchum Ben, the festival of the dead. Celebration dishes are favorites at the Water Festival in the fall and the plowing ceremony at the end of May.

K. ROMANO-YOUNG

A Cambodian market trader sells fresh vegetables, herbs, and spices from the street in Phnom Penh.

DAILY LIFE

Religion

The majority of Cambodians or Khmer identify themselves religiously as Theravada Buddhists. It is not uncommon to hear Khmer people suggest that being Khmer means being Buddhist.

Although small numbers of Khmer practice Christianity or Islam, the ideas and practices of Buddhism are fundamental to the definition of Khmer culture. Buddhist ideas underlie history, art, literature, education, shared moral values, and ritual practices. The exercise of political power, too, remains at least symbolically tied to Buddhist religion.

BUDDHISM

Buddhism was brought to Cambodia from India in the second century CE. Khmers adopted many Indian religious, philosophical, and political ideas and art forms, blending them with their indigenous animist and spirit-based beliefs. As Khmer chiefdoms grew into a larger, unified kingdom, the Khmer may have been attracted to Buddhism's more cosmopolitan worldview. Between the ninth and fourteenth centuries, Khmer kings built the kingdom of Angkor, which dominated much of mainland southeastern Asia. A strong link between religion and the state began to develop during this period.

After the thirteenth century, the Khmer were increasingly drawn to the Theravada interpretation of Buddhism, which included a strong emphasis on karma and merit making. One of the Buddha's most central theories concerned karma, which refers to any action performed with the body, speech, or thought. Thus, understanding right ways of behaving, speaking, and thinking is important to Khmer Buddhists.

RELIGION IN MODERN CAMBODIA

In Cambodia today, Buddhism is important for its central role in moral and ritual life, as well as in education. Monks living in monasteries, along with a growing number of lay people, practice meditation to help them achieve mindfulness.

A statue of the Buddha is honored with offerings of incense and flowers.

Meditators believe that the practice will help them recognize the results of their karma, or actions, and be more attentive to doing what is right. Many Khmer people also participate in merit-making ceremonies at their local Buddhist monastery, called a *wat*. At the *wat*, they come together at festivals throughout the year to earn merit by offering gifts of food, robes, or medicine to the monastery. Merit making is also seen as a way to help ease suffering. Giving gifts to the *sangha* (the community of monks) honors and helps loved ones who have died. Merit earned through giving can be dedicated to deceased relatives to help them achieve a better life when they are reborn.

Since substandard education is a problem in many parts of Cambodia, especially for poor and rural people, some young men and boys ordain as Buddhist monks or novices in order to obtain a better education. Women and girls are not admitted to the Buddhist order in Cambodia, although some live in monasteries, observe monastic rules, practice meditation, and look after the monks.

In 1975, the extreme Communist Khmer Rouge movement led by Pol Pot (1925–1998) took power. Along with massive forced migration and the deaths of more than one million people (possibly many more) from violence, disease, and starvation, the Khmer Rouge executed many monks and forcibly expelled others from temples. Although the Khmer Rouge tried to eradicate Buddhist institutions, practices, and influence entirely, many survivors of Khmer Rouge camps report that they secretly remained Buddhist in their hearts. After the regime was ousted in 1979, Buddhism slowly reemerged in Cambodia under the subsequent Communist-led governments. Restrictions on religious practice were finally lifted after 1989, and since then monasteries have been rebuilt and Buddhist life has been widely reconstituted. Politicians continue to patronize the *sangha* as a means of demonstrating their fitness for leadership.

A. HANSEN

Family, Society, and Welfare

Cambodia is a poor country that is unable to afford comprehensive health, social security, and modern education systems. Decades of civil war and the destructive dictatorship of the Khmer Rouge in the late 1970s destroyed much of the nation's fabric. In modern times, Cambodia is gradually rebuilding, and there is considerable reliance upon international aid.

The Khmer Rouge period had a destructive effect upon Cambodian society. Hardly a family was untouched by the genocide practiced by the regime. Large numbers of people were also uprooted through a policy of city evacuation to establish a classless rural society. Millions of people became refugees within their own country. The resettlement of the cities began in 1979, when Vietnamese forces overthrew the Khmer Rouge. However, the disruption to city life left a legacy, and today's urban communities have, in part, been formed from new groupings of peoples. The old urban society was destroyed.

STATUS

The revolution that the Khmer Rouge attempted to impose upon the people of Cambodia was particularly difficult in a conservative society in which status is important. The hierarchical nature of Cambodian society is reflected in the Khmer language. There are many pronouns that reflect the status of the person who is speaking and the person who is being addressed. The pronoun used instantly indicates a person's position in society. Age is the most important determinant of status: an older person is treated with respect, and children are taught to honor the elderly from infancy. Siblings are called "older" or "younger" rather than "brother" or "sister." People are commonly referred to by kinship names: a tradesman might be called "uncle" and an old woman is called "grandmother." The form of address also reflects social position: family wealth, the job of the individual, the reputation of the family, and even religious observance. Someone of a much higher class will be addressed by a term that implies age and

Traditional Cambodian family homes are made from wood and are often raised on stilts above flood level. The roofs and walls are often made of thatch.

therefore seniority. Determination of a person's position in the social structure is complex. In Cambodia's Buddhist society, a person's status reflects his or her merit in this life, and a high-ranking person is assumed to be reincarnated in a higher status in the next life if he or she is benevolent to those who are less fortunate.

FAMILY

The center of Cambodian society is the nuclear family: a mother, father, and their children. In many southeast Asian nations, the extended family—the nuclear family plus older generations, cousins, and other kin—is the most important kin group. In Cambodia, ties with more distant relatives tend to be looser than in many Asian societies, and Cambodians have no tradition of family names. Few families can trace their forebears back beyond two generations. The smaller family unit forms an economic unit on the land, growing sufficient food for the family group, cooperating, and sharing resources.

In the villages, where the majority of Cambodians live, neighbor relations are also important. Rural communities cooperate in many tasks, including house building. Community

A United Nations official examines a child at a field health center. In 1991, the UN began to reconstruct Cambodia's health system.

life revolves around the temple (*wat*), many of which have been reconstructed since their neglect or destruction under the Khmer Rouge regime. There is a strong feeling of community and local pride.

Two unique Cambodian adoptive relationships also establish strong ties outside the nuclear family. An individual of any age may formally establish an adoptive relationship with someone with whom she or he has no kin ties. This traditional practice allows a person to acquire a patron or guardian. Similarly, a person may establish a sibling relationship with a person who is not related. These relationships, called *thoa*, extend the family through nonlegal adoption. A different relationship, called *kloeu* (loosely translated as "blood brothers"), is established between two male friends. The tie is solemnized by ceremonies. However, these relationship are no longer common.

WELFARE

Lack of funding prevents Cambodia from operating a social security system. At the start of the twenty-first century, the government spent only $1 a head on health and welfare. There is no state pension program except for civil servants, whose small pension, which is paid irregularly, is insufficient to live on. Workers are required to retire at age 65 and are then dependent upon their families for support. There is no unemployment benefit.

A member of a land-mine clearance unit works in a Cambodian village. In a survey in 2002, around one-half of Cambodian villages had mines that needed clearing.

Approximately 2 percent of Cambodians are disabled, including an estimated 40,000 victims of land mines that were laid by all sides during decades of civil war. Soldiers who were disabled in service receive a small monthly pension, and the families of service personnel killed in the wars also receive a small payment. Other casualties of the wars do not receive social security payments.

HEALTH

The provision of health care in Cambodia is poorer than in neighboring countries. The health system was destroyed under the Khmer Rouge in the late 1970s. Reconstruction is slow and hampered by the nation's poverty. There are few modern hospitals and an insufficient number of doctors—there is only one doctor for every 1,700 people. Treatment is not free, and the majority of Cambodians are unable to afford anything more than the most basic treatments. Access to hospitals and health centers is difficult, and large areas of the country have no health facilities. The sick often travel to the cities for medical treatment.

The Sihanouk Hospital Center for Hope in Phnom Penh, the Cambodian national capital, is a magnet for the sick from country districts as well as from the city itself. The hospital is funded by international donations and staffed by local and foreign doctors. Unlike other hospitals in Cambodia, the Sihanouk Hospital does not charge for treatment. However, the center is so popular that it cannot treat the large number of prospective patients that flock to it daily.

Pharmacies are more common than health centers, and most medicines can be bought without a prescription. However, the high cost of medicines places them beyond the reach of the poor majority. Preventive medicine is uncommon in Cambodia, in part because the Cambodian health care system cannot afford to offer a comprehensive program of preventive medicine but also because the Cambodians have a traditional belief in not interfering with the natural course of events.

In the absence of an available and effective national health care system, Cambodians often resort to traditional healers known as *kru Khmer*. Traditional healing includes religious ceremonies and the widespread use of herbal medicines, the ingredients for which are readily available in gardens and forests. Practitioners of traditional medicine are totally unregulated in Cambodia.

EDUCATION

School attendance is around 65 percent, but some 30 percent of adults have never attended school. At the beginning of the twenty-first century, 90 percent of children were attending primary school until age 10, but large numbers of girls drop out of school after that age as parents are unable to afford their education. Many families believe that girls should stay at home to help their mothers rather than attend school. Books, pencils, and other equipment must all be purchased by the family. By age 18, male students outnumber female students by almost three to one. Poor families cannot pay school enrollment fees, and their children do not attend school at all. The education system is still recovering from the years of the Khmer Rouge regime, when an entire generation grew up illiterate. Universities and other institutions of higher education began to reopen through the 1980s with aid from foreign governments and international organizations.

P. FERGUSSON

Phnom Penh

In 1975, when the extreme left-wing Khmer Rouge regime seized power in Cambodia, Phnom Penh became a ghost town. The Khmer Rouge sought to create a rural classless economy with no cities and no commerce. As a result, the authorities forcibly evacuated almost the entire population of Phnom Penh.

Tradition states that in the fourteenth century CE an elderly woman named Penh found five statues of the Buddha beside the Sab River and built an artificial mound (Wat Phnom) topped by a temple to house them. The settlement that grew around the temple was named for her and the mound.

EARLY HISTORY

In the mid-fifteenth century, the Khmer kingdom was attacked by Siam, and the king moved his court to the safety of Phnom Penh. The town grew and walls, canals, and temples were built. Over the following four hundred years, the city was favored and then abandoned several times. In 1865, King Norodom (reigned 1860–1904) reestablished the Cambodian capital there.

The royal palace in Phnom Penh, begun in 1886, combines elements of traditional Khmer architecture with Thai and French influences. The building was restored after 1993.

France proclaimed a protectorate over Cambodia in 1863, and the French colonial authorities established their administration in Phnom Penh. Phnom Penh was a strategic site and natural route hub. It is located beside the confluence of the Mekong and Sab rivers, high enough above the floodplain to escape flooding and close to a wide fertile lowland that could produce rice, vegetables, and other crops to feed a growing urban population. In the middle of the nineteenth century, Phnom Penh was little more than three villages: one inhabited mainly by Chinese, another by Vietnamese, and a third settlement of Cambodians surrounding the new royal palace. From 1870, the French began to build schools, public buildings, hospitals, and other buildings. Gardens, boulevards lined with European-style villas, canals, and industries developed, and by 1900 Phnom Penh was a city of around 50,000 inhabitants.

At independence in 1953, Phnom Penh was home to about 350,000 people. It was the center of Cambodia's highway and railroad network, as well as an industrial and commercial center.

However, throughout the 1970s, Communist insurgency threatened the stability of Cambodia, and refugees poured into the city from the countryside. When the Khmer Rouge invaded Phnom Penh in 1975, it was home to more than two million people who were subsequently ejected.

Between 1975 and 1979, when Vietnamese forces intervened to overthrow the Khmer Rouge, Phnom Penh remained empty except for government officials and the military. Since then, a long reconstruction program has slowly restored the city and its infrastructure. Many former residents of Phnom Penh returned, but because the Khmer Rouge targeted educators, doctors, business people, and other professionals, the city has since suffered a shortage of skilled labor and middle-class residents.

RECONSTRUCTION

By 1985, the population of Phnom Penh was estimated to be around 425,000, and five years later, more than 600,000 people were living in the city. In 1995, Phnom Penh had nearly 825,000 residents. At the 1998 census, Phnom Penh metropolitan area had a population of 1,078,000, with 999,000 living within the city limits. The reconstruction of the city continues with new roads and public lighting, water supply, and drainage systems, schools, hospitals, public buildings, pagodas, and other facilities.

Wat Phnom remains the center of Phnom Penh. The artificial hill is regarded as the birthplace of the city, and it receives a constant flow of visitors. The temple on the summit was rebuilt in 1998. Other prominent buildings have been reconstructed or restored since 1979, including the royal palace, which was built in 1866. The palace has tiered concave roofs and is decorated with a small central stupa, or dome. Outside the walls is a pavilion in which lives the white elephant that takes part in royal parades. The Silver Pagoda within the palace compound is named for 5,000 silver tiles that cover its floor. The restored temple houses a solid gold Buddha that is decorated with 9,584 diamonds. Near the pagoda, the Wat Phnom Mondap temple contains a footprint of the Buddha.

North of the palace, the national museum contains a reassembled collection of Cambodian art. The museum houses art from the Khmer Empire dating from between the seventh and thirteenth centuries, including many statues, court costumes, and richly painted royal barges. The shaded central courtyard, where palm trees line the ponds, is a popular meeting place.

This typical street scene in Phnom Penh reveals a city that is slowly coming back to life after years of neglect.

Some of the city's monuments commemorate Cambodia's recent turbulent history. The Independence Monument was erected in 1958 to celebrate the recovery of national sovereignty. The monument now doubles as a memorial to the dead of Cambodia's wars. The Genocide Center at Choeung Ek marks the "Killing Fields," where the Khmer Rouge murdered thousands of Phnom Penh's citizens. Toul Seng High School was used by the Khmer Rouge as a torture facility. The building, whose walls are now lined with photographs of victims of the Khmer Rouge, has otherwise been left as it was when the Khmer Rouge were expelled. Toul Seng is preserved as the Museum of Genocidal Crime.

RECOVERY

New hotels and restaurants cater to the increased number of foreign visitors to Phnom Penh. The sidewalks are busy again with kiosks and cafés. Part of the tree-lined river bank has been restored as a public park. New shops, office buildings, and housing projects rise in the city. The university and colleges have reopened, and industry is once again active. The river port is operational, and barges trade with Ho Chi Minh City in Vietnam. The international airport receives tourists traveling to Angkor, and the railroads and highways to Thailand and the Cambodian coastal port of Preah Sihanouk (formerly known Kompong Som and as Sihanoukville) transport exports and imports.

C. CARPENTER

ECONOMY

The extreme left-wing Khmer Rouge regime that ruled Cambodia from 1975 through 1979 sought to create a rural peasant economy in the country. In their efforts to reshape the nation, the Khmer Rouge virtually destroyed the Cambodian economy, which has been slowly but not fully rebuilt.

In 1975, the population of Phnom Penh, the Cambodian national capital, was forcibly evacuated and other cities were also depopulated. Some three million Cambodians became refugees in the countryside. Industries and businesses were closed, schools and hospitals shut, and a classless society was proclaimed in which there were no distinctions, no more than basic education, and no money. People associated with the previous regime were killed. An unknown number of people lost their lives, at least one million, possibly far more. As a result, when Vietnamese forces intervened to overthrow the Khmer Rouge in 1979, Cambodia had been reduced to abject poverty and starvation, and apart from subsistence agriculture there was virtually no other economic activity. Immediate recovery was impossible, in part because of the civil war that continued for a decade. In 1993, a multiparty system and a market economy were reinstated and the long road to economic recovery began.

Cambodian workers plant rice in a paddy field north of Prey Veng. Rice is the most important food crop of Cambodia.

ECONOMIC CHALLENGES

As a result of the Khmer Rouge dictatorship and decades of civil war in the second half of the twentieth century, much of Cambodia lacks a basic modern infrastructure, particularly in the countryside. Transportation and communications networks are inadequate, and the educational system has had to be completely rebuilt. Industries were destroyed under the Khmer Rouge, and reconstruction has been slow. The nation suffers a considerable skills shortage, in part because so many qualified people were murdered by the Khmer Rouge.

Standard of Living

Cambodia has a low standard living, with 40 percent of the population living below the official poverty line. There is great inequality, with the poorest 10 percent of the population receiving only 3 percent of national income. The per capita GDP was $2,200 in 2005; this figure is adjusted for purchasing power parity (PPP), a formula that allows comparison between living standards in different countries.

Cambodia requires large-scale foreign investment and aid for reconstruction and development, but political instability discourages potential foreign partners. Political violence and corruption also deter donors and investors. Recovery was hit by an economic slump in southeastern Asia in the late 1990s and by a (temporary) contraction in tourism after the terrorist attacks in New York City and Washington, D.C., in 2001. However, tourism once more plays a major role in economic development.

Cambodia faces a major demographic challenge: around 60 percent of the nation's population is less than 20 years old. Large numbers of young people are entering the labor market, and there are too few jobs for them. The official unemployment level was 2.5 percent in 2002, but the real total is believed to be much higher. Some job creation programs have been made possible through government measures, but only a flourishing public commercial and industrial sector will be able to provide sufficient employment in the future. Development will depend upon diversification away from a revived industrial sector that is heavily dependent upon clothing and textiles and a service sector that relies upon tourism. The authorities face the twin challenges of tackling poverty—some 40 percent of Cambodians live below the official poverty line, many in extreme hardship—and of creating stable political conditions in which investment in industry and the infrastructure is encouraged.

The different armies and regimes that fought over Cambodia during decades of civil war laid millions of land mines across the country, nearly all of which were uncharted. It is estimated that more than 40,000 Cambodians have been killed by mines, and around 40 mine victims are still reported each week. Large areas of farming land cannot be used because of land mines, and international agencies estimate that, at current rates, it may take a century to clear all the land mines from Cambodia. The legacy restricts development, particularly in rural areas, and is costly because clearance diverts scarce resources.

RESOURCES

Cambodia has very limited natural resources. The nation has minor reserves of oil and natural gas at offshore sites adjoining Vietnamese coastal waters. Gemstones are mined near Battambang, and there are deposits of iron ore, manganese, coal, and phosphates that are not large enough to be economically important. The major rivers, particularly the Mekong and upper Sab, have some potential for the construction of dams to supply hydroelectric power. However, suitable sites are limited owing to annual floods along the Mekong River that reverse the flow of the Mekong's major tributary, the Sab River, for several months each year. As a result, most of Cambodia's electricity is generated at power plants that use imported oil.

AGRICULTURE

Cambodia remains a largely agricultural society in which farming, fishing, and forestry supply 35 percent of the GDP (gross domestic product; the total value of all the goods and services produced in a country in a set period of time, usually one year). At least 75 percent of the labor force works on the land.

Rice is the major food crop, with production concentrated along the Mekong River valley and in the lowlands that surround Tonle Sap lake. Production was hampered in the past due to a lack of irrigation facilities and, as a result, Cambodians have traditionally grown only one rice crop a year rather than the two or three annual crops that characterize the farming systems of neighboring countries. The Khmer Rouge regime that ruled Cambodia from 1975 through 1979 developed new irrigation systems in some lowland regions, and rice production initially increased. However, the projects were poorly constructed and soon fell into disrepair. In some places, the irrigation systems have been replaced or reconstructed, allowing some farmers to grow two or even three rice crops annually. Elsewhere, the size of the rice crop depends upon rainfall. Farmers plant rice in July when rainfall increases and harvest the crop between late fall and the following January. Rice farming in Cambodia is labor intensive and there is very little mechanization. Much of the rice crop is grown by subsistence farmers, and a large proportion of the crop does not enter the commercial market.

Cambodian farmers also grow fruits (oranges, bananas, papayas, mangoes, and pineapples) for local consumption, as well as vegetables, particularly beans and sweet potatoes, that are consumed on small family farms or marketed locally. Corn is also grown. Most farms keep cattle, mainly water buffalo, as draft animals and to pull the plow. Hogs and chickens are also raised.

Fishing is an important activity. Fishers catch freshwater fish in the major rivers and lakes, and most farmers supplement their family's diet with catches of carp, perch, and smelts from local ponds and waterways. Sea fishing is not well developed, and along the coast the destruction of mangrove swamps threatens fishing stocks. Illegal fishing and overfishing also reduce stocks.

Timber is a major resource. There is great demand for tropical hardwoods in North America and Europe, but the exploitation of Cambodia's forests is, in theory, restricted by legislation. However, illegal logging activities occur throughout the country, destroying the forest and increasing soil erosion. Timber produced both legally and illegally is a major export.

EMPLOYMENT IN CAMBODIA

Sector	Percentage of labor force
Agriculture	75
Industry and Services	25

Source: Government of Cambodia, 2003

In 2000, government figures showed that 2.5 percent of the labor force was unemployed. This figure is widely considered to be an underestimate, with the real total much higher.

Freshwater fishing is an important activity in Cambodia. These traditional fishing boats ply the Mekong River at Kompong Cham.

INDUSTRY

In the 1950s and 1960s, the Cambodian authorities encouraged the development of small industries. However, the period of Khmer Rouge rule in the 1970s as well as decades of civil war destroyed most of the industrial base. By the 1980s and 1990s, most of the remaining industrial plant was out of date. Lack of investment and the lack of a trained workforce have restricted industrial development.

Most Cambodian industry is concentrated in the capital, Phnom Penh, which has food processing (including rice milling), timber processing, cigarette, paper, and building materials industries. The principal industry in Phnom Penh and in other major centers is textiles and clothing. Cambodia's clothing industry expanded rapidly after the late 1990s, when the U.S. and Cambodian governments drew up a textile trade agreement. The trade agreement also served to improve working conditions for textile workers in Cambodia.

Instability still restricts industrial growth, and Cambodia does not have the flourishing modern industrial base that characterizes the economies of some of the neighboring countries. When nations such as Thailand and Malaysia developed consumer goods and electrical and electronic industries, Cambodia was wracked by civil war. Cambodian industry has since been unable to compete with the mass production of goods by its neighbors.

SERVICES

The service industries of Cambodia have been slowly rebuilt since 1979. Banking, commerce, and retail services had ceased to exist in the late 1970s in an economy in which there was no money. By the beginning of the twenty-first century, the service sector provided 35 percent of the GDP, and tourism was Cambodia's fastest growing industry. Western and Japanese

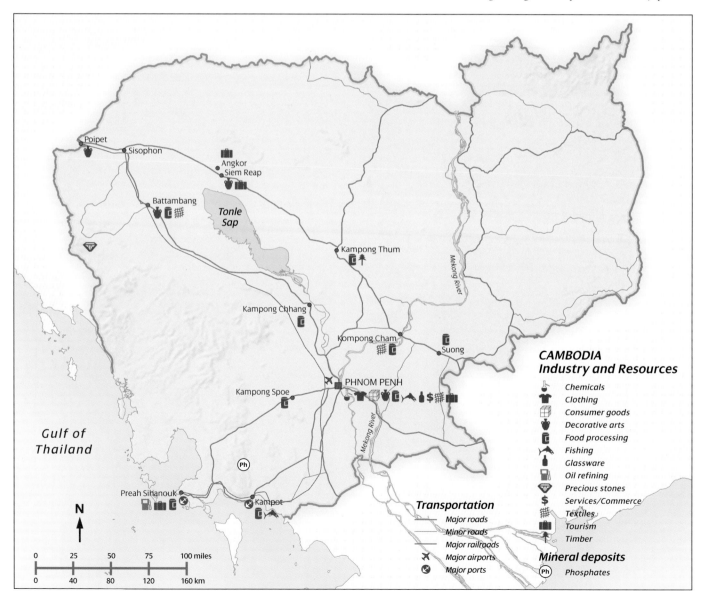

Tourism is Cambodia's fastest growing economic sector, with Angkor Wat the country's main tourist attraction.

CAMBODIA'S GDP

Cambodia's gross domestic product (GDP) was $31 billion in 2005. The figure is adjusted for purchasing power parity (PPP), an exchange rate at which goods in one country cost the same as goods in another. PPP allows a comparison between the living standards in different nations.

MAIN CONTRIBUTORS TO CAMBODIA'S GDP

Agriculture	35 percent
Industry	30 percent
Services	35 percent

Source: CIA, 2004

tourists visit the spectacular ruined temple complex at Angkor; by 2003, Cambodia received more than one million foreign tourists. Although tourism is centered in Angkor, almost all foreign visitors pass through Phnom Penh and spend some time in the city.

TRADE

Before 1975, Cambodia exported timber and agricultural surpluses to Europe and to other countries in the region. By 1979, foreign trade had virtually ceased. By the time Cambodia reentered the international trading arena in the 1990s, other nations had taken its markets, and Cambodia was no longer a significant food exporter. In modern times, Cambodia exports clothing and textiles, timber, rice, fish, rubber, footwear, and tobacco. The United States receives nearly 60 percent of Cambodia's exports in 2005. Other important trading partners included Germany (which took 10.4 percent of Cambodian exports), Vietnam (4.7 percent), Great Britain, and Singapore. Cambodia imports petroleum, construction materials, machinery, motor vehicles, gold, and cigarettes. The nation's main suppliers of imports are China including Hong Kong (which provided 27.8 percent of imports), Thailand (24.6 percent), Vietnam (11.3 percent), Taiwan (8.7 percent), South Korea, and Singapore. In 2005, Cambodia exported goods worth $2.4 billion and imported goods and services worth $3.5 billion.

TRANSPORTATION AND COMMUNICATION

Inland waterways supplement the nation's highway network. Some 1,492 miles (2,400 km) of waterways are navigable, including the Mekong and Sab rivers and their major tributaries. There are 7,659 miles (12,323 km) of highways, but only 1,241 miles (1,996 km) are paved. The national highway system is inadequate, and seasonal flooding regularly restricts and sometimes damages the network. The improvement of the nation's highways is widely perceived as a priority. A limited railroad system of 374 miles (602 km) links Phnom Penh with Battambang (the second largest city) and Thailand in the west and with Cambodia's main coastal port, Preah Sihanouk (formerly Kompong Som and previously known as Sihanoukville), in the south. Phnom Penh has an international airport.

Cambodia's communications system is underdeveloped. In 2003, there were 36,400 telephone lines in the country, mostly in Phnom Penh. The cellular mobile phone system is expanding, and nearly 500,000 Cambodians had cellular phones in 2003. About 41,000 people in Cambodia had Internet access in 2005.

C. CARPENTER

Laos

Although the Lao people have a long history, the nation-state of Laos is relatively modern. Colonized by the French toward the end of the nineteenth century, Laos comprised several small Lao states, which were eventually united into a single kingdom that gained complete independence in 1954. Independent Laos suffered civil war in which royalists fought Communist Pathet Lao forces. Vietnamese Communists used Laos as supply route during the war in Vietnam in the 1960s and 1970s, and the withdrawal of U.S. forces from Vietnam allowed the Pathet Lao to seize power in Laos in 1975, establishing a Communist dictatorship. Since the 1990s, Laos has undertaken economic reform, and the nation's economy is now dominated by that of its larger western neighbor, Thailand.

GEOGRAPHY

Location	Southeast Asia, between Thailand and Vietnam
Climate	Tropical climate with little seasonal variation in temperature; wet monsoon season from May through November; dry season from December through April
Area	91,429 sq. miles (236,800 sq. km)
Coastline	None
Highest point	Phou Bia 9,248 ft (2,819 m)
Lowest point	Beside the Mekong River 230 ft (70 m)
Terrain	Mountains interspersed by plains and plateaus
Natural resources	Timber, gypsum, tin, hydroelectric power potential

Wat Sayaphoum is the main temple of the city of Savannakhet.

FLAG

The national flag of Laos has three horizontal bands: red at the top, blue in the center, and red at the bottom of the flag. The blue band is wider than the red bands. There is a white circle at the center of the blue band. Red represents the blood shed by the Communist Pathet Lao in their armed struggle; blue represents national wealth. The white circle is variously said to represent national unity, the future, or the full moon shining over the Mekong River.

Land use	
Arable land	4.0 percent
Permanent crops	0.3 percent
Other	95.7 percent
Major rivers	Mekong, Ou, Banghiang
Major lake	Ngum reservoir
Natural hazards	Flooding, drought

NEIGHBORS AND LENGTH OF BORDERS

Cambodia	338 miles (541 km)
China	264 miles (423 km)
Myanmar (Burma)	147 miles (235 km)
Thailand	1,096 miles (1,754 km)
Vietnam	1,331 miles (2,130 km)

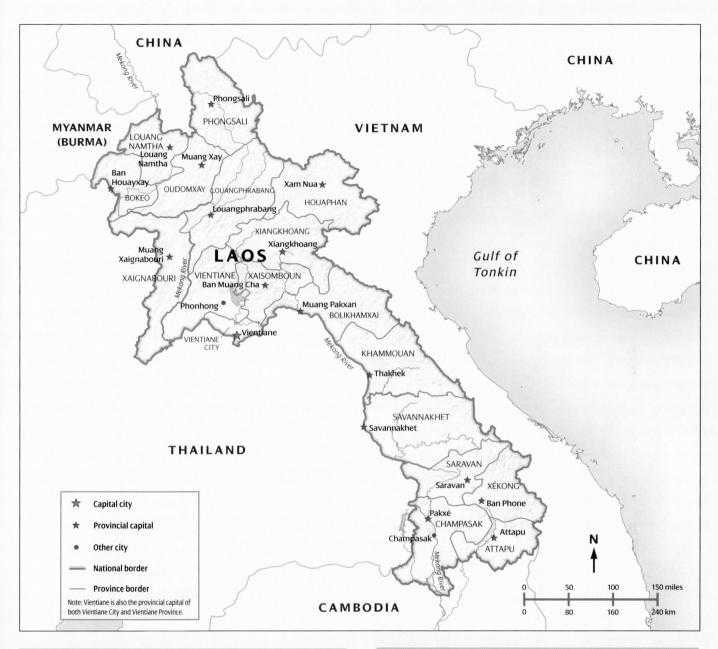

METROPOLITAN AREAS, 2005 POPULATIONS

Urban population	15 percent
Vientiane	695,000
Vientiane City	200,000
Pakxé	95,000
Savannakhet	68,000
Louangphrabang	50,000
Xam Nua	40,000
Muang Xaignabouri	32,000
Thakhek	26,000
Muang Pakxan	22,000

Source: Laotian census, 2005 (provisional figures)

POPULATION

Population	5,610,000 (2005 census)
Population density	61 per sq. mile (24 per sq. km)
Population growth	2 percent a year
Birthrate	35.5 births per 1,000 of the population
Death rate	11.6 deaths per 1,000 of the population
Population under age 15	41.4 percent
Population over age 65	3.1 percent
Sex ratio	98 males for 100 females
Fertility rate	4.7 children per woman
Infant mortality rate	83.3 deaths per 1,000 live births
Life expectancy at birth	
Total population	55.5 years
Female	57.6 years
Male	53.5 years

ECONOMY

Currency	New Kip (LAK)
Exchange rate (2006)	$1 = LAK 10,446
Gross domestic product (2005)	$12.1 billion
GDP per capita (2005)	$1,900
Unemployment rate (2005)	2 percent
Population under poverty line (2002)	34 percent
Exports	$379 million (2005 CIA estimate)
Imports	$541 million (2005 CIA estimate)

The Louangphrabang region of Laos has many waterfalls, some of which have become popular visitor attractions.

GOVERNMENT

Official country name	Lao People's Democratic Republic
Conventional short form	Laos
Former name	Kingdom of Laos
Nationality	
noun	Lao, Laotian
adjective	Lao, Laotian
Official language	Lao
Capital city	Vientiane
Type of government	Communist republic
Voting rights	18 years and over, universal
National anthem	"Pheng Xat Lao" (Hymn of Lao People)
National day	Republic Day, December 2, 1975

TRANSPORTATION

Railroads	None
Highways	20,273 miles (32,620 km)
Paved roads	2,852 miles (4,590 km)
Unpaved roads	17,421 miles (28,030 km)
Navigable waterways	2,859 miles (4,600 km)
Airports	
International airports	1
Paved runways	9

POPULATION PROFILE, 2000 ESTIMATES

Ethnic groups	
Lao Loum (Lowland Lao)	68 percent
Lao Theung (Upland Lao)	22 percent
Lao Soung (Mountain Lao), Hmong, and Yao	9 percent
Vietnamese, Chinese, and others	1 percent
Religions	
Buddhist	58 percent
Traditional beliefs	34 percent
Nonreligious	5 percent
Christian (mainly Roman Catholic)	2 percent
Sunni Muslim	1 percent
Languages	
Lao	80 percent
Khmer	10 percent
Vietnamese, Chinese, and other minorities	10 percent
Adult literacy	66.4 percent

CHRONOLOGY

5th century CE	The Kha, the indigenous people of the region, are subjugated by the Khmer (Cambodians).
8th century	Tai-speaking peoples from southwestern China migrate south into present-day Laos, supplanting the indigenous Kha.
12th–13th centuries	Much of Laos comes under Siamese control.
1354	Lao prince Fa Ngum (1316–1374) founds the first Lao state, Lan Xang (the "kingdom of the million elephants").
16th century	Laos struggles against invasions by forces from Burma, Vietnam, and the Thai kingdom of Ayutthaya.
1637	Souligna Vongsa (1613–1694) becomes king of Lan Xang. He restores order and secures the borders with Vietnam and Siam.
1707	Lan Xang is divided into Louangphrabang and Vien Chan (modern-day Vientiane). In 1713, the south secedes to form Champasak.
18th century	The three Lao states face persistent Siamese attacks.
late 19th century	Siam gradually cedes control of the Lao states to the French. Laos becomes part of French Indochina in 1893.
1941	Japanese forces invade Laos. They allow the French adminstration to remain in place but force the French to restore territory to Thailand.
1945	Japan takes control of Laos and encourages King Sisavang Vong (1885–1959) of Louangphrabang to declare independence from France.
1946	French rule is restored and the different Lao territories are united into the Kingdom of Laos.
1950	Prince Souphanouvong (1909–1995) founds the Communist Pathet Lao movement and cooperates with Vietnamese Communists against French rule.
1954	Laos gains complete independence. Civil war breaks out between royalists and Communists.
1960s	Extensive U.S. bombing of Laos to destroy North Vietnamese supply lines into South Vietnam causes widespread loss of life.
1975	Pathet Lao forces seize control and establish a Communist republic.
1979	Widespread food shortages encourage many Lao peasants to seek refuge in Vietnam.
1986	A cautious program of economic reform begins and foreign investment is encouraged.
1991	A new constitution restates the Communist Party's leading role in Lao national life.
1997	Laos joins ASEAN, the southeast Asian trading block.
2000	Thailand dominates the Lao economy and increasingly influences Lao culture.

GOVERNMENT

Since the overthrow of the monarchy in 1979, Laos has been a Communist dictatorship in which the Revolutionary People's Party of Laos has alone held the reins of power.

The political leadership of Laos was little changed from 1979 through 2001, when members of a new generation gained important posts in the administration. During the last decade of the twentieth century, economic reforms began to transform Laos, but there was no suggestion that the changes would be accompanied by political reforms. Laotians are unable to change their government through the ballot box. The government owns all broadcast and printed media, controls the labor unions (which have little power), and detains alleged dissidents. Personal communications are monitored, and party committees report the activities of Laotians in their neighborhoods and in the workplace. The activities of religious organizations are also watched, and the distribution and printing of non-Buddhist religious texts is tightly controlled.

A government propaganda poster exhorts Lao workers and the military to unite.

THE COMMUNIST PARTY

The (Communist) Revolutionary People's Party of Laos (PPPL) restricts the basic rights of Laotian citizens. It is the sole legal party and exercises power at all levels of the administration. The PPPL chooses all candidates for election, although independent candidates may apply to the party for approval to run for public office. The party rather than the National Assembly is the most powerful state body.

THE NATIONAL ASSEMBLY

The National Assembly (the Sapha Heng Xat) has 109 members, who are elected for a five-year term by universal adult suffrage. The voting age is 18 years. In the 2002 legislative election, the PPPL won 108 of the 109 seats. A "nonpartisan," who was approved by the PPPL, won the remaining seat. There is no real political debate in the National Assembly, which only approves decisions that have already been agreed by the PPPL party hierarchy.

THE PRESIDENT AND GOVERNMENT

The chief of state is a president, who is elected for a renewable five-year term of office by the assembly. The president also normally serves as leader of the PPPL and is the head of the executive. The president appoints a prime minister for a five-year term, upon the approval of the assembly. The prime minister chooses a cabinet of ministers and submits their names to both the chief of state and the assembly for approval.

LOCAL GOVERNMENT

Laos is a highly centralized country in which power is exercised by the chief of state and the ruling political party. The country is divided into 16 provinces, one municipality with the status of a province (Vientiane, the national capital), and one special zone (Xaisomboun) that has provincial status. The provinces, which are effectively administered by appointed officials, are divided into districts (*muong*).

C. CARPENTER

MODERN HISTORY

The Lao Kingdom

France established a protectorate over the Lao kingdom of Louangphrabang in 1893. The former Lao kingdom of Vientiane, which had been annexed by Thailand in 1827, became a French colony in 1883, and the southern Lao principality of Champasak became a French protectorate in 1904. In 1946, France recognized the union of these different territories to form Laos.

When Japanese forces invaded Laos in 1941 during World War II (1939–1945), they occupied a region that was divided into three separate territories: Louangphrabang, Vientiane, and Champasak. In April 1945, Japan took over the administration, encouraging Sisavang Vong (1885–1959), the king of Louangphrabang (northern Laos), to renounce French protection. but he also opposed Japanese rule. At the same time, Boun Oum (1912–1980), the former prince of Champasak, opposed Japanese rule in the south. In Vientiane (central Laos). the radical, anti-French Lao Issara movement, which took control when the Japanese surrendered, formed a governing committee with ambitions to unite Laos. When French forces reestablished control in 1946, the Lao Issara leaders fled.

France united Laos, granting internal self-government, with Sisavang Vong as king. While some elements of Lao Issara were prepared to compromise, most of the movement's leaders campaigned for independence. In 1950, the Lao Issara leader Prince Souphanouvong (1912–1995) founded the Pathet Lao ("land of the Lao") movement, cooperating with the Viet Minh Vietnamese Communists to fight French rule. By the early 1950s, Pathet Lao forces occupied most of northeast Laos. In 1953, France granted Laos increased autonomy, retaining control of only defense and foreign relations. However, the concessions were too late, and French rule in Indochina was crumbling. French forces were tied down in Vietnam, where the Viet Minh had gained an advantage.

INDEPENDENCE

In 1954, after the defeat of French forces by the Vietnamese Communists at Dien Bien Phu in northern Vietnam, France no longer controlled Indochina. The French signed the Geneva Accords (1954) to transfer sovereignty to the different regional governments in the former French Indochinese empire. In Laos, sovereignty passed into the hands of the Lao royal government. A coalition government was organized and headed by the leader of a neutralist faction, Prince Souvanna Phouma (1901–1984), half-brother of Prince Souphanouvong. The government included the right-wing military leader General Phoumi Nosavan (1920–1985). Backed by the Thai government, Phoumi reflected the views of the wealthy, landlords, army officers, and the largely ethnic Chinese and Vietnamese commercial interests that were centered in Vientiane and Louangphrabang. However, these elements were relatively weak compared to an overwhelmingly poor peasant society that was based on subsistence rice and corn farming.

The left wing in the new government was led by Prince Souphanouvong, who, although he was a member of the royal family, was a French-trained engineer, a Communist, and a radical nationalist. As head of the Communist-dominated Pathet Lao during the French war in Indochina (1946–1954), he and his Viet Minh allies had brought much of Laos under their control. Pathet Lao influence was strong among the upland ethnic minorities, while the royal government and right-wing elements exercised controlled the majority Lowland Lao population along the Mekong River valley. Both sides claimed the mantle of Lao nationalism, and the right-wing leaders denounced the close ties between the Pathet Lao and the Viet Minh.

A FLAWED NEUTRALITY

The 1954 Geneva Accords had proclaimed Laos to be neutral. However, the possibility of neutrality for Laos was imperiled from the beginning by the encroachment of the war in neighboring Vietnam and the international power politics of the Cold War (the struggle for supremacy between the West, led by the United States, and the Communist states, led by the Soviet Union from 1945 through 1990–1991).

Pathet Lao guerrillas detain villagers suspected of being unsympathetic. In the 1960s, Pathet Lao gradually took over most of eastern Laos.

Despite the neutral status of Laos, U.S. influence increased in conjunction with a growing American military presence in South Vietnam, where the pro-Western government faced insurgency by the Viet Minh from North Vietnam and by local Communists. The South Vietnamese government was aided by U.S. military advisers. The evolving war in neighboring Vietnam changed the course of Lao history. The United States saw Laos as a forward outpost in the struggle to contain Communist Chinese influence in Indochina. Economic aid from the United States helped to keep the right-wing forces in Laos united while bolstering U.S. political influence.

The power of the left was greatly strengthened by elections in 1958, when leftists won 13 of the 21 contested assembly seats. Left-wing candidates won about one-third of the popular vote. With U.S. support, a Committee for the Defense of the National Interest attempted to rally the right wing. Its leader, Phoumi Nosavan, broke up the coalition government, and in the ensuing war the Pathet Lao were forced to take refuge in the countryside.

THE LAO CIVIL WAR

Between 1958 and 1962, the Communists gained control over approximately one-third of the Lao population. The Pathet Lao effectively ruled the upland plateaus and mountainous regions to the east of the Mekong Valley. The rich bottom lands in the Mekong Valley, including the main cities, remained in the hands of the royal government, which was dominated by the military

under Phoumi Nosavan. The right-wing hold on the royal government was shaken in 1960 as a result of the rebellion by nationalist army officers who supported Souvanna Phouma while calling for Lao unity and neutrality. As a result, the neutralists entered negotiations with the Pathet Lao.

U.S. financial aid and a CIA (Central Intelligence Agency) presence buoyed the royalist government's military forces, which included not only Laotians but also Thai regular and irregular troops. Communist influence among the ethnic minorities in eastern Laos was countered by a U.S. alliance with some elements of the Hmong (a mountain people with a warrior tradition, whose subsistence living was bolstered by the production and sale of opium, of which Laos was a major producer). The United States justified its growing presence in Laos by the fact that it had never signed the Geneva Accords that had stipulated Lao neutrality. Furthermore, the Southeast Asia Treaty Organization (SEATO) pact, a regional Western defense organization created by the United States in the immediate wake of the Geneva Accords, identified Laos and Cambodia as countries to be defended from external aggression. The United States considered Pathet Lao militancy to be under Soviet, Chinese, and North Vietnamese influences. Indeed, the Soviets helped finance the Pathet Lao by flying in military supplies and regular shipments of silver, a metal that was of special value in the Lao society.

Despite U.S. aid to the government, by 1962 the Pathet Lao seemed close to victory. In the spring of that year, government forces were routed in the battle of Namtha, a heavily fortified town 19 miles (30 km) south of the Chinese border. Some government troops and city dwellers fled Vientiane to Thailand, fearing the imminent triumph of the Pathet Lao. In response, U.S. president John F. Kennedy (in office 1961–1963) threatened direct

U.S. intervention to prevent such a takeover. Kennedy was concerned not only with the situation in Laos; a growing Communist offensive in South Vietnam threatened the survival of the U.S.-backed government there, too. However, the location of Laos close to the Chinese border and the landlocked nation's difficult topography caused Kennedy to rethink his strategy. Concluding that South Vietnam would be more easily defended militarily as a barrier to Communism, he opted for a policy of attempting to neutralize Laos. Moving to restore the situation to that which existed between 1954 and 1957, Kennedy sent an experienced U.S. diplomat, W. Averell Harriman (1891–1986), to Switzerland to negotiate an agreement. The resulting accord allowed the neutralist Prince Souvanna Phouma to form a second coalition government, which lasted from 1962 to 1966.

FOREIGN INTERVENTION

The prospects for Prince Souvanna Phouma's coalition administration were directly determined by the situation in neighboring Vietnam. Growing political chaos in Saigon (the capital of South Vietnam), increasing Communist insurgency in the South Vietnamese countryside, and an expanding presence of North Vietnamese troops and advisers in the South led to the U.S. bombing of North Vietnam and a massive intervention by American ground troops in 1965. In support of the effort, the United States stepped up its assistance to the Lao military and political elite.

Massive inflows of U.S. aid and money totaling half a billion dollars became the determining factor in Lao politics. Prince Souvanna Phouma could not avoid coming under the influence of the United States. While American intervention in South Vietnam attracted worldwide attention, U.S. activities in Laos were deliberately kept as secret as possible. Considerable control over the Laotian government passed into the hands of the United States' ambassador to Laos, and the prince was kept in power in order to preserve a facade of neutralism. The activities of the CIA, Protestant missionaries, and American anthropologists among minorities assured the continued support of a large number of the Hmong, and through a clandestine airline the CIA allowed the Hmong to market their opium through Laos and the rest of southeast Asia.

As the ground war in Vietnam reached its peak in the late 1960s, U.S. policy concerning Laos had several goals. First, the United States endeavored to build up the Laotian royal army to contain the Pathet Lao. Government forces eventually reached 60,000 personnel. A second objective was to protect a series of sophisticated electronic listening posts set up on mountain tops close to the border with North Vietnam. These heavily fortified U.S. facilities provided vital intelligence and communication links with U.S. airplanes operating over North Vietnam.

Another goal of the United States was to interrupt the flow of North Vietnamese personnel and munitions along the Ho Chi Minh Trail, a network of north-south roads that ran through Laos and connected North and South Vietnam. It was constructed by the North Vietnamese though the foothills of the Annamese Cordillera near the border between Laos and Vietnam and was used to supply Communist forces in South Vietnam. The North Vietnamese considered continued access to the Ho Chi Minh Trail critical to their effort to topple the U.S.-backed government in South Vietnam and to reunify the two halves of Vietnam. Several divisions of the North Vietnamese army and tens of thousands of peasant laborers maintained and defended the route.

In the late 1960s, air strikes on eastern Laos by U.S. forces caused widespread destruction, leaving a landscape of bomb craters.

The North Vietnamese military presence in Laos bolstered the increasingly successful efforts of the 35,000-strong Pathet Lao against the royal Laotian army. The problems of the right-wing Lao government grew with the ousting of Phoumi Nosavan from his military command and his flight to Thailand in 1965. By 1968, the Lao army had ceased to be an effective force. Thai troops and some 30,000 Hmong fighters constituted the major elements of the government forces. Unable to sustain a successful ground campaign against Pathet Lao advances, the United States instead relied on massive air assaults to keep the Communist forces in check between 1964 and 1973. Some 2 million tons (1.96 million metric tons) of bombs were dropped on Laos in this period—almost as much as the United States expended during World War II. Some 3,500 eastern Lao villages were wiped out as a result of these bombardments, and the historic remains on the Plain of Jars were damaged by air assault.

In addition to blocking the Ho Chi Minh Trail and defending U.S. radar stations, the U.S. bombing campaign was also intended to try to empty the countryside of the peasantry by driving them into the cities. By the early 1970s, some 750,000 peasants had been forced to take refuge in relocation centers in urban areas. However, the Pathet Lao and their supporters held out against the U.S. attacks, sheltering in caves and forests against the bombing campaigns.

King Savang Vathana of Laos, here with President John F. Kennedy in 1963, may have starved to death as a Communist prisoner.

PATHET LAO ADVANCES

The United States began to withdraw its troops from the ground war in South Vietnam from 1969. The last major campaign of U.S. ground forces was the invasion of Cambodia in 1970. This campaign temporarily disrupted Vietnamese base areas and supply lines in Cambodia. As a result, Pathet Lao and North Vietnamese control of southern Laos became more important, and in 1970, Pathet Lao forces seized the provincial capitals of Attapu and Saravan in southern Laos. In an effort to cut the Ho Chi Minh Trail and prove their mettle in battle, 20,000 South Vietnamese struck west across the border into Laos in January 1971 in operation Lam Son 719. They were met and routed by heavily entrenched North Vietnamese troops.

Meanwhile, to the north, the Pathet Lao launched devastating attacks on Hmong regular and irregular troops. The whole fabric of Hmong society in Laos began to disintegrate. Displaced Hmong villagers on remote hilltops came to depend on U.S. air drops for food supplies. Men and boys were taken to serve in the war while women were left to tend the young. As the tide of the war began to turn decisively, those Hmong who had collaborated with the Americans were in danger from Communist reprisals.

THE END OF THE WAR

By the early 1970s, Laotians were deeply weary of a seemingly endless war, the loss of national sovereignty due to foreign intervention, and the corruption rife in the cities, especially among the elite. Peace negotiations between the Lao government and the Pathet Lao began in mid-1972. A peace agreement between the United States and the North Vietnamese in January 1973 facilitated the process. A cease-fire agreement was concluded in Laos in February 1973, and a third coalition government headed by Prince Souvanna Phouma was organized. The enhanced influence of the Pathet Lao, who gained an important foothold in the two major cities for the first time, was notable. While U.S. presence declined, the North Vietnamese redoubled their activity along the Ho Chi Minh Trail.

In the cities, militancy grew among workers and students. At the beginning of 1975, there were protest meetings and demonstrations by these elements for the first time. The overthrow of the U.S.-backed governments of Cambodia and South Vietnam in April 1975 paved the way for a Pathet Lao takeover. The Pathet Lao renamed itself the Lao People's Revolutionary Party. Amid popular demonstrations throughout the country, Communist ministers took over the government while the commercial and other elites fled into Thailand. At the beginning of December 1975, the monarchy was abolished. King Savang Vathana (reigned 1959–1975) and the senior members of the royal family were taken to "re-education camps" in northeastern Laos, where they probably perished. The monarchy was abolished and a People's Democratic Republic proclaimed, with Souphanouvong, no longer a prince, as president.

H. HELLER

Communist Laos

The 1975 seizure of power by the Communist Pathet Lao had widespread support among the majority of poor Laotians. Although the Communist revolution swept away the trappings of monarchy, a prince was still chief of state. The first leader of Communist Laos was Prince Souphanouvong (1912–1995), a cousin of the deposed king.

Prince Souphanouvong led the radical Pathet Lao for three decades; in the early 1950s, he had cooperated with the Communist North Vietnamese Viet Minh to drive the French from Indochina. After the Pathet Lao takeover in 1975, the movement renamed itself the Lao People's Revolutionary Party (usually known as the Communist Party), and after his long struggle to power, the Communist prince became president of the new republic.

Souphanouvong, the "Red Prince," was president of Laos from 1975 to 1986.

STATE SOCIALISM

In its first ten years, Communist Laos nationalized the banks and most of the rest of the commercial sector and established state-owned farms. An increase in rice production to 1,200,000 tons (1,090,000 metric tons) insured self-sufficiency in the staple crop. The Lao authorities maintained close ties with Vietnam—many Lao Communist leaders had family and other ties with their neighbor. In French colonial times, some had been members of the Vietnamese-dominated Indochina Communist Party alongside the leaders of Vietnam's government in the 1970s. As a result, Vietnam heavily influenced Communist Laos. To reduce dependency on pro-Western Thailand, a road to the Vietnamese port of Da Nang was opened to the east as well as an oil pipeline linking Laos with Vietnam. Around 40,000 Vietnamese troops remained in Laos to counter the threat of insurgents from Thailand and resistance by the Hmong hill people.

A NEW DIRECTION

By the early 1980s, political repression and economic hardship had led about one-tenth of the population of Laos to flee to Thailand. Economic reform became essential to stem growing discontent. In 1986, the Lao authorities moved to liberalize the economy to speed economic development in a move that paralleled developments in Vietnam. The next year, the regime accepted International Monetary Fund (IMF) advice to open the economy to foreign private investment. Relations with Thailand improved, and Vietnamese troops were withdrawn in 1988. Lao-Chinese relations, which had soured following the Chinese attack on Vietnam in 1978, also improved. The suspension of Soviet assistance in 1989 represented a serious setback, but the Lao government successfully multiplied its efforts to establish ties with other Asian governments. Liberalization of the economy spurred economic growth through the early 1990s.

Economic reforms were matched by a reinforcement of Communist control over political life. Replacing Souphanouvong as leader, Kaysone Phomvihane (1920–1992) became both secretary general of the Communist Party and prime minister in the 1980s. A new constitution in 1991 reenforced the Communist Party's monopoly over political life. After 1991, a social democratic trend emerged as a result of developments in the Soviet Union, where the Communists fell from power, but the more liberal tendency was swiftly crushed.

In April 1994, the first bridge across the Mekong River between Thailand and Laos was opened. By then, Thai capital investment in Laos was greater than that of any other country. Vietnamese political leverage in Laos was partially offset by the growing Thai economic influence. The traditional role of Laos as a buffer between the more powerful Thais and Vietnamese reappeared. At the same time, growing contacts with Thailand also opened further prospects of investment, trade, and tourism with other Asian and Western countries. Foreign investment increased, and in 1997, Laos became a member of ASEAN, the southeast Asian trading block. However, economic development was not matched by political development. Concern grew over a perceived threat from tourism, and the Lao authorities feared that Thai popular culture would undermine the Lao cultural heritage and traditional way of life, as well as the influence of the Communist Party. Early in the twenty-first century, uncensored news was increasingly available through Thai television, radio, and newspapers. Lao economic reforms appeared half-hearted, and some foreign investors withdrew because of official restrictions. As unrest grew, the low-level Hmong insurgency increased.

H. HELLER

CULTURAL EXPRESSION

Literature

Early Lao literature was oral but, by the fourteenth century, written literature, drawing on Hindu and Buddhist sources, evolved. French influences were strong from the late nineteenth century, while state control now shapes Lao literature.

Lao is part of the Tai-Kadai language group and shares some characteristics with Thai and Shan. When Buddhism came to Laos over 700 years ago, its teachings were written in Pali, a southern Indian language. Modern written Lao developed from this source, and there are Pali words in Lao.

Early Lao literature comprised folk tales that were passed from one generation to the next by word of mouth. As knowledge of writing spread, some stories were recorded on palm leaves. Early Lao folk poetry and prose includes stories about the Buddha, records of historical events, myths, and folk tales. Myths relate the lives of gods and the origins of humankind. Legends tell of the origin of settlements and the naming of places and physical features. Folk epics relate events in the foundation of the Lao state and the lives of its rulers.

Written Lao literature that owed much to Buddhist sources evolved from the fourteenth century CE. Buddhism was the primary source, and temples were the only centers of education. As a result, Lao literature was Buddhist in character and in subject (for example, life stories of the Buddha and his followers), and written literature was stored at temples. Stories from Buddhist literature were performed as plays by monks, particularly at religious festivals.

The most famous Buddhist epic in the Lao tradition is the *Vetsantrasadok*, the story of the life of the Buddha before his Enlightenment. *Thao Hung*, another well-known traditional epic, relates the struggle of two noble families. *Sin Xay*, a sixteenth- or seventeenth-century poem, is the tale of a boy called Sin Xay, who is born clutching a bow and arrow. He has two brothers: one is an elephant, the other a snail. Together, these works are often said to be the classics of early Lao literature. Other popular early works are translations, often adaptations, of Indian Hindu epics.

FRENCH INFLUENCES

Toward the end of the nineteenth century, the French established control in the Lao lands east of the Mekong River and eventually merged their territories to form Laos. By the 1930s, Laotians

educated in schools established by the colonial power studied French literature. Wealthier, upper-class Laotians read French novels, rather than traditional Lao literature. Under the influence of French literature, Laotians also began to write fiction in prose whereas Lao fiction had been only in verse.

French literary culture had no influence on the majority of the poor rural Laotians. The spread of printed literature in Laos was slow: printed books did not appear in the country until the 1930s, and the first regular newspapers were not published until the 1940s. Modern literature was initially confined to wealthier people in the cities of Vientiane and Louangphrabang, and the ruling elite tended to converse in French rather than Lao. As a result, the small upper class read French literature, wrote in French, and became divorced from traditional Lao literary culture.

MODERN LITERATURE IN LAOS

The first novel written and published in Lao was *Phra Phoutthahoup Saksit* (The sacred Buddha) by Somchine Nginn (1892–c. 1984), published in 1944. In the 1940s, the French colonial authorities encouraged indigenous Lao culture to counter growing Thai influence. More prose and poetry in Lao appeared, but after independence in 1954, two distinct Lao literatures evolved.

Through the 1950s and 1960s, rival political factions fought over Laos; most of the cities and the Mekong Valley were controlled by the royalist government, while much of the countryside, particularly the east, was under Communist Pathet Lao rule. In government-controlled areas, French-language education continued, and a variety of fiction in Lao was published. Among a limited number of authors writing in Lao, Outhine Bounyavong (1942–2000) was a dominant figure. Maha Sila Viravong (1905–1987) was a noted Lao historian who founded a literary magazine that lasted until a few months after the Communist takeover in 1975. At the same time, in areas controlled by the Pathet Lao, a radical literature developed

Outhine Bounyavong

Some of the works of Outhine Bounyavong (1942–2000) have been translated and published abroad. A collection of his stories is published in English under the title *Mother's Beloved*. In the mid-1960s, Outhine published a collection of stories, *Sivith Ni Ku Lakone Kom* ("Life is like a short play"), that was different in its tone from previously published Lao literature. At the time, foreign (mainly American) influence was strong, the country was wracked by corruption, and a large U.S. military presence in Vientiane, the national capital, had introduced a culture and social behavior that were at odds with conservative Lao society. Civil war raged between royalist government and Communist Pathet Lao forces. Into this volatile situation, Outhine's stories introduced social criticism into literature. Outhine stayed in Laos after the Communist takeover in 1975 and continued to publish a variety of work, including children's literature and stories that illustrate simplicity, the wisdom of Lao country people, and the beauty of the natural world.

Shop and hotel signs in Vientiane use the Lao language and English to advertise their businesses. Modern written Lao is based on the dialect of Vientiane, the national capital.

using traditional Lao forms to promote socialist ideas and revolution. The Pathet Lao largely rejected French cultural influence and promoted new and historic Lao verse as a vehicle of resistance to foreign rule and interference.

In modern Laos since 1975, literature has been government-controlled. Some works are translations of Communist literature from China and the former Soviet Union. Original works are created by three groups of writers: revolutionaries who were part of the Pathet Lao movement; established writers who remained in Laos after the Communist takeover; and a new generation that has grown up under Communist rule. Among writers who remained in Laos after the Pathet Lao took power were Outhine Bounyavong and Dara Viravong (born 1943). Dara Viravong is the author of short stories, novels, and poems, and she is also a noted scholar of religious literature.

In the late 1980s, the Communist authorities introduced a program of economic reforms but determined to maintain a hold on the nation's political life. There was a brief partial relaxation in censorship and, for a time, constructive criticism was allowed. However, the government quickly reimposed controls. Publishing in Laos is no longer subsidized by the state. Most new literature appears in newspapers and magazines, and the cost of book production is prohibitively expensive for most new works.

P. FERGUSSON

Art and Architecture

Lao art and architecture reflect the nation's changing history as well as influences from neighboring countries and regions. Styles date from several major cultural periods: pre-Lao, Lao kingdoms (1353–1892), the colonial years (1893–1954), the independent kingdom (1954–1975), and the Communist era (after 1975).

No architecture survives from the pre-Lao period (before the fourteenth century CE) in central and northern Laos. For the first six centuries of the common era, a people about whom little is known lived on the Plain of Jars, named for their custom of burying their dead in large stone jars, many of which remain.

Southern Laos was part of the Khmer Empire, and the ruined temple complex of Wat Phou near Pakxé was a major Khmer center. Wat Phou was built on six levels or terraces that were connected by steps and a central walkway. Built and maintained by Khmer kings between the seventh and fourteenth centuries, it was one of the most important Hindu sanctuaries in the empire from the ninth through the thirteenth century. Wat Phou was designed to express the Hindu vision of the relationship between nature and humankind, using an axis from a mountain top to a river bank to lay out a geometric pattern of temples, shrines, and waterworks that extend over some 6 miles (10 km). Most of the remains at Wat Phou that can be seen today date back to the eleventh century. The main shrine was originally dedicated to the Hindu god Shiva but now houses a statue of the Buddha. The site was declared a UNESCO World Heritage Site in 2001.

Wat Phou, in southern Laos, is home to a Hindu Khmer temple complex that is older than Angkor Wat in Cambodia. For a time, Wat Phou may have served as the capital of the Khmer Empire.

TRADITIONAL ARCHITECTURE

The Lao migrated into the region from southern China, and in 1353 they founded a kingdom called Lan Xang (literally, "a million elephants"). The typical Lao architectural medium was hardwood, preferably teak. Traditional Lao wooden houses are rectangular with a simple ridged roof covered with thatch or bamboo. They are built on high stilts and usually contain a large single room. Richer families have more elaborate structures of several interlocking rooms with shaded indoor and outdoor spaces. The stilts prevent flooding, enable better air circulation, and stop animals from entering. The shaded space beneath the house is used for cooking and keeping animals, such as pigs and chickens, and in modern times to park cars or motorcycles.

The finest buildings of the Lao kingdoms are found in Vientiane, the present national capital, and Louangphrabang, the former capital. In 1995 UNESCO declared Louangphrabang a World Heritage Site, calling it "the best preserved city of Southeast Asia." Louangphrabang has a mix of traditional Lao dwellings, former royal palaces, French colonial architecture, and long riverside promenades, as well as more than 30 Buddhist monasteries.

Since the fourteenth century, most Lao art and architecture relates to Theravada Buddhism, the main Lao religion. In addition to the royal palaces, the architectural structures of greatest interest are *wats* (temples or monasteries). A *wat* usually consists of several buildings, including the *sim* (the hall where monks are ordained), the *that* (a tower- or bell-shaped reliquary containing Buddhist relics), the *haw tai* (the library where old scripts are stored), the *haw kawng* (the drum tower), and the *kuti* (the monks' dwelling place). The large sweeping roofs are high peaked and culminate in decorative metal devices, called *dok so fa* ("pointing to the sky"), which are characteristic of Lao *wats*. Few early wooden buildings survived the frequent wars with neighboring countries, but many were rebuilt in the traditional manner. However, two famous temples were spared: Wat Xieng Thong in Louangphrabang and Wat Si Saket in Vientiane.

Wat Xieng Thong ("Temple of the Golden City") was constructed in 1559 and 1560 by Lao King Setthathirat (reigned 1548–1571). The temple is located at the junction of the Mekong and Nam Khan rivers. During the 1960s, Wat Xieng Thong was remodeled and finely redecorated. Until 1975, it was a royal temple, supported by the royal family, and the place

Wat Xieng Thong ("the Temple of Golden City") in Louangphrabang is the former royal temple where Lao kings were enthroned.

where Lao kings were crowned. It is considered the most beautiful of Louangphrabang's monasteries and represents typical Lao art. Its buildings have carved and gilded wooden door panels with motifs from the natural world, mythical creatures, or scenes from the Buddha's life. Inside the *sim*, richly decorated wooden columns support a ceiling vested with *dhammachakkas* (dharma wheels that symbolize Buddhist law and the endless cycle of reincarnation). The outer walls depict Lao legends. The rear gable is decorated with a famous glass mosaic of the "tree of life." Mosaics are also found on the exterior walls of the Sanctuary of the Reclining Buddha, known more commonly as the Red Chapel.

Wat Si Saket was built by King Anouvong (reigned 1803–1828) in 1818. The main buildings are in an early Thai style, surrounded by a thick-walled cloister. The interior walls are riddled with small niches that contain over two thousand silver and ceramic representations of the Buddha. Another three hundred seated and standing figures of the Buddha, some of them several hundred years old, rest on long shelves below the niches. The total number of Buddhas at Wat Si Saket is 6,840.

The most famous temple in the country, however, is the Phra That Luang (or "Great Sacred Reliquary") in Vientiane. The building can be traced back to an eleventh-century Khmer monastery, and it may have been a religious site before then. Rebuilt and considerably enlarged several times, the temple became the symbol of Lao nationhood when the capital moved from Louangphrabang to Vientiane in the sixteenth century. Today's buildings are early twentieth-century French reconstructions, regilded in 1995 to celebrate the twentieth anniversary of the Communist Lao Republic. The square temple has four arched gates at each side, opening onto four stairways leading to the upper levels. Each level has different architectural and ornamental features reflecting the Buddhist worldview. Believers are intended to walk around the building at all levels, contemplating these features. The main structure is the central stupa (dome) that rises 148 feet (45 m) and is crowned by a stylized banana flower and parasol. Surrounded by a thick wall, the temple also served a defensive purpose.

THAI, FRENCH, AND COMMUNIST INFLUENCES

Lao art and architecture were strongly influenced by Siamese (Thai) culture in the eighteenth and nineteenth centuries. French colonization from the end of the ninteenth century did not replace Thai influence but added another layer to Laos's cultural heritage. French colonial architecture can be found mainly in cities, where thick-walled buildings with shuttered windows and pitched tile roofs reflect French provincial style. Many colonial buildings decayed after independence, but some have been renovated to serve as government offices or company headquarters. The presidential palace (once the residence of the French colonial governor) in Vientiane is a vast building in the Beaux Arts style popular from 1885 through 1920. French influence is also evident in the colossal Patuxai monument in the capital. Reminiscent of the Arc de Triomphe in Paris, it was built in 1960 to commemorate the Lao who had died in the wars before independence. The former royal palace in Louangphrabang is a fine example of blended French and Lao architectural styles. Constructed between 1904 and 1909, it is now a national museum housing royal regalia and religious treasures.

Architecture in the Communist era has been strongly influenced by Soviet plans and designs, because many modern Lao architects were educated in the Soviet Union. Soviet-style buildings tend to be large, grandiose structures quite different from traditional local styles and their surroundings. Characteristic Soviet-style public buildings include the monumental National Assembly and the Lao National Culture Hall, both in Vientiane.

DECORATIVE ARTS

Traditional Lao decorative arts include sculptures and ornaments made of wood, bamboo, stone, bone, or bronze. The most popular sculptures depict the Buddha in different positions: standing, sitting, walking, or reclining in a style close to Thai or Khmer Buddhas. Many old sculptures survived wars and fires in the caves in the many limestone cliffs that dot the mountains of Laos. The most famous caves, some of which have been used for Buddhist worship for centuries, are Pak Ou, north of Louangphrabang, where two large caves are filled with hundreds of wooden and metal Buddha statues of different sizes. Many monasteries display statues of Kinnari, a female creature with a human upper torso but the wings and legs of a bird. The *naga*, a snakelike mythical creature, is frequently used as architectural ornament, flanking entrances in *wats* or beside stairs. Decorative art objects include woven mats and baskets, metal boxes and textiles such as the *phaa nung*, a characteristic Lao wraparound skirt, and the shawl-like *phaa biang* that is worn over the shoulders at weddings or festivals. The Hmong people in Laos also have their own distinct styles of decorative arts.

P. ZILTENER

Festivals and Ceremonies

The national day of Laos is December 2, the anniversary of the overthrow of the monarchy in 1975 and the establishment of the present Communist dictatorship. Celebration of the event is compulsory and the day is marked by parades and speeches.

Although Laos uses the Western calendar, most of its traditional holidays are marked according to the lunar calendar and fall on a different day in the Western calendar each year. Many Laotians celebrate traditional, mainly Buddhist, holidays rather than the secular and political holidays decreed by the authorities.

TRADITIONAL HOLIDAYS

In many rural areas, celebrations for the festival Bun Nam, which falls in October, are combined with the national day on December 2. By combining the two festivals, poor people save money and also add a popular reason to celebrate alongside the enforced public holiday. Bun Nam, the water festival, ends three months in which relatively little rain falls. The day is marked by boat races along the Mekong River, particularly in Vientiane, Savannakhet, and Louangphrabang. In smaller towns, the races are generally postponed until December 2.

Bun Nam is preceded by Awk Phansaa, a major public celebration that marks the full moon. At Awk Phansaa, Buddhist monks journey through the area around their temple receiving gifts of food, cloth, bowls, and other items from local people. On the day before Awk Phansaa, villagers make small banana-leaf boats, place candles in them, and float them on rivers at night.

A street parade in Vientiane marks the lunar New Year. At temples, people coat statues of the Buddha with flower petals.

The Bun Pha Wet festival in January is the traditional time for young men to become Buddhist monks. In each neighborhood, the ceremony is staggered by several days so that local people can witness the ordination of more than one friend or relative. Magha Puja, in February, marks a historic spontaneous gathering of monks to hear the Buddha preach. The festival is commemorated by offerings and candlelit parades around temples.

Boun Bang Fai, the May rocket festival, is a popular event. Monks make decorated rockets from bamboo. After being carried in a parade, the rockets are lit and sent skyward to invite rain. In larger towns, the celebrations lasts two days. The Buddha's birthday, in May, is combined with a commemoration of the Buddha's enlightenment and celebrated by candlelit prayers and ceremonies at temples. At the festival of the dead in August, people honor their ancestors, and the bones of those deceased in the previous year are exhumed for cremation.

NEW YEAR

Although New Year's Day, January 1, is marked as a public holiday, the traditional lunar New Year celebrations (Boun Pai Mai), which fall in spring, are more enthusiastically celebrated. The New Year holiday, the most important in the year, normally lasts for three days. Because the holiday falls when the spring rains are beginning, the festival is celebrated by the use of water. Statues of the Buddha are soaked to encourage rain, and boisterous groups of people throw water at passersby. Worshippers make small decorated stupas (domes) of sand in temple courtyards and leave offerings of flowers and fruit to ensure health and good fortune during the coming year. Laotians thoroughly clean their homes for Boun Pai Mai and usually wear new clothes. At Louangphrabang, an elephant parade marks the holiday, a reminder of court celebrations in the days of the monarchy before 1975. Family groups may sing folk songs and a traditional circle dance, *ramwong*, is popular.

The Chinese and Vietnamese communities in Laos celebrate their new year festivities in spring with noisy firework displays in Vientiane and Savannakhet. Chinese and Vietnamese residents close their workplaces for the holiday. Other public holidays in Laos include Labor Day, May 1, and Children's Day (June 1). In the cities, people attend fairs on public holidays and play music, and beauty pageants are increasingly popular on holidays in Vientiane.

K. ROMANO-YOUNG

Food and Drink

The culture of Laos has much in common with that of its western neighbor, Thailand, and Lao cuisine resembles Thai food in some respects. However, while Thai food makes use of more oil, curry, coconut, and other fragrant flavorings, Laotians prefer fresh, simple, often uncooked ingredients.

Lao food is typically seasoned with soy sauce, the characteristic galangal herb, garlic, coriander, lemongrass, chilies, mint, ground peanuts, ginger, and basil. Galangal, which is also known as laos root, is used in Thai cooking but is a signature flavor of Lao food. A member of the ginger family, galanga has a distinctive pungent quality. Sesame oil, vegetable stock, or vegetable oil form the base of many Lao dishes. Cider vinegar, distilled white vinegar, rice wine vinegar, lime juice, or tamarind juice may be added to dishes.

RICE

Most Laotians live in the country, and the majority grow rice. Laotians favor sticky rice, *klao niaw*, which is seldom used as a staple anywhere else. *Klao niaw* is served in a basket, and diners scoop it out with their fingers, either eating the rice on its own or with meat or freshwater fish. Each person forms a ball of rice, which is then dipped into condiments. A basket of rice can be carried into the fields by agricultural workers, and there is room inside the basket for fish or meat that is served to accompany it. Laotians also favor noodles that are served with caramelized sugar. *Pa daek*, an unmistakable sauce, may be used as a dip for rice, and it is served with a variety of Lao dishes. The sauce is made from fermented fish that is usually kept in a clay jar stored outside because it is so highly pungent.

FAVORITE DISHES

Traditionally, many Lao foods are often served raw. *Laap seua*, or tiger *laap*, is made of the finely chopped meat and organs of duck, chicken, pork, beef, water buffalo, deer, other game, or fish, along with chilies, onions, and mint. Although *laap* is usually raw, it may also be cooked. *Channam touk*, a beef salad, is served at the New Year festival and other celebrations, such as weddings. To make *channam touk*, finely chopped beef is minced with onion, lime, garlic, *pa daek*, cilantro, and other seasonings. It is served with lettuce leaves. Diners load the beef mixture onto the lettuce, along with rice, and roll the leaves into little parcels that can be dipped in sauce.

Laotians also stir fry, roast, and steam their foods. A popular dish is *khua my*, made with noodles, soy sauce, and beef. Chopped raw vegetables may be served along with thin rice

Laos grows a wide variety of fruit, including limes, that are used to make flavorful sauces and vinegars.

noodles or vermicelli called *klao poun*. The most popular fast food in Laos is *feu*. a soup of meatballs and vermicelli. Sidewalk *feu* sellers are common in the downtown areas of the few cities in Laos.

Popular dishes include vegetable soups made from bamboo shoots or mushrooms, and salads, such as the green papaya salad *tam mak hung*, which is made with a characteristic Lao deep mortar and pestle. Favorite vegetable dishes include eggplant, cucumber, mushrooms, carrots, bell peppers, cabbage, and broccoli, sometimes cooked with pineapple. Beef and chicken are the most commonly used meats, and catfish (*pa ling*) is the most common fish to appear in Lao dishes. Tofu, which is made of soy bean curd, may be served in a variety of ways, including sweet and sour.

The northern area around Louangphrabang, the former royal capital, is home to a memorable stew that is made from water buffalo meat, eggplant, fish sauce, and lemongrass, garnished with pork skin and basil. Other delicious Laotian stews are based on quail, cabbage, and coconut milk.

K. ROMANO-YOUNG

DAILY LIFE

Religion

Before 1975, when Laos was a monarchy, Buddhism was the state religion. When the Communists seized power in 1975, they were obliged to reach an accommodation with the religion that was followed by the majority of the citizens of Laos.

Buddhism arrived in Laos in the eighth century CE, and by the fourteenth century, most Lao Loum (Lowland Lao) were Buddhists. In the early twenty-first century, 58 percent of Lao are Buddhists, around 34 percent follow traditional beliefs, and 5 percent are nonreligious. Small groups of Christians and Muslims account for the remaining 2 percent. The majority of Lao Theung (Upland Lao) hold traditional beliefs in spirits (*phi*) and practice ancestor worship. Although spirit worship is banned, the practice continues. A belief in spirits underlies the Buddhism of some Lao Loum, who believe that they are protected by *khwan* (32 spirits), and some *wats* (Buddhist temples) have a hut that is thought to be home to the spirits.

THERAVADA BUDDHISM

Theravada (the school of Buddhism practiced in Laos) differs from other Buddhist schools in its beliefs about the Buddha. Theravada Buddhists hold that the Buddha was the only enlightened teacher; other schools teach that the Buddha was only one of many enlightened people. Buddhists believe in reincarnation and that the cycle of reincarnation can only be ended when all desires are extinguished. This state is called nirvana. Theravada Buddhists believe that only monks and nuns can attain nirvana.

Buddhist rites are an integral part of Laotian life, either as a tradition or a belief system. The *wat* is the center of village life and the place for ceremonies and festivals. Around 5,000 temples serve Lao Buddhists, who bring food to monks at their local *wat*. In Vientiane, a few large *wats* have been confiscated by the state and turned into museums. Laos is home to about 22,000 Buddhist monks, around 40 percent of whom are senior monks who will not return to secular life. A typical *wat* has an

adjoining building for monks and novices. Despite official discouragement, many Lao men spend a short period, often only a few weeks, as a monk. However, few Lao women become nuns. Buddhists believe that acts of benevolence (merit) help an individual toward enlightenment. Most Lao Buddhists believe that support for the local temple and participation in its ceremonies earn merit. Many Lao Loum attend prayers at the *wat* at the phases of the moon and major Buddhist festivals.

LAO BUDDHISM UNDER COMMUNISM

The Lao Buddhist heritage survived Communism. Monks were once the only village teachers, but in modern times, secular teachers appointed by the Communist authorities instruct children. Before 1975, Lao Communists attempted to enlist the support of rural monks. Popular resentment concerning great inequality in Lao society contributed to the partial success of this campaign, and by the time the Communists took power, many *wats* had been politicized. Lao Communists hold that Communism and Buddhism are compatible because both teach equality. The authorities tolerated Buddhism but sought to control it by restricting the activities of monks. In the late 1970s, Communist officials attempted to replace monks in their leading role in the villages. Some monks fled to Thailand, but the majority joined the (Communist) Lao United Buddhists Association, which replaced the former religious hierarchy. Buddhist practices revived from the late 1980s, and more people attended *wats*. Since the late 1990s, the authorities have encouraged Buddhism and some elements of Buddhist ritual have been incorporated into public ceremonies. Other religions operate within strict limits and restrictions on Christianity have increased.

P. FERGUSSON

A Buddhist monk chops wood at a temple. Monks' lives consist of meditation, chanting, and labor.

Society, Welfare, and Education

Lao society was traditionally hierarchical, with much emphasis placed on status. There were also many regional differences, particularly those between the Lowland Lao and the Upland Lao. Since the Communist takeover in 1975, political decisions have had a profound effect upon Lao society, particularly among city-dwellers.

In Lao society, age and experience provide status. Wealth, employment, and knowledge (particularly religious knowledge) also enhance the status of an individual. Historically, village communities elected a chief, but in modern times villagers elect a committee, headed by a president. Communist Party officials ensure that all candidates for election are ideologically acceptable. However, despite the imposition of egalitarian political structures, the concept of status remains embedded at the core of Lao society. The Lao language reflects the traditional hierarchy by having four different constructions for use when speaking to people in different levels of society.

Many Lao schools, particularly those in rural districts, have insufficient classrooms and school buildings for all their students' needs. These children break for a meal in the school yard.

MARRIAGE AND EQUALITY

Until the second half of the twentieth century, most Lao marriages were arranged, and a bride price covered the cost of the wedding. This practice still exists in some rural areas. A newly married couple often lives with the bride's family for several years, and the groom helps the bride's family farm the land. After a few years, the couple may set up their own home. Sometimes the youngest daughter and her husband remain in the bride's home to care for elderly parents. In a typical Lao home, gender determines who will perform different household tasks. Women clean, wash clothes, cook, raise children, and tend gardens and poultry. Men plow, harrow, maintain buildings, and look after larger animals. Both men and women prepare rice fields (paddies) for planting. The family remains at the center of Lao society. In small villages, the entire community often functioned as an extended family because, until recently, nearly everyone was related through marriage.

Although the constitution of Laos guarantees equal rights for women, discrimination—much of it rooted in tradition—persists. Nevertheless, many women in the cities have responsible positions in higher education, civil service, and with private corporations.

EDUCATION

Education became compulsory in 1951, but not all children attend school, particularly in the remote mountainous regions. Attendance rose from 63 percent of children of school age in 1988 to more than 90 percent by 2000. The education system is beset with funding difficulties. Village schools are often inadequate, poorly constructed, and lack textbooks and other equipment. Many schools have too few classrooms, and some districts do not have enough schools. Because of overcrowding, some village schools teach only two or three grades. There is also a considerable shortage of teachers. In secondary classes, there are insufficient computers and laboratory apparatus. The national curriculum is not innovative enough to prepare students for modern life: information technology is not taught. English, rather than French, is now taught as a second language.

Lao children are legally required to attend school at primary level for four years from age six. Compulsory attendance at junior high school level for three years and high school level for another three years is not yet effective. After lower-secondary education, some students opt for vocational education rather

Lao women wash clothes in a small waterway. Gender still determines many domestic responsibilities in Laos.

than higher secondary school. Secondary school students work toward a baccalaureate that, in theory, gives entry to higher education. However, only the wealthy can afford to put their children through college. Most higher education institutions, including the national polytechnic and university-level colleges, are in Vientiane, the Lao national capital.

Schoolteachers are poorly paid and often have second jobs. As a result, classes may be held for only several hours a day, and students may take two or more years to complete a grade. Large numbers of students drop out of school. Enrollment varies by region. School attendance is higher in the cities and among Lowland Lao (Lao Loum). In rural areas, attendance, particularly by female students, is much lower, and in some ethnic minorities in upland areas, there is little tradition of education. Students must usually travel to provincial capitals or local district centers for secondary education. Secondary schools are particularly short of staff. Many vocational and secondary teachers left Laos when the Communists took over in 1975. In the 1990s, teachers from the Soviet Union, East Germany, and Vietnam made up some of the shortfall of suitably qualified staff. Since the fall of Communism in the former Soviet Union and in central and eastern Europe, the flow of teachers from abroad has diminished.

Since the 1990s, a UNESCO- and state-sponsored adult literacy program has enrolled educated people in village communities to teach those adults who are unable to read or write. The program nearly doubled the number of literate adults in Laos, but some newly literate Lao later lost their ability to read and write because they had no access to written materials after taking part in the program.

WELFARE

Laos introduced a state social security system between 1999 and 2001. The system does not yet operate through the whole country, and only workers in state-owned or private enterprises with more than 10 employees are covered, but employees in smaller companies may participate in the program on a voluntary basis. The system is funded by employer contributions, a 5 percent levy on the monthly payroll. A separate social security system provides benefits for civil servants, members of the army and air force, and the police.

Several benefits are paid: an old age pension, a disability pension, a survivor's pension for widows, and a maternity benefit. The usual retirement age is 60, but retirement may be deferred. Disability benefit is paid to workers who suffer a permanent or long-term inability to earn an income. There is also provision for a caregiver's benefit, payable to those caring for the long-term sick or disabled. To receive a survivor's pension, a widow must be 44 years of age or over or have children under 15 years of age. Orphans' benefit is paid to children 15 years of age and younger (and up to age 25 in the case of full-time students). A death grant is paid toward funeral expenses. All of these payments or pensions are modest, but they represent a greater social security provision than in some countries in the region, for example Cambodia.

HEALTH

The provision of health care in Laos is inadequate, largely because of lack of funds. In most years, the government allocates less than 5 percent of a limited national budget to health care. As a result, modern hospitals are found only in the major cities, and in some rural areas, people do not have access to a doctor or a health center. Laos suffers shortages of doctors, health care facilities and equipment, and medicine.

Many health problems remain, particularly preventable communicable diseases. The authorities have prioritized vaccination against diseases and various measures to attempt to eliminate malaria, including the destruction of mosquito breeding grounds. However, although the incidence of malaria has been greatly reduced, the disease still remains widespread. Childhood diseases (particularly respiratory diseases) and diarrhea account for many infant deaths. Poor sanitation and vitamin deficiency add to the nation's health problems.

The Lao authorities are increasingly dependent upon aid from foreign governments, international organizations, and nongovernmental bodies to invest in improvements in health care provision. Bureaucracy sometimes hinders the distribution and availability of medical supplies, and people in the cities have come to use (unregulated) private pharmacies that sell Western drugs imported from Thailand. In rural districts, many people still use traditional herbal medicines and consult spirit healers.

P. FERGUSSON

Vientiane

A port on the Mekong River, Vientiane is the only large city in Laos. Although Vientiane was the capital of a Lao kingdom from 1707 through 1828, the city only gained preeminence toward the end of the nineteenth century, when it was chosen as the center of French colonial administration in Laos.

Vientiane had a population of 200,000 within the city limits at the national census in 2005 (provisional returns). In the same year, the metropolitan area was home to 695,000 people. The city is the only major center of industry and commerce in Laos.

A TURBULENT HISTORY

Toward the middle of the sixteenth century, the rulers of the Lao kingdom of Lan Xang moved their capital from Louangphrabang to Vientiane. Lan Xang divided in the eighteenth century, and Vientiane became the center of one of three Lao kingdoms. As Thai power increased across the Mekong River, the city became vulnerable to foreign intervention. In 1778, the Thais crossed the Mekong, annexing parts of the east bank and incorporating Vientiane within Siam. Thai rule continued into the nineteenth century, and when the ruler of Vientiane attempted a revolt against Siam in 1828, the city was sacked by the Thais who destroyed all but one of its ancient temples (*wats*).

French colonial rule began in Laos at the end of the nineteenth century. The Mekong River was established as the border between Thai and French territory along much of its course, and the new border placed Vientiane under French control. The French colonial authorities governed Laos in two colonies and two states, Louangphrabang and Champasak, that retained their own hereditary rulers. However, from 1899, the colonial administration was based in Vientiane, which soon surpassed all other Lao centers in size and status.

Vientiane grew rapidly. The city gained some European-style boulevards lined with French colonial villas and administrative buildings. The river port flourished and industries were developed. New temples were built and older buildings reconstructed. Vientiane became the commercial, industrial, administrative, and cultural center

of Laos. During World War II (1939–1945), Japanese forces invaded but left the French authorities in place until the final months of the war. After the war, French colonial rule soon returned. However, increased Lao nationalism would not permit a restoration of the pre-war situation. The French reorganized Laos as a united kingdom with the king of Louangphrabang as sovereign but with Vientiane as the national capital. The country gained independence in 1954.

A NATIONAL CAPITAL

Vientiane became the capital of an independent nation but the chief of state, the king, remained in residence in the small city of Louangphrabang. A limited number of foreign embassies opened in Vientiane and new government departments established offices. The city's industries grew and employment opportunities attracted people to the city from the surrounding countryside. However, the development of Vientiane was restricted by civil war among three different factions that wracked Laos through the 1960s.

Modern Lao buildings, such as the National Cultural Hall in downtown Vientiane, display a mixture of traditional Lao, Thai, and modern international styles.

Thirty-nine small stupas surround the central stupa of Phra That Luang in Vientiane. The main stupa contains a relic of the Buddha.

when the Thai-Lao Friendship Bridge was constructed, communication across the Mekong River was by ferry. A highway now crosses the bridge, and although a railroad track was laid beside the road, it has not begun service. Laos still has no railroads, and Vientiane's connection with the Thai railroad system is several miles away within Thailand. Vientiane airport has a new international terminal, but the facility is not large and receives a relatively small number of international flights.

ANCIENT AND MODERN

Despite the presence of some modern government buildings and other official buildings and growing industrial facilities, Vientiane does not have the atmosphere of a major city. Large areas of traditional wooden structures remain, and surrounding villages have been incorporated into the metropolitan area by the expanding urban growth. Many parts of Vientiane have the appearance of a huge village, and even close to the downtown area, plots of vegetables and rice grow behind tree-lined boulevards. City dwellers keep hogs, chickens, and other domesticated animals.

The city lies near the center of the most important lowland in Laos, beside a sweeping bend along the Mekong River. The district produces rice and other crops that form the basis of Vientiane's industry. Factories mill rice, brew rice beer, and process food. Local tobacco is the basis of a cigarette industry, while local cotton was the original spur to the development of a textile and garment industry that greatly expanded at the end of the twentieth century. Timber brought to the city by river is cut and processed, and the lumber and furniture industries flourish. Other industries include matches, detergents, rubber, footwear, and building materials. Cautious economic reforms since 1986 have encouraged foreign investment in Vientiane, and the city now has foreign-owned clothing, consumer goods, and information technology factories, largely Thai-owned.

The economic power of Thailand across the Mekong River is evident. Thai culture and influence are increasing, and the Lao Communist authorities are uneasy about the growing Thai presence in the Lao capital. In the 1980s and 1990s, the bulk of Lao trade shifted toward the west, and Thailand became the nation's major trading partner. Vientiane, strategically placed on the Thai border, benefited as a result.

Laos has a poorly developed highway system, but Vientiane is the center of the main north-south land routeway. River transportation supplements the basic road network, but natural obstacles in southern Laos prevent barges from sailing between Vientiane and Cambodia and Vietnam. Until 1994,

For a national capital city, Vientiane has relatively few large modern buildings or multistory constructions. The few tall buildings in the modern international style appear out of place. The city has a university, a polytechnic school, and other institutions of higher education, and public buildings include the national library and the assembly building. The city's museums include the Lao Revolutionary Museum, which records the history of the Pathet Lao movement and the Communist takeover of Laos.

Vientiane's most famous landmark is the Phra That Luang, the former royal stupa (dome). Originally built in 1566, the elaborately decorated stupa, which was reconstructed in the 1930s, has a large distinctive central spire that is surrounded by a cluster of smaller spires. The stupa has become the unofficial symbol of the city.

A ceremonial arch rises above the northern end of Vientiane's principal boulevard, Lan Xang Avenue. The arch, which was built in 1960, is known as the Patuxai or Victory Monument and resembles an interpretation of the Arc de Triomphe in Paris, France. Visitors can climb steps to the top of the arch to obtain a view across the city. The Wat Si Saket temple complex contains 6,840 images of the Buddha in niches along its walls. The oldest surviving temple in Vientiane, it was the only one of the city's temples to escape destruction by the Thais in 1828.

C. CARPENTER

Louangphrabang

Sited along the Mekong River, Louangphrabang had a population of 50,000 people at the 2005 national census (provisional returns). Louangphrabang city is, however, the nation's major tourist center and the former royal capital of Laos.

Louangphrabang lies 130 miles (210 km) northwest of Vientiane, the national capital, but feels far removed from the modern world. Proclaimed a UNESCO World Heritage site in 1995, the city is protected from inappropriate development, and the size and style of new buildings are strictly limited.

A HISTORIC CITY

In the fourteenth century CE, Louangphrabang (then known as Muong Swa) became the capital of the Lao kingdom of Lan Xang. In the sixteenth century, the kings of Lan Xang moved their court to the rival city of Vientiane, downstream along the Mekong River. Lan Xang divided in 1707 and Muong Swa, by then renamed Louangphrabang, became the center of a new Lao kingdom named for the city. The kingdom of Louangphrabang became the strongest Lao state, and the city became the national religious center for Laotians. The city gained finely decorated temples (*wats*), a royal palace, and administrative buildings. When the French colonized Laos toward the end of the nineteenth century, the colonial authorities governed from Vientiane, which soon surpassed Louangphrabang in size and status.

In 1946 and 1947, the French reorganized Laos as a single entity, and Laos became a united kingdom with the king of Louangphrabang as the sovereign. However, Vientiane became the national capital and the center of the administration. When Laos gained complete independence in 1954, the king remained in Louangphrabang, which functioned as the Lao royal capital until the Pathet Lao Communists seized power in 1979 and imprisoned the principal members of the royal family, who probably did not survive. Deprived of its national role, the city stagnated and became a backwater.

MODERN LOUANGPHRABANG

In 1986, Lao Communists cautiously began to reform the nation's economy. The secular state relaxed its attitude toward Buddhism, and the fortunes of Louangphrabang, the national center for Lao Buddhists, began to revive. By the 1990s, foreign tourists visited Laos in increasing numbers, and Louangphrabang became an attraction for visitors.

The city lies at the foot of Mount Phousi, which occupies a peninsula between the confluence of the Mekong and Khan rivers. There are dozens of temples, including the Phu Si, which is said to contain a footprint of the Buddha. Wat Xieng Thong, the largest and most spectacular temple, has a tiered concave roof and is decorated with gold and colored glass. The temple lies near the confluence of the city's two rivers. Wat That Chom Si, atop Mount Phousi, gives a view across the city's ancient monuments. The temple has a gold spired stupa (dome) that is a landmark. The former royal palace is now a museum.

As a royal capital, Louangphrabang was home to artists who worked for the court. In modern times, decorative arts and textiles remain the main industries. Metalworking, particularly in gold and silver, had a long tradition in the city and has revived with the advent of tourism. Many residents earn their living catering for tourists. There are growing numbers of small hotels, and many small restaurants perch above the banks of the Mekong River. The city has several teacher-training establishments, a legacy of its role as the national religious center. Louangphrabang is small enough for the main sights to be accessible by foot. Farther afield, the Kuang Si waterfalls, 19 miles (30 km) to the south, and the Pak Ou caves, 16 miles (25 km) upstream, also attract tourists.

C. CARPENTER

Wat Xieng Thong in Louangphrabang is the former royal temple. It was completely redecorated and restored during the 1960s.

ECONOMY

For centuries, the Lao people were politically and economically overshadowed by their more numerous neighbors, the Thais and the Vietnamese. In modern times, the Lao government hopes to use to its advantage the nation's strategic location at the crossroads between the larger economies of its more powerful neighbors.

Laos is one of the ten poorest countries in the world, and around 40 percent of Laotians live below the official poverty line. The nation has limited land suitable for agriculture, a poor transportation and communications infrastructure, few natural resources, and very little industry. Until the mid-1980s, Laos was also politically isolated.

ECONOMIC CHALLENGES

Through the 1960s, civil war damaged the Lao economy and held back the nation's development. The Communist Pathet Lao movement took power in Laos in 1975 and nationalized the nation's infrastructure. Business people fled abroad, and the state took control of agriculture, industry, and the banks. The government implemented strict central planning and regulated production, trade, and the pricing of goods and services. Initially, Laos drew close to its Communist neighbor Vietnam, but by the mid-1980s, the contrast between living standards in Laos and capitalist Thailand across the Mekong River to the west was stark. Circumstances forced the Lao authorities to attempt economic reforms.

In 1986, the Lao government introduced the New Economic Mechanism (NEM) program, a cautious range of reforms that, it was hoped, would encourage limited private-sector development and foreign investment. State-run cooperative holdings were broken up, and small farmers were again allowed to own land and to sell surpluses through local markets. Retail prices were no longer fixed by the state but were allowed to find their own level through market forces. Autonomy for individual businesses replaced central planning, but at the same time,

Lao textile factories tend to have out-of-date machinery. The low wages of textile workers make the industry competitive, however, and textiles and garments have become the main Lao export.

state-owned enterprises lost their access to government subsidies. Formerly, the import of some manufactured goods was banned to protect Lao industries; after the reforms, a tariff system on imports safeguarded the nation's industries by making some imports artificially expensive.

At first, Laos achieved rapid growth thanks to the economic reforms. Foreign investment began in the late 1980s, and the textile and garment and furniture industries expanded as a result. Tourism also developed on a small scale. However, a regional economic crisis in the late 1990s slowed the growth of the Lao economy. Rapid inflation reduced the value of the national currency, the kip, and foreign investors began to favor more advanced economies within the region rather than invest in Laos. By the beginning of the twenty-first century, the Lao reform program began to falter. Official caution has been part of the problem. The Communist authorities were unwilling to relax controls enough to allow the economy to develop, perceiving that reduced economic control might lead to reduced political control. Although the government attempted to attract exiles to return to invest in Laos, many of the foreign corporations that set up businesses in the country in the 1990s have withdrawn, frustrated by officialdom and the lack of an efficient market economy.

Standard of Living

Laos has a low standard of living, with 34 percent of the population living below the official poverty line. There is great inequality, and the average wage is less than $1 a day. The per capita GDP was $1,900 in 2005; this figure is adjusted for purchasing power parity (PPP), a formula that allows comparison between living standards in different countries.

Although many farmers benefited from a modest relaxation of government controls, only a small minority of urban Laotians have gained from the reforms. The authorities seem unwilling to permit a faster expansion of tourism, and foreign tourists, and many other outside influences such as Thai corporations and television, are treated with suspicion. The authorities are particularly uneasy about the growing influence of Thailand over the Lao economy.

Whereas Communist governments in China and Vietnam loosened economic controls to allow their citizens to become more prosperous, and thus more willing to consent to continuing political restrictions, the Lao authorities were less radical in their reform program. As a result, international aid organizations now play a greater role in development than foreign investment through corporations. The country is dependent upon support from international donors, in particular to meet a growing budget deficit. However, even aid agencies are becoming disillusioned with restrictions and some international bodies have withdrawn from Laos. The reforms have achieved some success, however, and Laotian export earnings were around 600 percent higher in 2000 than they were in 1986.

RESOURCES

Laos has very few natural resources. The nation has reserves of tin that have been mined commercially since the early twentieth century, and Laos also mines precious stones. However, deposits of iron ore, coal, copper, gold, gypsum, and lead are not large enough to be economically important. The Mekong River and its major tributaries have considerable potential for the construction of dams to supply hydroelectric power. At present, the principal hydroelectric power dam is on the Ngum River north of Vientiane, the national capital. The Ngum power plant produces enough electricity to supply the needs of Vientiane and to provide a surplus to export to neighboring Thailand across the Mekong River. A second large hydroelectric dam project is due for completion on the Nam Theun River, a tributary of the Mekong River, in 2009. Around 90 percent of the electricity produced by the Nam Theun project will be sold to Thailand. This World Bank–funded project is, however, controversial because a large area of environmentally important forest, the home of several endangered animal species, will be drowned by the new reservoir. Electricity exports are an important foreign-currency earner for Laos. However, almost all of rural Laos is still without electricity, and only the main cities have a regular electricity supply.

AGRICULTURE

Laos is a largely agricultural society in which farming, fishing, and forestry supply almost one-half of the GDP (gross domestic product; the total value of all the goods and services produced in a country in a set period of time, usually one year). More than 80

EMPLOYMENT IN LAOS

Sector	Percentage of labor force
Agriculture	80
Industry and Services	20

Source: Government of Laos, 2002

In 2005, government figures showed that 2.4 percent of the labor force was unemployed. International observers consider that this figure is an underestimate, and that the real total is considerably higher.

percent of the labor force works on the land. The agricultural sector is traditional, unmechanized, and—because the majority of farmers are subsistence growers who produce food only for their own families—the industry largely operates outside the money economy.

Economic reforms that began in 1986 stimulated growth in agriculture. Small farmers were once more allowed to own the land and to sell any surpluses through local markets, and as a result, production increased. The agricultural sector grew unevenly, but in most years production of the major crops has increased by around 5 percent. The nation is now self-sufficient in rice, the principal food crop. Vegetables, corn, and sweet potatoes are also grown on small holdings, while coffee, sugar-cane, cotton, and tobacco are grown commercially, mainly on state-owned land. In the northwest, adjoining Thailand and Myanmar (Burma), farmers from the Hmong hill people cultivate illegal crops of opium and cannabis.

Rice production is concentrated in limited lowlands along the Mekong River valley, but production is restricted by a lack of irrigation facilities and frequent floods and droughts. Many Lao

Small boats transport sacks of rice seedlings to farmland along the Mekong River.

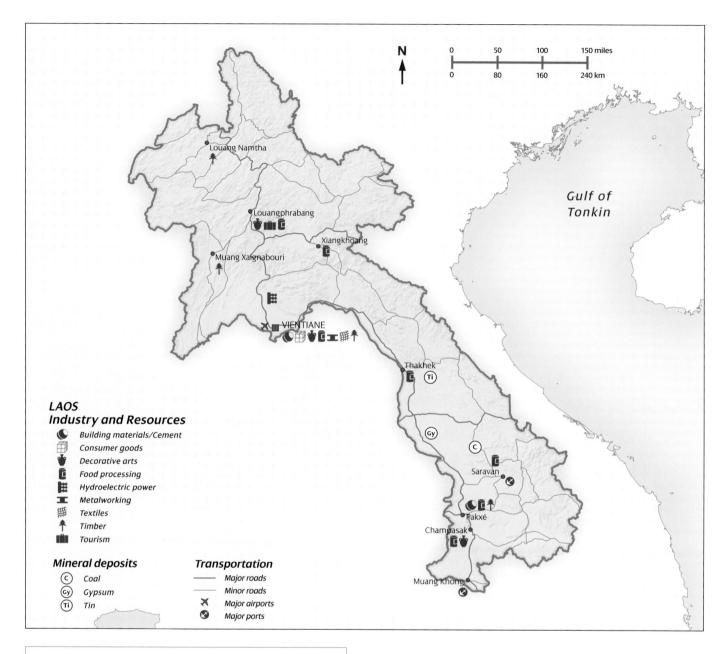

LAOS
Industry and Resources

- 🌙 Building materials/Cement
- ⊞ Consumer goods
- 🏺 Decorative arts
- 🗲 Food processing
- ⊞ Hydroelectric power
- ⚒ Metalworking
- ▦ Textiles
- ↑ Timber
- 📖 Tourism

Mineral deposits

- Ⓒ Coal
- Ⓖy Gypsum
- Ⓣi Tin

Transportation

- —— Major roads
- — Minor roads
- ✈ Major airports
- ⊗ Major ports

LAOS GDP

The Lao gross domestic product (GDP) was $12.1 billion in 2005. The figure is adjusted for purchasing power parity (PPP), an exchange rate at which goods in one country cost the same as goods in another. PPP allows a comparison between the living standards in different nations.

MAIN CONTRIBUTORS TO LAO GDP

Agriculture	45 percent
Industry	29 percent
Services	26 percent

Source: CIA, 2005

farmers grow only one rice crop a year, rather than the two annual crops that are possible in some other Southeast Asian countries. Unlike farming systems in neighboring states, where rice is an irrigated lowland crop, a proportion of the crop in Laos is grown by an upland dry rice method that relies solely upon rainfall. Cultivators in hill country fell areas of forest to cultivate rice for several seasons before abandoning the land once the soil is exhausted. Farming communities then move on to clear another piece of land for cultivation. The Lao authorities try to discourage this method of cultivation, perceiving it to be a major cause of deforestation and soil erosion, and the government has initiated programs to resettle hill people in the lowlands as fixed farmers.

Fishing is an important activity along the Mekong River and other major waterways. Most rural people catch fish from local ponds and rivers. Timber is also a major resource. Western nations import tropical hardwoods, and Laos produces large quantities of teak. Although felling is, in theory, tightly controlled, illegal logging activities occur throughout the country, as poor communications make oversight difficult. Illegal logging destroys the forest and increases soil erosion, yet the practice is expanding. Timber is a major export and is the basis of a rapidly growing furniture industry.

INDUSTRY

Laos is often said to be the least industrialized nation in Asia. The country's few industries, which supply only one-quarter of the GDP, are mainly based on processing agricultural and forest products. Most industries are centered in Vientiane (the only large urban area in the country), Louangphrabang, Savannakhet, and Pakxé. Food processing, particularly rice milling and making beverages, is an important industry. Furniture making and decorative arts industries, as well as sawmills, are centered in the main cities and in some smaller towns. A small but growing number of consumer goods factories have been established in Vientiane, including garment factories whose foreign owners were attracted to Laos by low local wage costs. Garments have now overtaken timber as the main Lao export.

SERVICES

The service industries of Laos were under government control until the late 1980s. The state still owns most of the banking sector, but privately owned banks are encouraged, and there are joint ventures between state-controlled Lao corporations and foreign investors. The retail sector is not highly developed outside Vientiane, where Thai, Vietnamese, and Chinese communities are active in commerce. Unlike neighboring Thailand and Cambodia, Laos has relatively few tourist attractions, but the tourist industry is expanding and has become an important foreign-currency earner. The nation's principal attractions include Vientiane, the Wat Phou temple complex, and in particular the temples and palaces of the former royal capital, Louangphrabang. Laos is still not widely known as a tourist destination and the tourist industry is still in its infancy. Growing numbers of Western tourists to Thailand also visit Laos—Vientiane is easily reached from Thailand.

TRADE

Timber and various wood products were formerly the nation's major export, but clothing is now the principal foreign-currency earner in Laos. The country also exports tin and coffee. In 2005, Laos exported goods worth $379 million and imported goods and services valued at $541 million, giving the nation a substantial balance of payments deficit. The main imports are machinery and equipment, transportation equipment (particularly motor vehicles), fuel, and consumer goods. In 2005, Thailand took 29.5 percent of Lao exports, followed by Vietnam (12.5 percent), France, and Germany. The principal suppliers of goods and services to Laos were Thailand (which provided around 66 percent of Lao imports), China (including Hong Kong), and Vietnam.

TRANSPORTATION AND COMMUNICATION

Landlocked Laos has an underdeveloped transportation system. The nation has one international airport at Vientiane, and only eight other small airports have paved runways. There are no railroads, but the Thai railway network extends to Nong Khai, a Thai town situated a few miles downstream from Vientiane on the opposite bank of the Mekong River.

Waterways supplement the limited Lao road system. Some 2,859 miles (4,600 km) of waterways are navigable, including much of the Mekong River, which forms most of the western border with Thailand. Barge traffic and smaller boats carry goods along most of the length of the Mekong River in Laos, but seasonal variations in flow restrict passage in some places, and two major natural obstacles block shipping and prevent barges from sailing the length of the Mekong. The Khone Falls in southern Laos, the world's second-largest waterfall in terms of volume of water, cuts off the Mekong River in Laos from the waterway downstream in Cambodia and Vietnam. Farther north, the Khemmarat Rapids, near Savannakhet, complete the barrier that cuts the navigable Mekong in Laos in two. Major tributaries of the Mekong are also navigable, and local people transport produce to towns using small boats and rafts.

Laos has 20,273 miles (32,620 km) of roads, only 2,852 miles (4,590 km) of which are paved. The road system is basic, comprising a main north-south highway that joins Vientiane with Savannakhet and Pakxé in the south and onward into Vietnam and a number of east-west routes that connect Vientiane with northern Vietnam. During the war in Vietnam in the 1960s and 1970s, the North Vietnamese built a road running from north to south through the Annamese Cordillera mountains in the border region between Laos and Vietnam. The route, which became known as the Ho Chi Minh Trail, was constructed as a supply line to bring troops and munitions from North Vietnam into South Vietnam. In modern times, the Ho Chi Minh Trail forms a second north-south route through Laos.

The Lao communications system is underdeveloped. In 2006, there were only 90,000 telephone lines in the country, mostly in Vientiane and the three other main cities. The cellular mobile phone system is not well established, and around 520,000 Laotians have cellular phones. Internet access is limited because of economic and political reasons, and by 2005 approximately 21,000 people in Laos had access to the Internet.

C. CARPENTER

Vietnam

Before French intervention in the region in the nineteenth century, central Vietnam was the empire of Annam. After the Japanese invaded in World War II (1939–1945), a Communist guerrilla force fought them in the north and attempted to establish a state centered on Hanoi. After the war, France struggled to regain control, and after the Communists defeated French forces in 1954, there were two independent Vietnamese states: a monarchy in the south and a Communist state in the north. South Vietnam (a republic after 1955) was unable to resist Communist infiltration from the north. By 1964, U.S. advisers supporting the southern government had grown into an army, and U.S. military involvement in the Vietnam War lasted until 1973. North Vietnam overran the south in 1975, and the two states united in 1976. After the late 1980s, Vietnam made economic reforms, but growth has been limited. Because it has a much larger population than its neighbors, except China, Vietnam has an influential role in the region.

GEOGRAPHY

Location	Southeast Asia, along the South China Sea between China and Cambodia
Climate	Tropical climate with little seasonal variation in temperature; wet monsoon season from May through September; dry season from October through March
Area	127,816 sq. miles (331,041 sq. km), excluding the disputed Spratly and Paracel islands
Coastline	2,153 miles (3,444 km), excluding the disputed Spratly and Paracel islands
Highest point	Fan-si-pan 10,306 ft (3,141 m)
Lowest point	Beside the South China Sea 0 ft (0 m)
Terrain	Flat delta regions in the north and south; central highlands; mountains in the northwest
Natural resources	Coal, phosphates, manganese, bauxite, offshore oil and natural gas, timber
Land use	
Arable land	20.1 percent
Permanent crops	6.9 percent
Other	73.0 percent
Major rivers	Mekong, Red River, Black River
Major lake	Hoa Binh reservoir
Natural hazards	Flooding, drought

FLAG

The national flag of united Vietnam was formerly the flag of Communist North Vietnam. The flag is red and there is a five-pointed gold star at the center. Red represents Communism. The five points of the star represent the different sections of Vietnamese society: industrial workers, farmers, intellectuals, the armed forces, and young people.

METROPOLITAN AREAS, 1999 POPULATIONS

Urban population	15 percent
Ho Chi Minh City	4,630,000
Ho Chi Minh City	3,320,000
Bien Hoa	360,000
Hanoi	2,610,000
Hanoi City	1,450,000
Haiphong	1,700,000
Haiphong City	550,000
Da Nang	750,000
Da Nang City	440,000

Can Tho	285,000
Can Tho City	240,000
Hué	265,000
Hué City	210,000
Nha Trang	260,000
Nha Trang	215,000
Buon Ma Thuot	230,000
Buon Ma Thuot City	130,000
Nam Dinh	220,000
Nam Dinh City	185,000
Long Xuyen	215,000
Long Xuyen City	150,000
Qui Nhon	210,000
Qui Nhon City	195,000
Rach Gia	195,000
Rach Gia City	190,000
Thai Nguyen	175,000
Thai Nguyen City	130,000
Tuy Hoa	160,000
Tuy Hoa City	65,000
Phan Thiet	150,000
Phan Thiet City	145,000

Source: Vietnamese census, 1999 (provisional returns). Apart from national and provincial figures, and figures for some cities, the results of the 1999 census have not been fully released.

NEIGHBORS AND LENGTH OF BORDERS

Cambodia	768 miles (1,228 km)
China	801 miles (1,281 km)
Laos	1,331 miles (2,130 km)

POPULATION

Population	82,070,000 (2004 government estimate)
Population density	642 per sq. mile (248 per sq. km)
Population growth	1.0 percent a year
Birthrate	16.9 births per 1,000 of the population
Death rate	6.2 deaths per 1,000 of the population
Population under age 15	27.0 percent
Population over age 65	5.8 percent
Sex ratio	98 males for 100 females
Fertility rate	1.9 children per woman
Infant mortality rate	25.1 deaths per 1,000 live births
Life expectancy at birth	
Total population	70.9 years
Female	73.9 years
Male	68.0 years

ECONOMY

Currency	Dong (VND)
Exchange rate (2006)	$1 = VND 16,752
Gross domestic product (2005)	$232.2 billion
GDP per capita (2005)	$2,800
Unemployment rate (2005)	2 percent
Population under poverty line (2004)	19.5 percent
Exports	$32.2 billion (2005 CIA estimate)
Imports	$36.9 billion (2005 CIA estimate)

A street market bustles with shoppers in a village by the Han River near Da Nang, in southern Vietnam.

GOVERNMENT

Official country name	Socialist Republic of Vietnam
Conventional short form	Vietnam
Nationality	
noun	Vietnamese
adjective	Vietnamese
Official language	Vietnamese
Capital city	Hanoi
Type of government	Communist republic
Voting rights	18 years and over, universal
National anthem	"Tien quan ca" (March to the front)
National day	Independence Day, September 2, 1945

TRANSPORTATION

Railroads	1,616 miles (2,600 km)
Highways	138,085 miles (222,179 km)
Paved roads	26,207 miles (42,167 km)
Unpaved roads	111,878 miles (180,012 km)
Navigable waterways	11,002 miles (17,702 km)
Airports	
International airports	3
Paved runways	26

POPULATION PROFILE, 2000 ESTIMATES

Ethnic groups	
Vietnamese	87 percent
Chinese	2 percent
Thai	2 percent
Khmer	2 percent
Hmong, Cham, and other minorities	7 percent
Religions	
Buddhist	67 percent
Nonreligious	19 percent
Christian (mainly Roman Catholic)	8 percent
Cao Dai	4 percent
Others	2 percent
Languages	
Vietnamese	87 percent
Tho	2 percent
Chinese	2 percent
Khmer	2 percent
Thai	2 percent
Other minorities	5 percent
Adult literacy	90.3 percent

CHRONOLOGY

111 BCE	The Vietnamese kingdom in the Red River Valley is annexed by the Chinese Han dynasty.
39 CE	The Trung sisters lead an unsuccessful uprising against Chinese rule.
3rd century CE	A Han-Vietnamese state, Dai Viet, subject to China, controls the north. In the south, the kingdoms of Funan and Linyi are part of the Indian cultural tradition.
939	The Vietnamese rise against the Chinese and secure their independence.
11th century	Ly Thai To founds the Ly dynasty (1009–1225) in northern Vietnam.
1225–1400	The Tran dynasty rules northern Vietnam.
1428–1788	The Le dynasty rules Vietnam, but after 1592, real power is in the hands of the Nguyen warlords (in the south) and the Trang warlords (in the north and center).
1771–1802	The Tayson peasant revolt breaks the stalemate between the Nguyen and Trang factions. Defeating the rebels, the Nguyen leaders reunite Vietnam and establish a new dynasty in Hué.
1867	Southern Vietnam becomes the French colony of Cochinchina.
1883	Tonkin in the north of Vietnam and Annam in the center become French protectorates.
1930	Ho Chi Minh (1890–1969) helps found the Indochinese Communist Party (ICP).
1940	Japan invades and occupies Vietnam.
1941	Ho Chi Minh establishes a Communist resistance force, the Viet Minh, to fight French and Japanese occupation.
1945	The Viet Minh declare an independent Communist state in the Red River Valley.
1946–1954	French and Viet Minh forces contest northern Vietnam.
1954	The Viet Minh defeat French forces at Dien Bien Phu. Vietnam gains independence but is divided into Communist-controlled North Vietnam and the monarchical State of Vietnam in the South.
1954–1975	North Vietnamese and local Communist forces attempt to undermine the pro-Western government of South Vietnam and force reunification.
1955	South Vietnam becomes a republic.
1960s and early 1970s	U.S. forces and South Vietnamese troops fight the Viet Minh.
1975	North Vietnam overruns the south, and in 1976 North and South Vietnam are reunited.
1979	Vietnamese troops enter Cambodia to oust the extreme Communist Khmer Rouge regime.
1986	The government introduces a program of economic reform, encouraging foreign investment.

GOVERNMENT

Vietnam is a Communist dictatorship. The Dang Cong San Viet Nam (Communist Party of Vietnam) exercises power through dominance of an electoral front called the Vietnamese Fatherland Front.

The Vietnamese Fatherland Front (VVF) comprises the Communist Party of Vietnam (DCSV) plus affiliated organizations that give the illusion of a multiparty system. The VVF allows some nonpartisans to contest elections. Economic reforms in the 1990s led to increased dissatisfaction concerning perceived corruption, disputed land rights, and the effective exclusion of ordinary citizens from the political process. In order to maintain a complete hold on power, the DCSV cracked down on critics, including dissident rural hill peoples and urban dissidents who communicated via the Internet.

Because of economic reforms, including the privatization of thousands of small businesses, the government no longer has absolute control over the Vietnamese economy. Communist Party hard-liners oppose additional liberalization, fearing that loosening the state's control of the economy may undermine the DCSV's political hold on the nation. The regime routinely detains perceived dissidents, restricts political and religious freedoms, controls the media, and prevents the establishment of free labor unions.

THE NATIONAL ASSEMBLY AND THE PARTY

Effective power rests with the 17-member politburo (central committee) of the DCSV. The assembly approves decisions that have already been made by the politburo and does not generally initiate legislation. The leading party official is the secretary general of the DCSV, who since 2001 has been Nong Duc Manh (born 1940). In practice, the secretary general exercises more power than the prime minister or the chief of state (the president).

The National Assembly (Quoc Hoi) has 498 members, who are elected for a five-year term by universal adult suffrage. The voting age is 18 years. In elections in 2002, 48 members were affiliated to the governing electoral organization, the VVF, but were not members of the DCSV, and an additional three members were independent candidates who were not members of the VVF. Since the late 1990s, some grievances have been allowed to be aired in the National Assembly as a means of providing an outlet for growing dissatisfaction.

THE CHIEF OF STATE AND THE HEAD OF GOVERNMENT

The Vietnamese chief of state is a president who is is elected for a renewable five-year term by the National Assembly. The chief of state has a ceremonial role and exercises fewer powers than the DCSV party leader. Since 2006, the chief of state has been Tran Duc Luong (born 1937).

The National Assembly elects a prime minister and other ministers who are responsible to the assembly in theory but who are responsible to the DCSV in practice. The prime minister exercises fewer powers than the party leader or the chief of state. Since 2006, the prime minister has been Nguyen Tan Dung (born 1949). Unlike the former common practice in the Communist states of eastern and central Europe before 1990, where the party leadership was often combined with the presidency or the prime ministerial office, the three main offices of state have remained separate in Vietnam.

Tran Duc Luong, Vietnam's president from 1997 through 2006, trained as a geologist.

LOCAL GOVERNMENT

Vietnam is divided into 64 provinces (*tinh*), including several municipalities that have provincial status. The provinces are administered by officials appointed by the DCSV. In 1996, 16 new provinces were created (including a municipality of provincial status). An additional three new provinces were created in 2003. The provinces are subdivided into municipalities (*thu do*) that are headed by elected mayors who are members of the Vietnamese Fatherland Front.

C. CARPENTER

MODERN HISTORY

Toward the Vietnam War

Defeat in the Battle of Dien Bien Phu in 1954 forced the French to negotiate a peaceful withdrawal from Vietnam at the Geneva Accords. The treaty, signed in 1954, temporarily split Vietnam into two until elections could bring reunification. However, partition would last a generation.

While the revolutionary leader Ho Chi Minh (1890–1969) became chief of state and head of the government in North Vietnam, the French confirmed Bao Dai (1913–1997), the former emperor of Annam (central Vietnam, which had been a French protectorate), as monarch of the State of Vietnam (South Vietnam). At the same time, Ngo Dinh Diem (1901–1963) was named as South Vietnam's prime minister.

NGO DINH DIEM

Ngo Dinh Diem quickly consolidated power. In October 1955, he displaced Bao Dai as chief of state and proclaimed Vietnam to be a republic, with himself as president. After the French withdrawal from South Vietnam, the United States, which had subsidized a major part of the French military campaign in Vietnam since the early 1950s, took their place as the main source of aid to the new South Vietnamese government. Diem concentrated upon building his power base in the south and continued to reject all efforts to reunify the two parts of Vietnam. The international community persistently refused North Vietnamese requests for nationwide elections and rebuffed a similar proposal from China in 1956. North Vietnam's pleas to Great Britain and the Soviet Union for help in fulfilling the terms of the Geneva Accords were ignored, and in 1957 the Soviet government proposed that both North and South Vietnam be admitted to the United Nations (UN) as separate countries. The seventeenth parallel that divided the two Vietnams appeared to have become a permanent dividing line.

From 1956 through 1959, the North Vietnamese did little to challenge the balance of power in Diem's South Vietnam, although there was low-level insurgency by Communists in the south. Efforts to reform land practices in the north had failed dismally, and North Vietnam was faced with food shortages and the consequences of political policies that included executions of landowners and the use of torture on political prisoners. However, the North Vietnamese abandoned such measures when it became clear that they did little to promote political cohesion or agricultural production. Diem was equally unsuccessful in the south, and he increasingly alienated more sectors of the South Vietnamese population. Diem faced major resistance among his own people. His problems stemmed from a

North Vietnamese Communist leader Ho Chi Minh holds a discussion with students at an exhibition in Hanoi in 1955.

number of factors. He was an uncompromising Roman Catholic in a predominantly Buddhist nation and was determined to promote Catholicism regardless of other religious traditions. Diem also allowed his brother, Ngo Dinh Nhu (c. 1910–1963), and his brother's wife, Tran Le Xuan (better known as Madame Nhu; born 1924), to exercise corrupt influence within the government. Land reforms failed, and Diem increasingly relied upon the military to maintain him as chief of state.

THE NLF

Political resistance in South Vietnam, fear of Communism on the part of U.S. government officials, and lack of international pressure to ensure free elections led to a gradual escalation of war from 1959. The North Vietnamese and insurgents in the south sought to undermine the southern government and reunite Vietnam.

Mounting guerrilla activity raised the pressure on Diem, and by 1960, dissatisfaction with Diem helped fuel the organization of a South Vietnamese movement to overthrow his government and unite South and North Vietnam under Ho Chi Minh. The National Liberation Front (NLF), created on December 20, 1960, allowed men and women to join regardless of political affiliations as long as they agreed to the reunification of Vietnam and the end of Diem's regime.

Despite this apparently broad condemnation of Diem, U.S. intelligence sources declared that the NLF was an instrument for the spread of North Vietnamese Communism. Even the terms applied to the organization revealed differing analyses: U.S. supporters of intervention on behalf of South Vietnam persistently used the label Viet Cong, short for Vietnamese Communist, for the NLF, a label that many in the NLF considered derogatory.

THE 1963 COUP

As Diem's government stumbled and its opponents gathered strength, U.S. officials publicly portrayed the South Vietnamese leader as a brave opponent of Communist opportunists. Within Washington circles, however, military and State Department officials acknowledged that despite extensive aid—South Vietnam was the fifth-largest foreign recipient of U.S. assistance by 1961, with $8 out of $10 earmarked for security—Diem had become a problem. When John F. Kennedy (1917–1963) assumed the U.S. presidency in January 1961, he increased financial aid to Vietnam and sent new advisers to assess political and military conditions. The resulting "December 1961 White Paper" called for more U.S. advisers to the South Vietnamese Army (ARVN), more money, and more equipment.

President Kennedy sent more "advisers," military personnel whose role would unofficially include active involvement in air and ground missions. U.S. advisers promoted the Strategic Hamlet Program, which attempted to eliminate NLF centers of support by removing villagers from their rural homes. The program became one of the major mistakes of U.S. planning in Vietnam because it disrupted centuries of village tradition and quickly alienated those faced with dislocation.

U.S. money and military prowess did little to win more support for Diem, and by the summer of 1963, the Kennedy administration warned Diem that he risked a coup. Matters worsened when Buddhist monks began to burn themselves alive in the streets of Saigon (modern Ho Chi Minh City), protesting the lack of religious freedom. When Army of the Republic of Vietnam (ARVN) generals secretly approached U.S. officials in Saigon for support, Kennedy made it known that he would not block the overthrow of Diem. On November 1, 1963, the coup engineered by ARVN generals ended with the assassination of Diem and his unpopular brother.

GROWING U.S. INVOLVEMENT

By the end of 1963, the United States had approximately 16,000 military advisers in Vietnam. In 1969, at the end of the presidency of Lyndon B. Johnson (1908–1973), the number had grown to well over 500,000 soldiers. During this period in the United States, Americans in the administration and in the general public argued constantly about the wisdom of continued military involvement in Vietnam.

When Johnson assumed the presidency in 1963, the war in Vietnam presented him with a major problem. If he withdrew or reduced troop strength and the United States appeared vulnerable to Communism on his watch, his reputation would be lost. If he pursued a war with no good hope of victory, he ran the risk of sacrificing his legacy as president. Johnson chose to escalate the war, and events in August 1964 marked his path to a dramatic change in the U.S. role in Vietnam.

On August 2, 1964, the U.S. destroyer Maddox was attacked by three North Vietnamese torpedo boats off the coast of North Vietnam, in the Gulf of Tonkin. All the North Vietnamese torpedoes missed, and the Maddox inflicted considerable damage on the torpedo boats before withdrawing. On August 3, the Maddox returned to the area with another destroyer. the USS C. Turner Joy. On August 4, the ships reported that a second attack was occurring. Although subsequently many participants questioned the accuracy of these accounts, Johnson immediately used the occasion to ask Congress for authority to proceed with military action without a declaration of war. The Gulf of Tonkin Resolution won unanimous approval in the House of Representatives. In the Senate, only two members objected to giving Johnson such unprecedented power.

The war in Vietnam continued as the president, in the words of the resolution, began to "take all necessary steps, including the use of armed force, to assist any member or protocol state of the Southeast Asia Collective Defense Treaty requesting assistance in defense of its freedom." By 1965, that included U.S. ground troops, aerial bombing by U.S. fighters, and America's first real battle in Vietnam.

M. MAY

The War for Vietnam

In 1965, the United States came more directly into conflict with North Vietnam. South Vietnam lurched from leader to leader after the assassination of President Ngo Dinh Diem (1901–1963), while in the United States, President Lyndon B. Johnson (1908–1973) increased U.S. involvement in the war in Vietnam after he succeeded to the presidency following the assassination of President John F. Kennedy in 1963.

President Johnson continued to follow the strategies of the Cold War (the rivalry between the Communist nations, led by the Soviet Union, and the Western world, led by the United States) of his predecessors. Johnson argued publicly that Vietnam was like a domino in terms of the spread of international Communism. If South Vietnam fell, he and his advisers claimed, so would the next country and the next, until the entire Pacific region risked a Communist takeover. Although such an analysis began to wear thin in the 1960s, both within the Johnson administration and among its critics, it was the basis of a dramatic expansion of the United States' role on the ground and in the air in Vietnam.

ESCALATION OF THE WAR

In March 1965, the United States initiated bombing raids over North Vietnam. Called Operation Rolling Thunder, the action continued, with some breaks, for three years. According to Johnson's officials, U.S. goals centered on improving South Vietnamese morale, halting supplies to North Vietnamese forces in the South, and demonstrating U.S. resolve. Some historians now argue that bombing primarily agrarian or less urban nations such as North Vietnam produces only limited military advantage, but during the war, U.S. reliance on bombing was a critical strategy. As a result, U.S. forces expended an unprecedented amount of bombs and explosives per capita in South Vietnam and Laos, and substantial amounts in North Vietnam and, from 1969 onward, Cambodia. The B52 Stratofortress, a staple bomber of the U.S. Air Force, was used from 1966 until 1973 for 124,532 missions. Civilian casualties were high.

In March 1965, President Johnson ordered the 9th Marine Expeditionary Brigade to Vietnam, as the first official ground troops of the war. Approximately 25,000 military "advisers" were already in South Vietnam. By August, U.S. troop numbers had risen to 125,000, and the 101st Airborne Division landed at Cam Ranh Bay. On August 18, U.S. troops clashed with National Liberation Front (NLF) forces (South Vietnamese organized to overthrow the nation's government; often called the Viet Cong) in Quang Ngai province. The first major battle involving U.S. forces came the following October and November, however, in the Ie Drang Valley. North Vietnamese forces (the PAVN; the People's Army of Vietnam) attacked a U.S. Army Special Forces camp at Plei Mai, in the Central Highlands. The U.S. 1st Cavalry Division (Airmobile) responded with a campaign, using the innovative technique of "air cavalry," in which helicopters, especially the UH-1 "Huey" and CH-47 Chinook, were used for rapid transportation of personnel and artillery, evacuation of the wounded, and resupply.

GROWING U.S. DISSENT

Some members of President Johnson's administration, including Assistant Secretary of State William Bundy (1917–2000) and Undersecretary of State George Ball (1909–1994), began to question the nation's deepening commitment in Vietnam. Outside the White House, dissent emerged from older foreign policy analysts and senators and members of the House of Representatives. Such critics offered careful nuanced reasons and possible plans for disengagement. On college campuses, in churches, and in city halls across the United States, an antiwar movement at grassroots level slowly gained momentum, protesting the American war in Vietnam.

U.S. bombing raids devastated large areas of North Vietnam during the period from 1965 through 1973.

Faced with more vocal opposition, yet still counseled by adherents of engagement, Johnson focused on what seemed to be a middle course: a limited war, in which the United States would continue its air and ground campaigns to bring the North Vietnamese to negotiations. Johnson defended his policies as a reflection of "America's solemn pledge" to the South Vietnamese people and a necessary protection against the still-present threat of Communist aggression in the region.

Supported by Secretary of Defense Robert McNamara (born 1916) and other advisers, Johnson rejected the requests of General William Westmoreland (1914–2005) and the Joint Chiefs of Staff for a significant increase in troop numbers, while agreeing to raise troop strength by 100,000. The president also authorized Westmoreland to proceed militarily as situations warranted, in effect fully Americanizing the war. These changes occurred without notification to Congress or any announcement of a new policy, which would later deepen the antagonisms between Americans supporting and opposing the war.

THE WAR ON THE GROUND

Between 1965 and 1968, the number of Americans serving in Vietnam rose from 23,000 to approximately 536,000, but the adversary proved tenacious. The North Vietnamese Army maintained supply lines via the 600-mile (960 km) Ho Chi Minh trail (or Truong Son Trail), which stretched along the Truong Son Range, part of the Annamese Cordillera, from Hanoi to near Saigon. The supply line ran in part through neighboring Laos. Repeated U.S. attempts to bomb or destroy the trail and its numerous way stations did little to discourage the so-called porters who carried hundreds of pounds of goods on specially fitted bicycles or on their backs. The tenacity of the porters earned them respect from their U.S. enemies.

The war in Vietnam was different from previous conflicts that the United States had undertaken. The Vietnamese climate, with extreme heat and monsoons, made fighting difficult, and many soldiers complained of an uncomfortable condition known as "immersion foot" caused by constant moisture. The nature of combat and the indecisiveness of victory were even more troubling for some Americans fighting in Vietnam. Unlike other wars, in which securing the enemy's territory indicated success, platoons routinely went on "search and destroy" missions in order to kill the opponent rather than to capture ground. It was, in other words, a war of attrition. This type of combat rapidly became demoralizing for U.S. troops because it focused warfare directly on killing. Many veterans cited the difficulty of determining which Vietnamese was an enemy, a sympathizer, or a friend. This psychological stress and uncertainty at times resulted in casualties that veterans would later recall with regret.

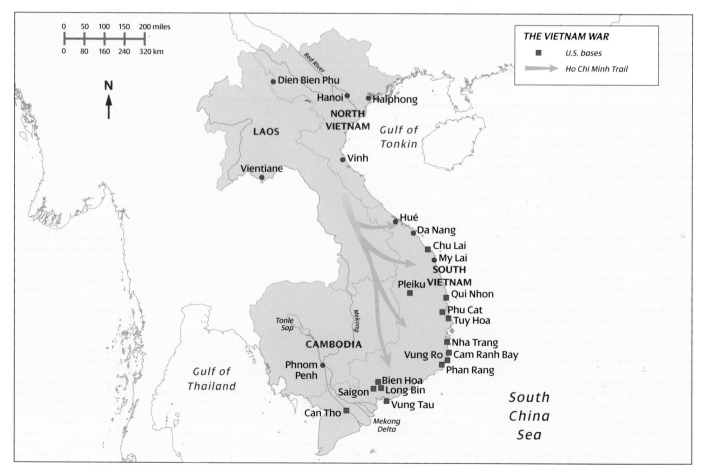

U.S. Marines place a casualty in a helicopter. Helicopters played an important role in the war, ferrying supplies and personnel.

The Protest Movement

In the United States, opponents and supporters of the war seemed to become ever more certain of their respective points of view. The antiwar movement expanded in 1966, as television coverage graphically brought the fighting into American homes. As early as August 1965, CBS News reported on Marines setting fire to the village of Cam Ne with their cigarette lighters. Although severely injured Americans never made the nightly news, the news from Vietnam seemed more and more disquieting. By early 1967, returning veterans organized Vietnam Veterans Against the War and protested in New York City. Dr. Martin Luther King, Jr. (1929–1968), already a Nobel Peace Prize winner, condemned the war, and student activists protested on college campuses. In October 1967, the March on the Pentagon attracted 100,000 for a rally, and afterward an estimated 35,000 descended on the Pentagon. The peaceful protest ended in violence that evening as federal marshals used tear gas to break up the remaining crowd. Almost 700 were arrested.

The March on the Pentagon was the first of numerous similar protests. In 1969, a Moratorium against the War attracted hundreds of thousands to the nation's capital, and *Time* magazine estimated that nearly two million Americans joined the protest in their respective towns and cities. While large assemblies gathering in Washington, D.C., or other U.S. cities riveted public attention on growing disapproval for President Johnson's policies, they also polarized the nation.

THE CONSEQUENCES OF WAR

Within Vietnam, the war had devastating consequences. Military and civilian casualties ran into thousands each month. Large numbers of civilians were forced to move. Some had to leave their homes as result of the "Strategic Hamlet" program in South Vietnam, in which villagers were relocated to barracaded villages patrolled by armed guards in an attempt to halt the influence of the NLF or those sympathetic to their cause. Others sought refuge in the cities of South Vietnam to escape the conflict. In North Vietnam, many civilians were killed or had to be evacuated because of U.S. bombing of urban areas. The infrastructure of both North and South Vietnam was badly damaged, and both parts of the country became poorer because resources that could otherwise have been used for development programs were diverted to fight the war or to address the consequences of war.

In the United States by 1967, doubt over the war grew even among those within the Johnson administration itself who had been its main advocates. Secretary of Defense Robert McNamara, who had been a key proponent of the war, urged President Johnson to reconsider his policies. When the president refused to do so, McNamara resigned. In 1968, both of the major U.S. political parties embraced presidential candidates who openly sought ways to disengage from the war in Vietnam.

THE TET OFFENSIVE

By 1967, the North Vietnamese were feeling the strain of an increasingly costly war against enemies who had superior weaponry. They decided on a drastic change in tactics. Attacks in the jungles and mountains of the western part of South Vietnam, mostly by PAVN forces, would draw the attention of U.S. forces to these remote areas. Then, during the Tet holiday (the Vietnamese lunar new year), when South Vietnamese forces would be at a low level of readiness, the NLF, along with some PAVN forces, would launch surprise attacks in urban areas.

Begun on January 30 and 31, 1968, the Tet Offensive ultimately ended with a technical victory for the U.S. and South Vietnamese. The NLF suffered devastating losses, although they were not so completely destroyed as some observers later claimed. The American military success ultimately mattered little, however. As Americans watched television reports of Tet engagements, including a devastating attack on the former imperial capital Hué, many concluded that the United States should withdraw. Then, on March 31, 1968, President Johnson stunned the U.S. electorate when he announced that he would not seek a second term in office.

TOWARD WITHDRAWAL

As the U.S. presidential campaign season continued, Johnson began to pursue new avenues for negotiations with the North Vietnamese. After the resignation of Secretary of Defense Robert McNamara, Johnson welcomed the careful diplomacy of new Secretary of Defense Clark Clifford (1906–1998). The North Vietnamese agreed to negotiations in Paris, and in order to further the talks, Johnson suspended bombing in October.

Republican Richard Nixon (1913–1994) won the presidential election in November 1968, promising to find "peace with honor" in Vietnam. Nixon's strategy became known as Vietnamization. The stated goal of Nixon's policy was to assist nations in fighting for themselves. In practice, Vietnamization meant that the United States would slowly decrease its troop numbers, use strategic bombing to reinforce secret peace talks with the North Vietnamese, and assume that the South Vietnamese would prepare for an eventual U.S. withdrawal. Nixon named Henry Kissinger (born 1923) as his National Security Adviser, and together Nixon and Kissinger also engaged the Soviet Union and China in discussions about an end to U.S. involvement in Vietnam.

While President Nixon's policies focused on reducing U.S. commitments in Vietnam, however, casualty rates remained high during his presidency. Questions of morality and covert operations also surfaced during the Nixon administration. While the CIA had begun activities such as Operation Phoenix as early as 1965, in which Vietnamese locals were targeted for assassination, the numbers increased dramatically by the last years of the war. The Church Committee of the U.S. Congress in 1976 received reports that Phoenix operatives killed more than 20,000 Vietnamese. The entry of U.S. forces into neutral nations was even more controversial. In 1970, an invasion of Cambodia by U.S. ground troops provoked campus protests in the United States. When troops fired on a crowd of protesters at at Kent State University, Ohio, killing four people. this led to even larger protests.

A disturbing incident became public in 1969, when U.S. reporter Seymour Hersh (born 1937) broke the story of My Lai. In March 1968, a platoon under the command of Lt. William Calley (born 1943) assembled and ordered the shooting of more than 300 Vietnamese villagers in the hamlet of My Lai. Several soldiers present attempted to stop the killings, and one soldier later alerted Congress. Military authorities indicted Calley, who was convicted by a military court of premeditated murder.

As the 1972 election approached, Nixon and Kissinger pushed the North Vietnamese for a peace settlement. When the North Vietnamese hesitated at the Paris negotiations, however, Nixon ordered renewed bombing. In the so-called "Christmas bombing" of 1972, the United States was more willing than ever before to risk B-52s in the area of the strongest North Vietnamese antiaircraft defenses. The 12 days of bombing, aimed mostly at targets in the region of Hanoi, the North Vietnamese capital, and Haiphong, its port, killed more than 2,000 civilians in what Kissinger called "jugular diplomacy."

THE PEACE AGREEMENT

On January 14, 1973, talks at the Paris peace conference reached an agreement. The South Vietnamese government had little choice but to accept the terms. In effect, the United States had won the right to expatriate its prisoners of war and for a peaceful withdrawal from Vietnam. The South Vietnamese government would be left to fight, or not, on its own. On January 15, 1973, Nixon announced the peace to the American people. The Paris Peace Accords, signed on January 27, 1973, officially ended America's war in Vietnam. In total, America lost 58,226 soldiers during the Vietnam War; the Vietnamese lost more than one million fighters and between two and four million civilians.

The South Vietnamese government remained unable to defend itself from the North Vietnamese or the NLF. By April 1975, North Vietnamese forces entered Saigon, and by the end of the month, the South Vietnamese government fell. Distraught South Vietnamese nationals who had worked with the Americans attempted to flee in a massive evacuation organized by the United States. The last American officials were airlifted to safety from the roof of the U.S. embassy.

The North Vietnamese had refused to negotiate surrender with the south. The end was a military conquest. A Communist republic was declared in South Vietnam and the "re-education" of public employees began. The infrastructure of the economy was taken into state ownership, and Saigon was renamed Ho Chi Minh City for the leader of Vietnam's revolution. On July 2, 1976, the Socialist Republic of Vietnam officially united what had formerly been North and South Vietnam since 1954.

M. MAY

Modern Vietnam

The fall of South Vietnam to North Vietnamese troops in April 1975 brought an end to a protracted series of wars that had cost the Vietnamese, French, and Americans millions of lives and billions of dollars. With the creation of the Socialist Republic of Vietnam in 1976, the reunified nation confronted significant political and economic challenges.

The Vietnamese faced the physical consequences of decades of combat. An estimated 1.1 million North Vietnamese and National Liberation Front (NLF, often known as the Viet Cong) soldiers had been killed between 1954 and 1975. More than two million civilian casualties throughout Vietnam added to the toll on families. Permanently injured soldiers and civilians also required support. Other battlefield dangers gradually became evident. Exposure to toxic chemicals such as Agent Orange, or dioxin, widely used by U.S. forces as a defoliant during the war, caused both disabilities among adults and significant birth defects in children. Unexploded land mines throughout South Vietnam posed an additional hazard; since 1975, an estimated 40,000 Vietnamese have been killed by remnant mines.

THE AFTERMATH OF WAR

Vietnam faced the difficult problem of how to deal with defeated adversaries. Former officials or supporters of the defeated South Vietnamese government had to be realigned to support or at least not oppose the new authorities. As many as half a million people were sent to "re-education" camps. Many high-level officials and business people had fled to the West before the fall of Saigon (renamed Ho Chi Minh City). More than 1.5 Vietnamese fled the nation, forcing an international refuge crisis. Many left in small boats and became known as the Boat People.

The extreme left-wing Khmer Rouge regime in neighboring Cambodia embarked on a program of genocide in 1975, murdering at least one million Cambodians (probably twice that number). The Cambodian genocide ended when Vietnam invaded in 1978 and forced out the Khmer Rouge in 1979. China, already disturbed by Vietnam's deepening alliance with the Soviet Union, retaliated with a brief invasion of Vietnam. The 29-day war, perceived by the Chinese as an appropriate chastisement, increased tensions between the neighbors. Following China's withdrawal of its forces from Vietnamese territory, both nations intensified troop strength along their shared borders, and their relationship remained hostile throughout the 1980s.

The Soviet Union provided the new Vietnamese government with its primary source of economic and trade support from 1978, when both nations signed a Treaty of Friendship and Cooperation. Vietnam, seeking to become a member of the Soviet Union's economic alliance, the Council for Mutual Economic Assistance (popularly known as Comecon), shifted from reliance on China, which in the past had given Vietnam nearly $2 billion in assistance. The shift of alliance continued to trouble the Chinese and ultimately may have harmed Vietnam, which struggled economically as one of the world's poorest nations—the Soviet economy to which Vietnam became linked performed poorly, while China experienced great economic development from the 1980s.

REFORMS AND RECONCILIATION

As reunited Communist Vietnam took shape, the government ordered a series of economic reforms. Land reforms in the south, similar to those that had failed in North Vietnam between 1954 and 1959, focused on collective production. The result was a decline in agricultural productivity, most significantly in the critical rice harvest. By the end of the 1970s, the Vietnamese people faced severe food shortages. As the government converted private enterprise in the former South Vietnam to a new socialist economy, Vietnam entered an economic crisis.

Economic revival came slowly. The collapse of the Soviet Union from 1989 through 1991 forced the Vietnamese to seek new partners for trade. In the late 1980s, Vietnam began to privatize its economy in the Doi Moi program to create a more viable trade environment. At the same time, relations between Vietnam and the United States began to thaw. In 1991, both nations agreed to discuss the question of remaining U.S. service personnel in Vietnam, or MIAs (Missing in Action). Bans on Americans traveling to Vietnam were lifted, and in 1994 trade relations between the two nations resumed. In 1995, President Bill Clinton (in office 1993–2001) announced the normalization of relations with Vietnam, and embassies opened in Hanoi and Washington, D.C.

Between 1990 and 1997, economic growth in Vietnam rose by 8 percent, and the country had become the world's third-largest exporter of rice. Growth in Vietnam remained steady, but for all the economic reform achieved, the Communist authorities maintained a firm hold on political life. There has been no suggestion that economic liberalization should be accompanied by political reform. However, the reformist Nong Duc Manh (born 1940) was appointed general secretary of the ruling Communist Party in 2001, but change has remained tentative.

M. MAY

Paracel Islands

The low-lying flat Paracel Islands lie in the South China Sea, east of central Vietnam, south of China, and west of the Philippines. The highest point is an unnamed location on Rocky Island (46 ft. or 14 m). There are more than 130 small arid coral reefs in the archipelago (most of which have little vegetation). The islands, which have a tropical climate with little seasonal variation in temperature, form two groups: the Amphitrite Group in the north and east, and the Crescent Group in the south and west. The sea surrounding the islands is a rich fishing ground, and there may be submarine deposits of oil and natural gas.

In 1932, France, then the colonial power in Vietnam, annexed the islands and established a weather station. During World War II (1939–1945), Japanese forces occupied the archipelago. The Paracel Islands were included in South Vietnam when Vietnam was partitioned in 1954; South Vietnam continued to maintain the weather station that had been established by the French and installed a garrison there. China claimed sovereignty over the Paracel Islands in 1951, and Chinese forces occupied the islands in 1974, dislodging the South Vietnamese garrison that was established in the 1950s. China bases its claims on the fact that Chinese fishers had visited the islands for centuries. Vietnam bases its claim on the fact that France annexed the islands to their colonial possessions in Vietnam. When China took the islands from South Vietnam, North Vietnam did not protest and, it is alleged, acquiesced. Several years later, when relations between China and reunited Vietnam became tense, the Vietnamese government reasserted its claim to the islands. Taiwan also lays claim to the islands.

The Chinese government has a program to develop the islands. As well as prospecting for hydrocarbons intermittently since 1976, China intends to establish tourist resorts. China maintains military bases on Woody Island, Rocky Island, and Duncan Island. Pattle Island, the largest island, houses a weather station, and there are signal stations on several islands. There is a Chinese air force base on Woody Island.

Area 62 sq. miles (160 sq. km)
Population The islands have no permanent population but there are Chinese military bases on Woody Island (Lin-tao) and Rocky Island (Shi-tao). The size of the Chinese military establishment in the Paracel Islands is not known.

Spratly Islands

The Spratly Islands in the South China Sea are the subject of one of the most complicated territorial disputes. All of the islands are claimed by Vietnam, China, and Taiwan. The Philippines and Malaysia each claim part of the archipelago, while Brunei claims a fishing zone around a single shoal. The different claims overlap, and in some cases, individual islands are claimed by four or five nations.

The archipelago comprises more than 100 very small low-lying islets (coral reefs and shoals) east of southern Vietnam, north of the Malaysian states of Sabah and Sarawak, and west of the Philippines. The Spratly Islands spread across some 160,000 square miles (410,000 sq. km) of ocean, although the total land area of the archipelago is less than 2 square miles (5 sq. km). The highest point is an unnamed location on Southwest Cay (13 ft. or 4 m). The islets are tropical, arid, and have little vegetation. The Spratly Islands are known to the Chinese as Nansha and to the Vietnamese as Truong Sa.

Control of the islands is an economic prize. Not only are the extensive territorial waters of the Spratly Islands a rich fishing ground, but there are large reserves of oil and natural gas below the sea bed. Chinese geologists claim that the region holds the world's fourth-largest reserves of oil. The Spratly Islands are also strategically important: one-quarter of the world's shipping passes through the area every year.

Archaeological evidence shows that Chinese fishers visited the islands in the first century CE. China bases its claim on this long-established connection. Various European expeditions came to the islands in the eighteenth and nineteenth centuries, but no power showed any territorial interest in the archipelago until the 1930s, when France annexed the islands to the French possessions in Indochina. During World War II (1939–1945), Japanese forces occupied the archipelago. The Spratly Islands were included in South Vietnam when Vietnam was partitioned in 1954. The Philippines became interested in the islands through the activities of Philippine fishers in the waters off the eastern part of the archipelago. After the discovery of oil off the nearby Philippine island of Palawan in 1968, the Philippines posted troops on three of the Spratly Islands. Chinese forces occupied some of the archipelago in 1974. China defeated Vietnam in a brief naval engagement there in 1988. There have also been clashes between Chinese and Philippine forces. China, the Philippines, and Vietnam have all granted oil exploration concessions to foreign oil corporations in the territorial waters of the Spratly Islands, despite their disputed status.

Today there are military outposts on 45 of the islands in the group. Three of the claimants have constructed airports in the archipelago, but there are no ports, and access to individual islands is from offshore anchorages. Some islands contain huts on stilts, built as shelters for passing fishers. Around 100 oil wells have been sunk in waters adjoining islets controlled by Malaysia, Vietnam, and the Philippines. In 2002, the nations that claim islands in the archipelago signed a "Declaration on the Conduct of Parties in the South China Sea," which has eased tension but not solved the dispute.

Area 2 sq. miles (5 sq. km)
Population No permanent population; about 2,200 forces from claimant nations (except Brunei) are stationed in the islands—around 450 Chinese forces, between 75 and 100 Malaysians, around 100 Filipinos, and 1,500 Vietnamese (2003 estimate).

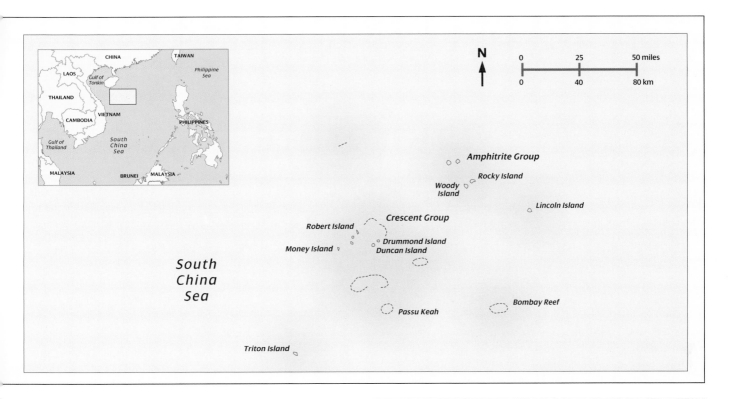

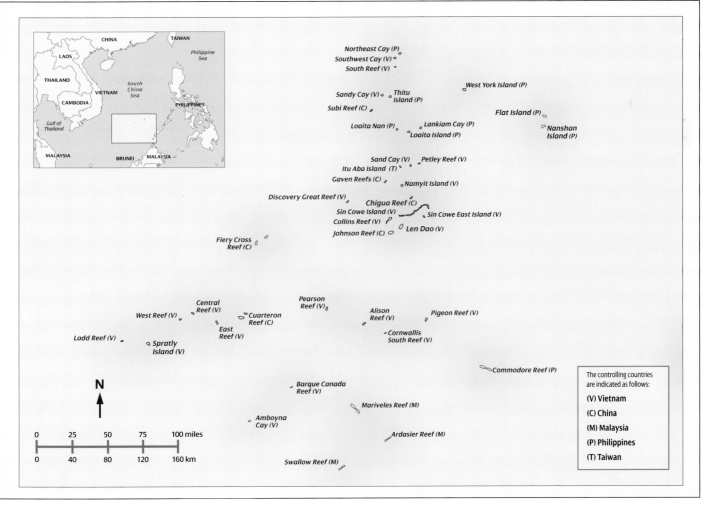

The controlling countries are indicated as follows:

(V) Vietnam

(C) China

(M) Malaysia

(P) Philippines

(T) Taiwan

CULTURAL EXPRESSION

Literature

Historically, Vietnamese literature had two traditions: an oral, Buddhist tradition in the local language and a Confucian court tradition in Chinese. From the nineteenth century, French influence brought Western literary traditions to Vietnam, while, in modern times, a state-sponsored literature promotes socialist ideas.

The Vietnamese emerged as a distinct group in southern China four thousand years ago. Known as the Viets, they were linguistically and ethnically separate from the Chinese. Eventually some Viets moved south, and people who regard themselves as Vietnamese have been living in the delta of the Red River for nearly three thousand years. The Viets established their own country, called Au Lac, south of the powerful Chinese empire, and the earliest surviving Vietnamese literature dates from the first millennium BCE.

THE FIRST FOLK TALES AND CHINESE INFLUENCES

The first Vietnamese kings, who were part of the semi-legendary Hung dynasty (before 208 BCE), established a complex government to administer the country—Au Lac practiced wet rice agriculture, which required a high degree of social organization. The Hung kings are still revered in Vietnam and many Vietnamese folk tales, which were originally passed on orally, are set in the Hung period. These tales tell of the creation of the Earth, the founding of the nation, and the early history of the Vietnamese people.

In the Vietnamese creation story, a heavenly princess, called Au Co, descends from heaven with her sisters, only to be stranded on the Earth when she tastes a sample of the soft, pink soil. Her sisters are forced to leave her behind and, in her sadness, she cries so much that her tears form a river that runs down the mountainside to the sea. The son of a dragon who lives in the sea goes to investigate, and when he meets Au Co, they fall in love. They become the mother and father of the people who refer to their land as "mountains and rivers," the Vietnamese.

In 208 BCE, a Chinese warlord overthrew the last of the kings of the Hung dynasty and established a kingdom called Nam Viet that lasted until 111 BCE, when it was incorporated into China by the powerful Han Dynasty. The Chinese occupied but never quite subdued Vietnam for the next thousand years. From the reign of the first Hung king through the period of Chinese domination, there were two kinds of literature in Vietnam: an elaborate court poetry written in Chinese, and an oral folk poetry sung by the illiterate peasants. There were also two great philosophies during this period, Confucianism at court and Buddhism in the countryside.

Confucius (551–479 BCE) was a Chinese philosopher who emphasized loyalty to the state and obedience to the king. In turn, the king was responsible for overseeing the welfare of the people. If he failed to do so, he would lose the "mandate of heaven" (his right to rule) and be overthrown. The mandarins, officials who made up the royal bureaucracies in both Vietnam and China, earned their rank by memorizing Confucian classics and demonstrating their literary ability by writing poems and essays that imitated the classics. During the period of Chinese rule, the Vietnamese absorbed Chinese political and literary practices, but they never fully submitted to Chinese authority. The Trung Sisters (died c. 42 CE), Vietnamese heroines whose deeds were immortalized in literature, led a revolt against the Chinese in 39 CE that was briefly successful, but the Chinese crushed the rebellion two years later. Every Vietnamese city has a street named Hai Ba Trung, which means "the two Trung sisters." Other rebellions followed, and their leaders are also remembered in poetry and popular culture.

BUDDHIST INFLUENCE

Buddhism entered Vietnam by two routes, first from India, then from China. Buddhism emphasizes release from suffering, a message that found a receptive audience among a people who worked the land in service to their rulers. Many of the folk songs (*ca dao*) of the time deal frankly with the difficulties of rural life but also exhibit a philosophical attitude toward existence that was clearly influenced by Buddhism. In 939 CE, the Vietnamese threw off Chinese rule for good, although they spent the next

The traditional art of storytelling with water puppets, or Mua Roi Nuoc, *has become an important element of Vietnamese culture.*

300 years fighting invasions from the north, most notably by the Mongol conqueror Genghis Khan (c. 1162–1227). The stories of heroes who defended Vietnam from invasion, such as the army commander Tran Hung Dao (1213–1300), have become part of the literary and cultural heritage of the Vietnamese people.

EIGHTEENTH- AND NINETEENTH-CENTURY LITERATURE

Three great works of Vietnamese poetry were written in the eighteenth and early nineteenth centuries. *Chinh Phu Ngam* (Lament of the soldier's wife) was written first in Chinese by Dang Tran Con (1710–1745). It was almost immediately translated into Vietnamese by Doan Thi Diem (1705–1748), whose own husband had been sent to fight by the emperor. The poem's 408 lines tell the moving story of a family torn apart by a husband's military obligation to the king. Many scholars believe that the imagery of the Vietnamese translation is finer than that of the original. By contrast, the poems of Ho Xuan Hung (c. 1775–c. 1842) are very different in character to *Chinh Phu Ngam*. Ho Xuan Hung's poems combine bitter social satire with humor and frank eroticism.

The most famous poem in Vietnamese literature is *Kim Van Kieu* (The tale of Kieu) by Nguyen Du (1765–1820). The 3,254-line poem tells the story of a young woman sold into sexual slavery, who triumphs in the end through purity of spirit, intelligence, and powerful ambition to be reunited with her true love. Phrases from *Kieu* are common in everyday Vietnamese, often serving as a verbal shorthand for complex emotions.

MODERN LITERATURE

Late in the nineteenth century, Vietnam was colonized by the French, who brought Christianity and Western ideas into the country, including Western literary forms. In the twentieth century, Vietnamese came to be written in the Roman script. French influence widened the scope of Vietnamese literature, and Vietnamese writers produced short stories and novels. At the same time, during the colonial period, many intellectuals refused to work with the French, preferring instead to write poems that slyly satirized the colonists and their Vietnamese collaborators. The essayist Ngo Tat To (1894–1954), for example, criticized colonialism. The novelist Vu Trong Phung (1912–1939) was controversial owing to his representation of sexuality.

The Communist political leader Ho Chi Minh (1890–1969) wrote poetry and had great respect for literature. When his movement came to power in the north in 1954, Ho Chi Minh supported literacy programs for all Vietnamese. The programs changed the character of the nation, and Vietnam has one of the highest literacy rates (90.3 percent) in the developing world.

After the Communists defeated the French in 1954, Vietnam was divided into a Communist northern state and a pro-Western southern state. In South Vietnam, a creative cosmopolitan literature developed; in North Vietnam a state-sponsored literature reflected socialist ideas. Writers active in the north included the story writer Nguyen Cong Hoan (1903–1977) and the poet Xuan Dieu (1916–1985). The war in Vietnam (1965–1973) produced a great deal of literature that is now finding publication in the West, and although state control characterizes the literature of modern Vietnam, more lively and individual works have appeared since the late 1980s.

J. DUEMER

Art and Architecture

From its beginnings, Vietnamese art has been shaped by foreign influences, most notably from China, Vietnam's powerful neighbor to the north, which ruled the country for more than a thousand years until the tenth century.

Vietnam has an ancient cultural legacy, but very few monuments or artworks survive in their original form. Many have been destroyed in the wars that have marked the nation's history, while others have decayed in the tropical climate or have been devoured by termites. Many buildings have also been continually rebuilt and remodeled by later generations. Some of the earliest artworks to survive date from the Dong Son culture, which flourished in the region between the third century BCE and the second century CE. A number of large, highly decorated ceremonial Dong Son drums survive.

TRADITIONAL TEMPLES AND PAGODAS

Some of the best examples of Vietnam's artistic heritage are its sacred buildings, temples, and pagodas. The majority of pagodas are Buddhist, although many accommodate elements of Taoism, Confucianism, and animism, which together have shaped Vietnamese religious life. In some temples, for example, sculptures of Confucius are venerated alongside those of the Buddha. Most provincial capitals also contain a Confucian temple of literature (*van mieu*). Another type of building that is central to the spiritual life of communities is the *dinh*, a communal meeting house and a place of worship that contains an altar dedicated to the guardian spirit of the village.

The position and orientation of all these buildings were traditionally determined by geomancers, people who interpreted features of the landscape in terms of religious and magical beliefs to find the most propitious site. The buildings themselves share certain fundamental characteristics. They are based on a large, single-story hall, built with wooden columns that support the heavy timber framework of the roof. These great roofs are low and tile-covered, often curling up at their lower corners to reveal a richly carved wooden framework. A typical pagoda comprises three separate halls—one for the public, one for the Buddhist monks, and one to house altars—arranged in an H-shaped plan. More important temple complexes include a bell tower, sacred pools, and gardens. Some also contain towers known as *thaps*, which mark the burial places of important monks.

Temples and *dinhs* contain some of the best examples of Vietnamese art. Sculptures of fearsome guardian figures, dragons, and lions are set at temple entrances, altar halls feature numerous statues of the Buddha and other deities, and *dinhs* are renowned for their richly carved woodwork, which sometimes includes scenes of daily life. Temples often contain lacquered furniture and altars inlaid with designs in mother of pearl or precious metals. The art of lacquerwork dates back to the fifteenth century in Vietnam. Lacquer is made from a natural resin, which is colored and then laboriously applied in thin layers to build up a hard glossy surface. Most temples also contain beautiful ceramic vessels and vases. As in neighboring countries, the production of sophisticated ceramics has a long history in Vietnam. Vietnamese ceramics were prized throughout East Asia, Southeast Asia, and as far away as the eastern Mediterranean from as early as the eleventh century.

CHAM TEMPLES AND SCULPTURES

Some of the oldest surviving temples and sculptures come from the kingdom of Champa, which between the second century CE and its decline in the thirteenth century occupied the central region of present-day Vietnam. Unlike the rest of country, which was under Chinese domination, Champa was much influenced by India, and its rulers adopted the Hindu religion. The best surviving examples of Cham architecture are temple ruins at Myson, a principal center of Cham power until the eleventh century, as well as in Nha Trang, Phan Rang, and Thap Chang in the south of the country.

Highly distinctive Cham temples take the form of brick-built towers, conceived to symbolize Mount Meru, the home of the gods in Hinduism. They are sited on raised platforms, are square or rectangular in plan, and have pyramid-shaped roofs with elaborate profiles—those at Myson were once covered in gold. Each side of the building is articulated with pilasters (columns attached to the wall) and decorative arched openings. There is usually just one entrance, facing east. Each temple contained a sculpture of the god to whom it was dedicated or a lingam (a stylized, phallic-shaped symbol of the god Shiva), which was set on a finely carved pedestal.

The elaborately built Cham towers were embellished by a profusion of carvings and sculptures. Carved sandstone panels were incorporated in the architecture, and after the towers were built, artists carved designs into the finished brickwork. Relief sculptures (sculptures carved against a flat background, rather than in the round) of Hindu deities often adorned niches above

▶ *Hindu tower-temples stand above the ruins of Myson, the principal Cham site in Vietnam. Most of the temples are dedicated to Cham kings.*

These lacquered pots and dishes were made using methods that developed in Vietnam in the fifteenth century.

the main openings, and other surfaces were decorated with scenes from sacred texts, as well as with carvings of plants, flowers, animals, musicians, and heavenly maidens (*aspara*s). While the style of Cham sculpture varies according to the period in which it was made, its full rounded forms, sinuous lines, and realism reflect Indian influences rather than the more formal, stylized traditions of China that otherwise dominate Vietnamese art and architecture.

IMPERIAL PALACES AND TOMBS AT HUÉ

The Chinese influence on Vietnamese art and architecture is seen at one of Vietnam's greatest historical sites: the imperial city of Hué. In 1802, Gia Long (1762–1820), the first emperor of the Nguyen dynasty, built a new capital for a reunited Vietnam at Hué. He sited the new city in a bend of the Perfume River, according to the advice of his geomancers, and enclosed it in massive defensive earthworks and a moat. The city was divided into a number of zones, the most important of which was the Inner City. The Inner City, which was also enclosed by a moat

and protective walls, contained the Imperial City, which included royal palaces and temples, and the Forbidden Purple City, containing the royal residences.

Two of the most magnificent of Hué's surviving buildings are the Ngo Mon Gate, the main entrance to the Inner City, and the Thai Hoa Palace, the most important of the ceremonial palaces. Both stand on stone podiums and are constructed from great wooden columns, beams, and rafters that are decorated with carvings, lacquer, and gilding. Each has two tiers of sweeping, low-pitched roofs, covered in brightly colored tiles and with elaborate ceramic dragons prancing along their crests and rearing up at their corners. Chinese influences can be seen in these and many other features, including the symmetrical layout of the city and the grandeur of its palaces, which were inspired by Beijing's Forbidden City.

Hué is also remarkable for the tombs that the Nguyen emperors built for themselves. Situated south of the city, these funerary monuments were inspired by imperial Chinese examples. They consist of a number of buildings scattered amid woods, streams, and gardens. Each tomb complex has a pavilion housing a stela (carved stone pillar or slab), which is inscribed with the biography of the deceased emperor. Behind the pavilion is a courtyard containing rows of statues of soldiers, mandarins, horses, and elephants that symbolize the spirit road. Behind the courtyard is the main temple, dedicated to the emperor. The emperor's body is interred elsewhere in a concealed place. The tomb complexes include other buildings, among them temples and pleasure pavilions for the enjoyment of the emperor while he was still alive. The tombs vary greatly in style, from the gracious architecture of the tomb (constructed 1841–1843) of Emperor Minh Mang (reigned 1820–1841) to the more overwhelming concrete structures of the tomb (constructed 1920–1931) of Emperor Khai Dinh (reigned 1916–1926).

THE FRENCH COLONIAL PERIOD

After the French completed their annexation of Vietnam in 1883, the appearance of the downtown districts of many Vietnamese towns and cities was transformed by new European-style buildings. The French colonists constructed imposing government headquarters, official residences, and cultural institutions in the classical style. In Hanoi, the headquarters of the governor general of French Indochina was a massive, four-story Italianate villa (built 1900–1906). It is now the presidential palace. In Saigon (modern Ho Chi Minh City), an enormous City Hall (now the People's Committee Building) was completed in 1908. It was modeled on the Hôtel du Ville (city hall) in Paris. The French used the Romanesque and Gothic styles for their churches and cathedrals. The red-brick Notre Dame Cathedral (built 1877–1880) in Ho Chi Minh City follows a traditional French design, with its soaring twin spires flanking its west front, as does the more austere stone-built, twin-towered Saint Joseph's Cathedral in Hanoi (completed 1886).

The city of Hué is now protected as a UNESCO World Heritage site. The Ngo Mon Gate has been restored, but some buildings suffered irreparable damage during the Vietnam War (1965–1973).

The French also had a strong impact on the visual arts in Vietnam, introducing Western approaches and materials, such as oil paint. Most significantly, in 1925 they founded the École des Beaux-Arts de l'Indochine (EBAI) in Hanoi. Initially, this art school offered a traditional French art education, with an emphasis on the realist and impressionist styles then flourishing in France. Soon, however, EBAI also began offering instruction in traditional Asian techniques and materials as well. At EBAI, young Vietnamese painters such as Nguyen Phan Chanh (1892–1984) began working with watercolors on silk, a method of painting that had a long history in Vietnam and also in China. Other EBAI teachers and students, such as Nguyen Gia Tri (1908–1993), developed the decorative technique of lacquer to create lacquer paintings.

THE COMMUNIST ERA

As Ho Chi Minh (1890–1969), leader of the Communist revolt against French rule, and his colleagues led the struggle for Vietnam's independence from 1946, they encouraged art with a strong nationalist message in the form of paintings, sculptures, and posters showing ordinary Vietnamese families, peasants, and soldiers working for the good of their country. After the reunification of Vietnam in 1976, the Communist government continued to exercise tight control over art and architecture, much of which reflected the country's close political ties with the Soviet Union. The Soviet style found its most famous expression in Ho Chi Minh's Mausoleum (1973–1975) in Hanoi, a stark, simple concrete building based on Lenin's tomb in Moscow.

Since 1986, the government's policy of Doi Moi, or opening up, has initiated a period of greater cultural freedom. One result of the measured economic liberalization has been a plethora of new commercial complexes and high-rises in Ho Chi Minh City and Hanoi, among them the Saigon Trade Center in Ho Chi Minh City (completed 1997), which at 476 feet (145 m) is Vietnam's tallest building. The prosperous elite who have profited from Doi Moi have also built new mansions in a flamboyant mixture of architectural styles, notably in the exclusive Ho Tay area of Hanoi. Although artists are still subject to censorship, there has also been a flowering of creativity, with painters such as the Group of Five embracing elements of modern Western art and traditional Vietnamese art.

National pride and the desire to attract tourism have also prompted the government to begin supporting the country's traditional decorative art villages—small communities whose inhabitants traditionally worked together to produce particular products. Bat Trang, the most successful of these villages, has become a major center for the production of ceramics.

The government has also begun to prioritize the restoration and preservation of Vietnam's historic monuments. The United Nations Educational, Scientific, and Cultural Organization (UNESCO) listed Hué and Myson as World Heritage Sites in 1993 and 1999, respectively.

R. BEAN

Music and Performing Arts

Although the majority of the inhabitants of Vietnam are Vietnamese, the country is home to 53 other ethnolinguistic groups. The music of the Vietnamese is well documented, and strong influences from elsewhere in Asia, particularly China, have been studied by musicologists. However, the diverse musical traditions of Vietnam's minorities are not as well known.

Based on the recent discovery of a set of tuned stone slabs that are currently housed at the musicology institute in Ho Chi Minh City (formerly Saigon), the Vietnamese can trace their music back nearly four thousand years. Written records of musical activity date from the first millennium BCE, when bronze drums were played for agricultural rituals, along with mouth organs. Several forms of theater, including water puppets and human music-dramas, developed over the last twelve hundred years, along with dance music, music for Buddhist ceremonies, and different forms of court music. Among the ethnic Vietnamese, cultural distinctions are often based on four regions: north, central, south central, and south Vietnam. Regional differences in music reflect these divisions.

PERCUSSION INSTRUMENTS

In modern times, the peoples of Vietnam use several hundred varieties of instruments, some played solo, others in small- and medium-sized ensemble combinations. Numerous kinds of percussion instruments are found throughout Vietnam. Single-headed drums include a small, hand-beaten drum called *trong cai* (in the south) or *trong boc* (in the north) and the hourglass-shaped drum, known as a *bong*. Among the many double-headed drums, the largest (variously known as the *trong chau* or *trong dai co*) is played for traditional theater, in court music, and in temples. Some other types of drums that differ from one another in pitch are played in pairs or sets.

A great variety of shaken and struck bamboo percussion instruments are found among Vietnam's many ethnic minorities, and the names of these instruments differ from one group to another. A set of three wooden planks, known as the *sinh tien*, is unique to Vietnam. One plank has a serrated underside with several Chinese coins attached at one end. The second plank has additional Chinese coins and a brass tip, while the third has a serrated edge. The instrument acts as a combined clapper, rasp and scraper, and *sistrum* (rattle) all at once. Other wooden clappers (the *sanh* and *phach*) and woodblocks (*song lang* and *mo gia tri*) are also widely used.

Chinese-influenced bells (*chuong*) are used in Buddhist and Confucian music, and assorted other gongs and cymbals are often used by the Vietnamese. In the highlands, percussion ensembles often consist wholly or largely of flat or knobbed gongs. The gongs are handheld or suspended, the percussionist usually striking the gong with the right hand and controlling the sound with the left.

STRINGED AND WIND INSTRUMENTS

Stringed instruments are the primary melodic instruments of the Vietnamese. Best known is the unique monochord (*dan bau* or *dan doc huyen*), which consists of a wooden-box resonator with a single metal string attached at one end to a peg and at the other end to a small, flexible stem of bamboo or wood sticking out of the box. The string passes through a tiny gourd-shaped or coconut-shell resonator that is also attached to the bamboo or wooden stem. The player plucks the string with a small bamboo stick held in the right hand and, with the edge of the same hand, lightly touches the string at different points to produce harmonics, and alters these tones to obtain other scale tones and ornaments by bending the flexible stem with the left hand. The sound is soft, and the instrument is usually played solo.

The *dan tranh* is another prominent stringed instrument. It is a zither with 16 metal strings, each passing over a wooden bridge. The fingers of the right hand pluck the strings as the left hand produces ornaments and raises pitch by pressing down on the portion of the string to the left of the bridge.

The Vietnamese also use a variety of plucked lutes, such as the two-stringed, long-necked *dan nguyet*, the short-necked *dan doan* or *dan tau*, the three-stringed *dan tam* and *dan day*, and the Vietnamese adaptation of the Western guitar, known as the *luc huyen cam* or simply *ghi-ta*. The main bowed lutes are the *dan nhi* or *dan co* and the *dan gao*, both with two strings. Among the wind instruments are a side-blown bamboo flute (*sao* or *dich*), an end-blown flute (*tieu*), and a mouth organ consisting of bamboo tubes (*khen*), which is similar to the Lao *khene*.

ENSEMBLES

Vietnamese ensemble music usually involves singing accompanied by one or more instruments. Historically, the main instrumental ensembles were the traditional court ensembles of the central district, based in the imperial city of Hué. They included the *dai nhac* (a large ensemble, with conch and water-buffalo horns, oboes, drums, and gongs), the *nhac huyen* (bell- and stone-chimes), and *nha nhac* (a small, mostly string ensemble, with several flutes). Despite the end of the imperial court in the middle of the twentieth century, the court music style continues. In the south, ceremonial ensembles called *nhac le* use fiddles, lutes, oboes, and a variety of drums, gongs, and cymbals. Chamber music, such as *hat a dao* (in the north), usually features singing with at least one melodic instrument and one percussion instrument, either clappers or a drum. The Hué songs (*ca hue*) of the central region and the so-called "skilled amateurs" music (*nhac tai tu*) of the south also feature singing accompanied by stringed instruments and occasional flute accompaniment.

THEATRICAL MUSIC

A major context for musical performance in Vietnam is theater. The classical *hat boi*, formerly a court genre, closely resembles Chinese opera in costuming, make-up, and staging. Characters speak and sing accompanied by an ensemble of wind instruments, strings, and percussion, among which an oboe (*ken*) and "battle drum" (*trong chien*) play leading roles. The dance theater form *hat cheo* originated in the north, away from the courts, and uses an accompanying ensemble of fiddles, lutes, flutes, drums, gongs, and cymbals, led by a drummer.

The major theater genre of the south, developed from *hat boi* in the early twentieth century, is *cai luong*. In addition to plays concerning Vietnamese and Chinese history, *cai luong* also presents contemporary stories, and stories derived from distant

Gongs, bells. handheld drums, cymbals, and a selection of other instruments play an important role in Vietnamese percussion.

countries, such as Egypt and France. Actors move smoothly between speaking and singing, accompanied by Vietnamese string instruments, as well as by Western-style pop music ensembles featuring electric keyboard, bass, guitar, and sometimes a saxophone or a trumpet.

TONES AND SCALES

Vietnamese music employs five-tone and seven-tone scales, varying according to the region and the individual instrument and genre. The two basic modes (*dieu*) are *bac*, which conveys happiness or solemnity, and *nam*, which conveys serenity, melancholy, and deep sorrow. The subtle differences within each mode are referred to as *hoi* (nuance). Because the Vietnamese language is tonal (like that of its neighbors, Laos and China), song melodies often maintain the tonal contours of speech, so that the word meaning is not lost. Rhythms are mostly duple (even counts) or free (no regular pulse). Vietnamese music is characterized by independent variations of a single melody, with each part sounding its own version of the basic melody. This use of different "voices" is known as a heterophonic variation.

Use of Western-style harmony was introduced during colonial times at the end of the nineteenth century. Western harmony is now sometimes applied to traditional Vietnamese pieces and to newly composed works. Vietnamese conservatories offer both Vietnamese and Western classical music, and the global music industry has introduced many varieties of foreign popular music, heard widely, along with Western-influenced Vietnamese pop music, known as *nhac moi*.

R. A. SUTTON

Festivals and Ceremonies

Public holidays in Vietnam are either anniversaries associated with the Communist Party or traditional celebrations that are mainly Buddhist. The majority of holidays are secular, but the most enthusiastically celebrated festival is the Vietnamese New Year, Tet, which falls in the dry season.

Although Vietnam uses the Western calendar, the nation's traditional holidays, such as Tet, are marked according to the lunar calendar. As a result, traditional holidays fall on a different day each year in the Western calendar.

TET

Although New Year's Day in the Western calendar is a public holiday, the major annual public celebration in Vietnam is Tet, the ancient New Year festival, which coincides with the traditional Chinese New Year. The festival falls in either January or February in the Western calendar, depending on the lunar cycle. The holiday lasts seven days, during which time families gather to share celebrations. Many people travel from the cities to their ancestral villages for the holiday.

Special meals play a major role in Tet festivities. It is believed that people who eat plenty of food during the festival will not go hungry during the coming year. For this reason, large meals are common throughout the holiday period. Noisy firework displays are held in towns and cities throughout Vietnam, and the authorities stage spectacular displays for public entertainment.

Worshippers burn incense at Thien Hau Temple in Ho Chi Minh City to celebrate the Tet festival.

At Tet, those Vietnamese who practice a religion visit a temple or church to pray and to remember their ancestors. Everyone, even nonreligious people, prepares a tray of cakes, fruit, and wine for the ancestors and puts the offering in a prominent place in the home. The tray is generally decorated with flowers. People burn incense to mark the passage of the old year. Children receive small presents of paper money, and people visit their parents on the first day of Tet. There are many Tet customs and superstitions, for example regarding the direction in which a person walks when first leaving their home at Tet.

SECULAR HOLIDAYS

February 3 is a public holiday commemorating the foundation of the predecessor of the Vietnamese Communist Party in 1930. The anniversary is marked by speeches and public ceremonies. A public holiday on April 30 marks the anniversary of the fall of South Vietnam to Communist forces from North Vietnam in 1975. Labor Day, on May 1, is a public holiday, and later in the same month, the birthday of Ho Chi Minh (1890–1969), the

Military parades, such as this one marking the fall of Da Nang, are common on Vietnam's major secular holidays.

founder of Communist Vietnam, is celebrated on May 19. Two major public holidays fall at the beginning of September: September 2 is National Day, which marks the declaration of independence by the Communists in Hanoi in 1945. The following day, September 3, commemorates the solemn anniversary of the death of Ho Chi Minh in 1969.

TRADITIONAL HOLIDAYS

An ancient holiday in March commemorates a rebellion led by the Trung Sisters against Chinese rule during the first century CE. Although widely marked, the festival is no longer a public holiday. The Buddha's birthday, enlightenment, and death are celebrated with a national holiday on May 28. The Day of the Wandering Souls (Thrung Nguyen), a traditional festival in August, is no longer a public holiday. On this day, the spirits of the ancestors are believed to leave their grave and journey to their childhood homes. People make offerings of food for the spirits and burn fake paper money to appease them. Thrung Thu, the moon festival that is celebrated in the fall, is a popular holiday for children, who join candlelit street parades. Traditional rice moon cakes are made for the festival.

K. ROMANO-YOUNG

Food and Drink

The Vietnamese say that their country is shaped like a carrying pole with a basket of rice hung from either end. The "basket" to the north is the Red River Valley (the Tonkin region), the "basket" to the south is the Mekong Delta region (formerly known as Cochinchina), and the carrying pole is the long narrow central region of Annam. The cuisine of each region has its own distinct flavors and dishes.

The Vietnamese hold that their diet is one of the healthiest and one of tastiest in the world. The great variety within Vietnamese cooking comes from the different culinary traditions of its three main regions, along with the cuisines of its ethnic minorities and influences from neighboring countries. Favorite dishes in northern Vietnam show the influence of neighboring China, and the Mongol invasion of the region in the thirteenth century introduced a taste for beef to the region. Southern Vietnam is characterized by the simplicity of its dishes, which reflect the tastes of the medieval Khmer Empire of Cambodia.

RICE DISHES

In all parts of Vietnam, the dietary staples are rice and vegetables. Rice-laden barges bring their cargo along the rivers to the cities. Rice may be eaten steamed, but it is also ground into flour, which is then made into noodles. Rice flour noodles are popular in a variety of forms and available for breakfast, lunch, and dinner. Noodles may also be made from wheat or bean starch. They may be cut into sticks, vermicelli (thin noodles), or "bean threads," also known as cellophane noodles. Rice flour is also used to make rice paper, the wrapping for rice paper rolls that may be filled with meat, noodles, shrimp or shrimp paste, fresh vegetables, and herbs. Rice rolls can be served uncooked, steamed, or deep-fried, and are usually served with dipping sauce.

REGIONAL VARIATIONS

Fresh vegetables and herbs are served at every meal. Meats, especially pork and chicken, as well as fish and shrimp, are important parts of the Vietnamese diet and are cooked, along with vegetables and a small amount of vegetable oil or pork fat, in traditional conical-shaped pans that are deep enough for deep-frying but wide enough to fit a whole fish or chicken. Stir-frying, in which the pan is heated first and the oil and ingredients added next, is more typical in the north, with its Chinese influences (although the characteristic Vietnamese pan differs from a Chinese wok). In southern Vietnam, gentle sauteeing is a more common cooking method.

The central region around the city of Hué owes its distinctive cuisine to the practice of combining salt and rice. Hué is known for a dish called clam rice, made from clams from the Huong, or Perfume, River steamed and added to vegetables, minced banana flowers, soy sauce, fish sauce, pounded sesame, fish, garlic, and salt. From Hué also come delicate pastries, such as *banh khoai*, a crepe with bean sprouts, shrimp, and meat. Southern Vietnamese cooking draws on some of the traditions of the Hué region but owes its most characteristic flavor to *nuoc mam*, a fish sauce made of fermented fish mixed with herbs. Other signature southern tastes include lemongrass, chilies, and curries.

A wide variety of street foods, such as dim sum, spring rolls, and cooked vegetables, is available on the city streets of Vietnam.

CELEBRATION MEALS

Celebration banquets for weddings, funerals, and the anniversaries of deaths are traditionally served in even-numbered dishes, four solid and four liquid, to groups of four people seated around round trays. The more unusual the dishes, the more popular they seem to be. Feast dishes may include abalone, sea-swallow's nest, fish bladder, or shark fin. Weddings also will include a rice dish colored red, the color of happiness and good fortune, with the juice of *momordica* (bitter Chinese melon). Before the wedding meal, a bride may receive *banh phu the*, a dessert traditionally given by a suitor and now part of many wedding banquets.

Many special dishes are served at Tet, the lunar New Year, including mung-bean pudding (*che kho*), pork sausage called *gio lua*, and pickled scallions, which can be gathered at this time of year. Tet, which falls in January or February, is celebrated with large meals. Tradition dictates that if a person eats plenty of food during the festival, he or she will not go hungry during the coming year.

A mother and daughter enjoy a typical Vietnamese meal of noodles and vegetables served in a bowl and eaten with chopsticks.

FAVORITE DISHES

Meals in Vietnam are served in bowls with saucers, along with little bowls of *nuoc mam* for dipping. Meats and vegetables are chopped into small pieces, and fish, shrimp, and beans may be mashed or ground for easier eating. Utensils are chopsticks and spoons, indispensable for Vietnam's many delicious soups, including chicken with rice noodles, spicy and sour shrimp soup, and *pho bo*, the famous hearty soup that is virtually a national dish. *Pho bo* (beef noodle soup) contains noodles, poached beef, and vegetables to form a delicate broth that is garnished with scallions and a slice of lemon.

Breakfast may comprise soup and noodles or rice cakes. Depending on the area, breakfast may be a fuller meal than lunch. Vietnamese meals typically have three courses: soup; salad or a fried or sauteed dish; and a salty dish, which is the main course of meat, fish, chicken, duck, shrimp, or crab. Plain rice, nowadays cooked in electric rice cookers that are imported from Japan, comes with each dish.

The first course of soup is followed by steamed, sauteed, or fried dishes. Favorites include steamed stuffed cabbage, Vietnamese rolls (*cha gio*), clams, shrimp paste (*mam tom*) made from fermented shrimp and served on bread or sugar cane, sweet and sour dishes, noodles sauteed with various meats and vegetables, spiced fried crab, and crepes. Popular main courses include beef with onion served with bell pepper and celery, chicken with spices in marinade, pork chops with five spices, lemongrass chicken with bean thread noodles, or *cha ca La Vong*, a grilled fish pie.

STREET FOOD AND RESTAURANTS

Not everyone eats at home. Street cafes are important as well. People line up for *chao*, a plain rice gruel that can be augmented with salty egg, herring, shredded meat, shrimp, or vegetables and herbs. Steamed rice pancakes and steamed noodles are also popular street food. Ho Chi Minh City (formerly Saigon) had many restaurants and other eating places before 1975, when the Communist north overran South Vietnam. In modern times, Ho Chi Minh City and Hanoi once more have a growing number of restaurants and street cafes. The French colonial period left its mark on city tastes, and croissants, French bread, coffee, and dairy products are popular with more affluent city dwellers. Vietnam's two large cities have French restaurants that are famously expensive because so many ingredients for classic French cuisine must be flown in from Europe.

DRINKS AND DESSERTS

Popular drinks in Vietnam include a rice wine similar to Japanese sake, wines made from soy beans and banana, rum, soft drinks, wine, and beer. Black tea is drunk at any time of day but particularly after every meal. Coffee is popular after dinner, when it is served with locally grown fruit: banana, watermelon, mangosteen, durian, starfruit, guava, mandarin oranges, pineapples, and mangoes. Prepared desserts feature cassava cake, fried bananas, mung bean cake, peanut cookies, and a Vietnamese flan.

K. ROMANO-YOUNG

DAILY LIFE

Religion

The Socialist Republic of Vietnam is a secular state guided by Marxist-Leninist principles, but its citizens are deeply affected by the religious traditions of Buddhism, Confucianism, and Taoism. Vietnam is also home to new religions: Caodaism and Hoa Hao, which are both based in part on Buddhism.

Official statistics show that one-third of Vietnamese citizens practice a religion, but government figures acknowledge that while only 12 percent are formally Buddhist, 67 percent are strongly influenced by Buddhist practices. Christians make up the second largest religious group: around 8 percent of Vietnamese are Christians, the majority of whom are Roman Catholic. Caodaism, a new religion that was founded in Vietnam, is followed by 4 percent of the population, although some estimates suggest that as many as 7 percent of Vietnamese follow Caodaism. Up to 2 percent of Vietnamese practice Hoa Hao, another new religion founded in Vietnam.

BUDDHISM

Buddhism was introduced to Vietnam in the fourth century BCE and became the state religion of the Ly dynasty in the eleventh century. Buddhism is separated into three schools: Theravada Buddhism, Tantrayama Buddhism, and Mahayana Buddhism. The schools of Buddhism differ in their beliefs about the Buddha. The Thien or Zen sect of Mahayana Buddhism is the most important form of Buddhism in Vietnam, but Southern or Theravada Buddhism is also found in the Mekong Delta and some central regions. Popular Buddhism is a mixture of some Zen elements and many practices of the Pure Land sect, including chanting the names of the Buddha.

During the thousand years that Vietnam was occupied by China (111 BCE–938 CE), its Buddhist monks absorbed Confucian and Taoist influences from China. Confucianism left a philosophical legacy, while Taoism encouraged meditation. After independence, the monarchy developed Confucian schools to train members in the bureaucracy, who assumed positions of authority. Confucian political philosophy prevailed among the elite, while Buddhist monks provided more basic education to the masses. At the same time, Taoist beliefs spread mystical traditions that linked humans to natural forces and popular practices of spiritism, divination, and magic.

CHRISTIANITY

Roman Catholic missionaries came to Vietnam in the seventeenth century led by the French Jesuit Alexandre de Rhodes (1591–1660), who developed a new phonetic Latin-based alphabet in which Vietnamese is still written. Several communities of early Catholic converts formed. In the nineteenth century, reports of the persecution of missionaries motivated French military expeditions and eventually French colonial conquest of Vietnam from the late 1850s. At present, the most Catholic areas are Bui Chu-Phat Diem in the northern province of Ninh Binh and Ho Nai-Bien Hoa in Dong Nai province to the South. Two-thirds of Protestants in Vietnam are ethnic minorities in highland areas, where evangelical Hmong missionaries have rapidly increased conversions since 1990.

NEW RELIGIONS

In the 1920s and 1930s, growing anticolonial movements awakened a sense of spiritual crisis that gave birth to several new religions in southern Vietnam. Caodaism is a monotheistic faith founded in Saigon in 1926 by a group of French-educated intellectuals who practiced spiritism, communication between spirits and the living. They combined the teachings of Buddhism, Confucianism, and Taoism with Roman Catholicism. Initial visions received by Ngo Minh Chieu (1878–c. 1926), the founder of Caodai, suggested that the Supreme Being (Cao Dai, "the highest power") should be worshipped, represented by the sign of the left eye of God. Later spirit messages described an elaborate hierarchy, including a pope as the religion's leader. A colorful hybrid architecture developed in the buildings of the new religion, which gathered more than one million followers in its first decade. Led by a charismatic spirit medium, Caodai Pope Pham Cong Tac (died 1959), and based in a complex of temples at the Holy See in Tay Ninh, Caodaism quickly became the third religion of Vietnam. It still commands between two and five

Worshippers pray at an elaborately decorated Caodai temple. Since the reunification of Vietnam in 1976, Caodai followers have suffered persecution.

million followers worldwide. Caodai disciples dress in white robes to pray, but the higher-ranking dignitaries wear saffron (for Buddhism), turquoise (for Taoism), and cardinal red (for Confucianism and Catholicism). A dozen denominations of Caodaism developed in the years between 1934 and 1964, spreading the religion's influence throughout the Mekong Delta and the central region of Vietnam. While the Tay Ninh Church was involved in political struggle and massive ritual ceremonies, the smaller groups stressed meditation, mysticism, and intimate spirit seances.

Hoa Hao Buddhism emerged in 1939 when the Vietnamese philosopher Huynh Phu So (1919–1947) drew on Buddhist apocalyptic traditions to preach that the world would end to make way for a new purified faith in the era of Maitreya, the future Buddha. Similar to Caodaism in its millenarianism (a belief in a future period of happiness and peace) and political activism, Hoa Hao was, however, opposed to ritual. The religion stressed purity and asceticism rather than ceremonialism. In 1947, Huynh Phu Su was ambushed by Communist forces and disappeared, but his followers expect him to return to guide them at some future time. In 1975, all Hoa Hao offices were closed, and the Communist Vietnamese authorities completely suppressed the activities of Hoa Hao until 1999, when a new Hoa Hao administrative council was formed under government supervision.

RELIGION AND THE STATE

Vietnam's many years of war and political upheavals left their mark on its religions. In 1963, after several Buddhist monks burned themselves to death to protest persecution by the United States–supported government of South Vietnam's President Ngo Dinh Diem (1901–1963), a national congress was held to unify southern Buddhists and northern Buddhists in the Unified Buddhist Church of Vietnam (UBCV). Buddhist leaders became active in the antiwar movement, sending a delegation to the Paris Peace Talks in 1973 and traveling around the world to seek international support. Growing Buddhist influence ended in 1975, when strict government controls were imposed on all religious organizations.

In 1977, the activities of all religious bodies in Vietnam were placed under control of the Communist-dominated electoral front, the Vietnam Fatherland Front. Many religious practices—

including spiritism and the use of mediums to confirm the promotion of Caodai religious officers—were banned as "superstition," and religious groups were no longer allowed to speak in public places or say prayers in private homes. Vietnamese Protestant groups have been most active in protesting these restrictions, arguing that they have been used to suppress unregistered house churches in ethnic minority areas.

In September 2004, Vietnam was named as a "country of particular concern" with regard to religious freedom by the U.S. State Department, because of reports of restrictions on the movement and freedom of expression of religious leaders. In 2005, the Vietnamese government released thousands of prisoners and allowed the long-exiled Buddhist monk and author Thich Nhat Hahn (born 1926), who worked throughout the Vietnam War to reconcile North and South Vietnam, to return to Vietnam and visit Buddhist temples. Government agencies monitor religious activities that they say could oppose state policies, but they have also permitted the renovation of many Buddhist pagodas and Caodai temples, and religious pilgrimages are hugely popular, attracting both tourists and foreign investment.

When Vietnam was divided in 1954 into Communist North Vietnam and pro-Western South Vietnam, the organization of the Roman Catholic Church was also divided. After 1976, the reunification of a more confident Church in the south and a cautious Church that suffered restrictions in the north was not easy. The authorities persecuted the Roman Catholics in former South Vietnam until 1989. The state recognizes the Roman Catholic Church, the UBCV, Caodaism, Hoa Hao, Islam, and Protestantism. The Catholic Church operates within restrictions, while the state attempts to undermine the UBCV, harrassing more independent members. Caodaism and various Protestant bodies suffer the greatest persecution.

J. HOSKINS

Family and Society

War in Vietnam in the 1960s and early 1970s profoundly influenced the nature of Vietnamese society. The conflict took many men away from their homes and widowed many women. As a result, traditional family roles changed, and women gained more responsibilities and rights.

The Vietnam War (1965–1973) affected everyone in all parts of the country: there was a huge displacement of the population, families were torn apart, and large numbers of people were forced or chose to leave their homes. Many people found shelter in refugee camps. In the south, thousands of people left the countryside for the greater security of the cities. Other Vietnamese chose to move either north or south, drawn toward the ideology in which they believed. Many of the leading Communist figures came from the south and had moved north to the Communist state. Business people and wealthier Westernized people from Hanoi moved south to Saigon (now Ho Chi Minh City), not wishing to live under a left-wing dictatorship. By breaking up families, the war also diminished kinship and its rituals.

As traditional roles change, women find work in new areas, such as road building.

This practice extends though Vietnamese society as a deep respect for elderly people and the knowledge that they have acquired through their life experiences. As a result, Vietnam's political leadership is elderly, and age and experience rather than ability are the keys to promotion.

A SOCIALIST SOCIETY

When South Vietnam fell to a combination of local Communist forces and invaders from North Vietnam, the Westernized society of the south was transformed. North Vietnam had been a Communist republic since 1954, and society was tightly controlled. The state assumed the same leading role in former South Vietnam after 1975. Throughout Vietnam, many younger women were urged to join the Communist Party, and girls became members of the Ho Chi Minh Communist Youth League. The assumption of political roles by more women contributed to a relaxation of the rigid traditional family unit.

From the 1950s in the north and the mid-1970s in the south, rural collectivization changed society. The demands and expectations of a wider group working together on state-owned collective agricultural units diminished the role of the male head of the family. Individual wishes could be overruled by the ruling party leadership in the collective. Whereas previously the individual was subordinate to the family, in the new Vietnam, the individual and the family were subordinate to the collective.

In 1986, a new family law defined the basic unit of society as the "socialist family," comprising a husband and wife, equal before the law in all respects, and their children. The law described rights and duties and sought to eliminate remaining Western and Buddhist practices. It also made legal the previously recommended minimum age at which Vietnamese can marry: a woman must be age 18 or over; a man must be 20 or over. Strengthening this provision was, in part, aimed at reducing the size of families. The 1986 law also made the practice of family planning an obligation.

P. FERGUSSON

THE TRADITIONAL FAMILY UNIT

Vietnamese society was traditionally patriarchal. The father of a household was responsible for providing for his wife and children. Although women were expected to submit to decisions made by their husbands, they had a strong and influential role within the family unit. A wife and mother was often called *noi tuong*, which translates as "general of indoors." Women were responsible for domestic chores and in the countryside shared agricultural tasks. When widowed, a woman was expected to defer to her eldest son. Every family member had a role defined by tradition, with older children helping to look after infants. Life revolved around the family, and divorce was almost unknown in the countryside and rare in the cities.

In the past, ancestor worship was widely practiced in Vietnam, and respect for ancestors remains widespread. It was believed—and is still believed by many—that the spirits of ancestors remain to influence events and must be honored. If the spirits become restless, ill luck will befall the family. Children are taught to honor their parents and the memory of their forebears.

Health and Welfare

Through the 1990s and into the twenty-first century, Vietnam made progress in the national health care sector. Life expectancy improved, infant mortality rates fell, and immunization levels rose. Advances were made in reproductive health and in combating communicable diseases. However, many major problems remain.

Some diseases that were once endemic have been eradicated. Cholera and polio have been eliminated, typhoid is rare, and malaria, which was once common, is confined to a small area and is no longer a problem in the most populated areas of the country. Several serious communicable illnesses are still endemic, including Dengue fever and gastroenteritis. Avian influenza (bird flu) spread through poultry flocks throughout much of Vietnam. In 2003 and 2004, outbreaks in the Mekong Delta caused many human fatalities. However, Vietnam has a good record in confronting major health issues: In 2003, it was the first country in the region to bring severe acute respiratory syndrome (SARS) under control.

HEALTH CARE PROVISION

The nation has a network of medical and pharmaceutical colleges to train doctors, pharmacists, and nurses, and other facilities to train paramedics. The major cities of Hanoi, Ho Chi Minh City, and Haiphong have modern hospitals that practice sophisticated procedures. Hospitals in smaller cities and rural areas are more basic. There are adequate pharmacies that dispense Western and traditional medicines.

Traditional medicine remains important, particularly in country areas. Official approval of traditional medicine, including herbalism and acupuncture, extends to funding the Institute of Folk Medicine in Hanoi. A shortage of drugs in the 1980s and 1990s led to greater reliance on herbal remedies, and some rural health centers prescribed more herbal cures than Western medicines.

Despite improvements achieved since the 1980s, shortages of funds and of physicians remain. Doctors are poorly paid, and some attached to city hospitals offer unofficial private health care. International aid, from individual foreign governments as well as international agencies, supports a number of Vietnamese health projects, including programs combating malaria, promoting reproductive health, and controlling the spread of HIV/AIDS. Particular emphasis has been placed upon family planning programs. The fertility rate dropped from 3.8 children per woman in 1989 to 2.2 in 2004, and is expected to be around 2.0 in 2010. Contraception is widely available.

Health care in Vietnam suffers from inadequate funding, and patients receive only the most basic treatments free of charge. Extra payments are common even for painkillers. The national health care system is effectively bankrupt, and hospitals cannot earn enough through charges to upgrade treatments or to improve equipment and facilities. The overwhelming majority of Vietnamese attend state hospitals and clinics, where a basic consultation costs $2.50. The state spends only 3 percent of its annual budget on health care and must increasingly look toward foreign aid donors. The Japanese International Cooperation Agency is the most active donor, and it has made grants to build and maintain hospitals in Vietnam for more than 30 years. The International Hospital in Hanoi is a joint-venture project with an Australian medical company. Several other joint ventures are planned. However, private medicine is limited.

SOCIAL SECURITY

Few Vietnamese have health insurance, although some state employees contribute 8 percent of their salary to the state medical fund. The state welfare system is not well developed. There is a minimum wage that is set at a very low level. There is also a state pension for the elderly, financed through contributions, but many employers do not contribute to the fund. The health care fund is too small and payments received by patients from the fund seldom meet medical costs.

V. MORRES

Children at a state-run orphanage in Ho Chi Minh City learn a trade, such as hairdressing, that will help them find work as adults.

Education

By regional standards, Vietnam has a high literacy rate: 90.3 percent. Most of those who cannot read and write live in remote areas or are members of ethnic minorities. More than 22 million students attend schools, colleges, and universities in Vietnam. Primary schools teach around 13.2 million students, while 4.3 million students attend secondary schools.

After 1954, different educational systems developed in North and South Vietnam based on a French school system. In both states, emphasis was given to Vietnamese language, literature, and history. In the south, greater variety was provided by private schools. In the north, state control ensured a curriculum that emphasized Marxism and socialist ideas. After the fall of South Vietnam in 1975 and the reunification of Vietnam in 1976, the diversity in the southern school system was eliminated and a unified state-school system was created. Teachers from North Vietnam were sent to southern schools to supervise the transition, and teachers in the south had to undertake "re-education" courses before they were able to resume teaching.

REFORM

By the late 1970s, it was evident that the Vietnamese education system required modernization. A reform program began in the academic year 1981–1982 to integrate the school system. Under the program, the whole country used the same curriculum and textbooks, and nine years of schooling became compulsory. To increase funding, the authorities asked agricultural cooperatives and private citizens to donate equipment and make contributions to local schools. A People's Educational Council in each neighborhood increases community involvement in its school.

The nine years of compulsory education correspond to primary and junior high school. An additional three years of schooling is offered at secondary schools, whose graduates either enter work or procede to college or vocational or professional schools. Reforms in the 1980s emphasized vocational training, but many middle-class children avoid vocational courses in favor of university, despite a shortage of university places. The major universities are in Hanoi and Ho Chi Minh City, but an expansion of the university system in the 1980s established new universities in regional centers. The reform of the education system, particularly the

expansion of higher education, relied upon foreign aid, initially from the Soviet Union and China. Vietnamese students also went to the Soviet Union and other Communist countries to study.

Since the collapse of the Soviet Union in 1991, Vietnam's education authorities have looked elsewhere for aid. In 1993, the World Bank loaned Vietnam $50 million to invest in a primary education project. Since then the World Bank, other international organizations, and foreign governments have provided aid for the modernization of the education system. The nation now has 214 universities and colleges, nearly 550 institutions that offer vocational training, some 26,400 schools, and more than 10,100 kindergartens. University enrollment increased by more than 50 percent between 1994 and 2004.

SHORTAGES AND TEACHING METHODS

The government regards education as important for its own sake—to ensure a skilled labor force and as an instrument of social and political control. However, the system faces major challenges, mostly the result of insufficient funding.

Vietnam suffers a shortage of teachers at all levels. Salaries are low, and many teachers are obliged to take on work outside school hours to earn enough to live on. Poor standards of education and a lack of basic skills by students reflect the shortage of qualified teachers, particularly in remote areas and among ethnic minorities.

Vietnamese schools and universities, use traditional teaching methods. The teacher usually gives a lecture and students gain little practical experience. The teacher-centered technique is, in part, the result of inadequate funds for equipment and materials. Many teachers offer extra private classes on school premises. Because education is valued, many parents are willing to pay for extra tuition. For the teacher, extracurricular lessons are a useful source of additional income.

Forty-two percent of students graduating from Vietnamese schools are female.

V. MORRES

Housing

After the reunification of Vietnam in 1976, the two halves of the country had very different housing stocks. In the former North Vietnam, housing was susidized and provided by the state, but many dwellings in the cities had been destroyed by U.S. bombing in the 1960s and early 1970s. The former South Vietnam had newer, privately owned housing stock.

In the south, the Communist authorities took over housing in 1975, and the program of state housing subsidies that had existed in North Vietnam spread across the country. State bureaus and departments provided housing for their employees in return for very low rents.

In North Vietnam, new housing before 1975–1976 was usually constructed in the Soviet style of the period. New homes were typically in two- to five-story apartment buildings in urban neighborhoods. The buildings were often poorly constructed, and because planning was inadequate, the supply of services (including water and drainage) was sometimes deficient. Because the state provided housing, tenants were sometimes reluctant to maintain their homes themselves. Maintenance was perceived as the responsibility of the state and, as a result, many properties rapidly deteriorated.

A high-rise modern building sits between an office building and a traditional pagoda in Hanoi.

THE NATIONAL HOUSING PROGRAM

In reunited Vietnam, a national housing program provided subsidized housing for state employees—in a nation in which the state ran most of the economy, state employees were numerous. New housing was typically in four- or five-story plain apartment buildings that were not well built and were poorly equipped. Overcrowding was common because families were large and apartments were small.

By the 1980s, however, new housing was of better quality and large numbers of new homes were built. In a huge expansion of the housing program, Hanoi increased its total number of homes by about one quarter. New construction was less evident in Ho Chi Minh City (formerly Saigon) because the city had a large stock of former private housing that was transferred to state ownership. At the time, the authorities also deliberately attempted to reduce the size and influence of the city.

By the 1990s, demand outstripped supply, and about only one-third of state employees received state housing. Most larger Vietnamese cities, where the state was virtually the sole provider of housing, suffered a housing crisis; there were not enough homes for the remainder of state employees, who were left to find somewhere to live on their own. In the countryside, on the other hand, many people own their homes, and individuals are largely responsible for finding their own accommodation. Much of the rural housing stock is traditional in design and construction.

A NEW ORDER

Since 1986, economic reform has introduced some elements of a market economy to Vietnam. The state abandoned its housing responsibilities. Instead, the government attempts to provide conditions in which people can construct their own homes. As a result, in the 1990s, more than one-third of new homes were privately built. A construction boom followed the end of the state-subsidized system for new housing in 1991. The number of new homes greatly increased, and a much wider variety of houses was constructed. With ownership, tenants began to take more responsibility for the upkeep and maintenance of their property.

Although the availability of housing has improved, many difficulties remain. In major cities, such as Hanoi, large areas of housing are still state-owned. Overcrowding is a problem: one-third of Hanoi's residents live in homes where there is less than 30 square feet (3 sq. m) of space per person. An infrastructure that is unable to support the growing urban areas also adds to the housing problem. Despite reforms, there remains much inequality between the quality of housing for rich and poor. While a new generation of professionals and business people live in modern homes, a greater number of poor people live in sub-standard accommodation. Ho Chi Minh City has around 150,000 temporary dwellings and poor slum districts, and the counry lacks the necessary capital to repair and replace poor housing.

V. MORRES

Hanoi

Hanoi, the national capital of Vietnam, was the center of administration for Indochina, the colonial union of Cambodia, Laos, and Vietnam ruled by France between the late mid-nineteenth century and the 1950s. In 1954, the city became the capital of North Vietnam, and since 1976, Hanoi has been the capital of a reunited Vietnam.

There has been a settlement on or near the site of Hanoi for several thousand years. The Chinese ruled the surrounding Red River Valley from the city on several occasions when they overran the region. The site of Hanoi is a natural route hub, set on the western bank of the Red River about 85 miles (140 km) inland from the sea.

This shop in the Old Quarter in the north of Hanoi sells a variety of religious goods and other artifacts.

A HISTORIC CITY

In 1010, Thai To (reigned 1010–1028), the first ruler of the Vietnamese Ly or Li dynasty, established his capital at Hanoi. The city was then called Thang Long, meaning "ascending dragon," named for the dragon that it was claimed the king saw rising from the Red River. Although different Vietnamese kings moved the capital to other cities, Hanoi remained the principal seat of Vietnam's monarchs until 1802. Wars and invasions from China destroyed many of the city's ancient buildings, and by the early fifteenth century, Thang Long was occupied by the Chinese. When the Vietnamese king liberated Thang Long from Chinese control in 1428, he renamed the city Dong Kinh, which was later transliterated into French as Tonquin. In time, Tonquin (in English, Tonkin) became the name for the entire Red River Valley. In 1802, the court of the Nguyen dynasty of Vietnamese emperors moved south to Hué. Dong Kinh remained an important city, and in 1831, it was renamed Hanoi, meaning "between two rivers."

Beginning in the 1860s, France built a colonial empire in the region. In 1862, the French formally proclaimed a colony in Cochinchina, the Mekong Delta region of southern Vietnam. The following year, France made Cambodia a protectorate. In 1883, Annam (central Vietnam) and Tonkin became French protectorates, and control over the Lao states followed. The French established the administrative, commercial, and military headquarters of their Indochinese empire in Hanoi. Their choice was influenced in part by the rich mineral resources of Tonkin, and Hanoi became a center for shipping minerals from the region. Hanoi's position, close to southern China, was another, greater attraction. France harbored commercial and other ambitions in southern China, and the French linked the Red River Valley with southern China by railroad and highway to facilitate their plans.

A CITY AT WAR

Hanoi remained the capital of French Indochina until World War II (1939–1945), when Japanese forces invaded. The Japanese also made Hanoi their administrative center in the region. In September 1945, Vietnamese Communists proclaimed an independent Democratic Republic of Vietnam in Hanoi. The French retook Hanoi in 1946 but struggled to reestablish control over northern Vietnam. When French rule in Indochina formally ended in 1954, following the defeat of the colonial army at Dien Bien Phu by the Vietnamese Communists in May 1954, Vietnam was partitioned. Hanoi became the capital of the Communist state usually known as North Vietnam.

Soviet and Chinese aid in the 1950s transformed Hanoi. New factories and industries developed, including metalworking, machine tools, generators, chemicals, and engineering. The food processing and textile industries expanded, and new housing projects began. Much of the new development was somewhat austere, contrasting with the French colonial-style architecture of the downtown area. However, many of the historic buildings and the city's new industries were damaged by war in the 1960s and 1970s, when North Vietnam attempted to subvert the pro-Western Vietnamese state based in Saigon (now Ho Chi Minh City). American military advisers aided South Vietnam, and by 1965, a U.S. army was fighting alongside the South Vietnamese against the North Vietnamese Army and South Vietnamese insurgents. During the war in Vietnam (1965–1973), U.S. forces bombed Hanoi in 1965, 1968, and 1972. Much of the city was destroyed.

A MODERN CITY

In 1976, when Hanoi became the capital of a united Communist Vietnam, reconstruction was a priority. Some colonial era buildings survived and others were replaced. Some ancient monuments remain, and damaged temples and pagodas have been rebuilt. The skyline is now punctuated by modern multi-story buildings in the international style, but much of modern Hanoi also has a large number of tree-lined boulevards, extensive public parks, and shaded lakes. Open spaces and trees characterize the city. Hanoi's avenues are lined by street cafés, and the pace of life seems slower than that in many large Asian cities. Traffic is relatively light and Hanoi's *cyclos* (pedicabs) are a quieter and more environmentally friendly method of public transportation than the automobiles that gridlock cities such as Bangkok in Thailand. Only three bridges cross the Red River in Hanoi. The oldest, the century-old Long Bien Bridge, now carries only pedestrians and bicycles.

The city is a river port served by small seagoing ships and also a land route hub. Highways converge on Hanoi from across the Red River Valley and from central and southern Vietnam, as well as from Laos to the west and China to the north. Hanoi has railroad links with Ho Chi Minh City and Annam, with the port of Haiphong, and with the major cities of neighboring China. The city has two airports, including an international airport that is relatively underused.

Hanoi had a population of 1,450,000 within the city limits at the 1999 national census, when 2,610,000 people lived in the metropolitan area. (This figure is from provisional returns of the 1999 census; final figures have not been released by the Vietnamese authorities.) In 2006, unofficial estimates suggest a population of around three million.

THE CITY SIGHTS

The principal focus for visitors to Hanoi is the Ho Chi Minh Mausoleum, where the embalmed body of the founder of Communist Vietnam, Ho Chi Minh (1890–1969), is displayed. The body lies in a large stark concrete structure that is guarded by the military. Nearby, Ho's house and garden are a national monument, with his possessions displayed just as he left them. The neighboring Ho Chi Minh Museum tells the story of Ho's life and his leadership of the Vietnamese independence movement.

Hanoi has many other museums and public buildings, including the National Assembly and government ministries, several universities and institutes of higher education, the Army Museum, and the Revolutionary Museum. The Museum of Ethnology houses a huge collection of costumes and artifacts from Vietnam's different peoples. The Fine Arts Museum displays ancient stone Buddhas, intricate decorative arts, and modern politically motivated paintings.

Some areas of traditional narrow streets remain in the Old Quarter, a market district where sidewalk kiosks sell food, spices, clothing, footwear, jewelry, and decorative arts. Van Mieu (usually called the Temple of Literature) is an eleventh-century complex of traditional Vietnamese buildings around five courtyards. Van Mieu is a college where students have studied Vietnamese literature for nearly one thousand years. The names of all the graduates since the fourteenth century are carved on the backs on stone turtles in one of the courtyards.

C. CARPENTER

The Bao Tang Quan Doi Army Museum on Dien Bien Phu Street houses objects and artifacts from Vietnam's twentieth-century wars against French and American forces.

Haiphong

Haiphong, the third-largest city in Vietnam, is the port for Hanoi, and for the Red River lowlands that form the northern region of the country. The city lies at the northeastern edge of the Red River Delta, 10 miles (16 km) from the open sea at the Gulf of Tonkin.

Haiphong had a population of 550,000 within the city limits at the 1999 national census, when 1,700,000 people lived in the metropolitan area. The Vietnamese authorities have not fully released population figures from the 1999 census, and these figures are provisional returns.

A MAJOR PORT

In the first century CE, the Vietnamese rebelled against Chinese rule. Tradition says that the Trung Sisters led the revolt and that one sister, Le Chan, founded the port of Haiphong. A port has existed on the site for centuries, but the city did not develop until the second half of the nineteenth century, after the region came under French colonial rule. The French authorities expanded the port in 1874 and developed its facilities to serve not only the northern region of Vietnam (Tonkin) but also adjoining regions of southwestern China, with which it was connected by railroad.

Haiphong became the main naval base for the French in Indochina (modern Cambodia, Laos, and Vietnam), and the city grew as a commercial hub and military center. The French developed industries in the port, including shipbuilding, construction materials, textiles, clothing, glass, porcelain, and food processing. The colonial authorities widened and deepened the narrow access to the port, which prospered as Hanoi developed as one the principal cities of French Indochina.

During World War II (1939–1945), the region was overrun by Japanese forces, and when the French attempted to reestablish control of the area in 1945 and 1946, Vietnamese Communists had already declared an independent republic centered in Hanoi. Haiphong port was shelled by French forces in 1946 when they unsuccessfully attempted to retake Hanoi. During the war between the French and the Vietnamese Communists, Haiphong's harbor silted.

After 1954, Haiphong was the principal port of North Vietnam, a Communist state that had close trading relations with China and the Soviet Union, which funded the reconstruction of the port. The port was modernized, shipyards were rebuilt, and canning plants, machine-tool factories, and chemical-fertilizer plants were constructed. However, war damaged the port again. Through the 1960s and 1970s, the North Vietnamese attempted to undermine pro-Western South Vietnam. The United States became involved in the war in South Vietnam, initially as military advisers and eventually with a large army. During the war, U.S. forces heavily bombed Haiphong harbor, destroying the shipyards and many industrial facilities and cutting the railroad link with Hanoi. However, the North Vietnamese managed to relocate factories and plants to other cities before the city's industries were completely devastated. In 1972, the port was closed to shipping by U.S. mines. When a cease-fire was signed in 1973, the reconstruction of Haiphong slowly began again.

MODERN HAIPHONG

Since 1973, Haiphong has rebuilt its port and its industries. The industries that had sought refuge from bombing returned to the port, initially being rehoused in ruined facilities. In the 1980s, aid from the Soviet Union and China allowed new industries to grow. New developments included an iron and steel industry, and the city now has a modern trade exhibition center. Despite repeated war damage in the twentieth century, Haiphong retains a few ancient monuments, including ornate pagodas and temples, such as the reconstructed Du Hang and Dong Thien pagodas and the Phu Xa temple. The metropolitan area includes the beach resort of Do Son.

C. CARPENTER

Haiphong is the largest port in northern Vietnam. Throughout its history the port has been repeatedly developed and destroyed.

Ho Chi Minh City

Ho Chi Minh City, until 1976 known as Saigon, is the largest city in Vietnam. It had a population of 3,320,000 within the city limits at the 1999 national census, when 4,630,000 people lived in the metropolitan area. Data from the 1999 Vietnamese census has not been fully published; the data is taken from provisional returns.

From 1954 through 1975, South Vietnam, whose capital was Saigon, was invaded by Communists from North Vietnam and local Communist sympathizers (the Viet Cong). U.S. forces aided the South Vietnamese in the 1960s and 1970s until a cease-fire agreement in 1973. During this period, Saigon was a major U.S. military base and a commercial and industrial center. Large numbers of people flocked into the city from the countryside, driven out by Viet Cong insurgents and attracted to the city by economic opportunities. Saigon had previously also attracted business people from Hanoi, who had fled from the Communist republic in North Vietnam in 1954. Saigon was a city of enterprise and energy, although war damage was a constant hazard. A Communist offensive in 1968 caused much damage to the city's infrastructure.

On April 30, 1975, North Vietnamese forces entered Saigon, and South Vietnam fell. The governing classes and the wealthy had already fled abroad, and the transformation of the city began. Saigon

International-style buildings rise up above downtown Ho Chi Minh City.

lost its name, its identity, and its status as a national capital. Much of the city's commerce was dismantled, and the bars, restaurants, and places of entertainment that had characterized Saigon during the Vietnam War were closed. The city's foreign trade links were severed, businesses were nationalized, and the authorities attempted to reduce the size and influence of the city through a forced reduction of its population. Despite these punitive measures, Ho Chi Minh City remains Vietnam's largest urban area and its principal commercial and industrial center.

SAIGON

The site of Saigon was on a low terrace along the Saigon River, a waterway that reaches the sea independently a short distance north of the Mekong Delta. The Mekong Delta was a swampland

that was mainly inhabited by fishers. The region was part of the Khmer Empire (ruled from Angkor) until Saigon came under Vietnamese control in the seventeenth century. Saigon was little more than a small fishing port until 1698, when it became a local center of Vietnamese administration. French interest in the Mekong Delta region, formerly known as Cochinchina, began in the eighteenth century when merchants and missionaries arrived from France. In 1862, the French proclaimed a colony in Cochinchina with Saigon as its capital. However, the French established the administrative, commercial, and military headquarters of their Indochinese empire in Hanoi in northern Vietnam.

Saigon prospered under French rule. The city became a major port, exporting the produce of southern Vietnam and the French possessions of Cambodia and Laos. Saigon became a route hub, focusing highway, railroad, and waterway traffic from the entire French-ruled Mekong Basin and beyond. Food processing, textiles, and other industries grew, and the city gained many public buildings, wide tree-lined boulevards, and elegant colonial villas in the French style. Poor rural people settled in large new urban districts that soon surrounded the city.

During World War II (1939–1945), Japanese troops invaded Saigon, but the French colonial administration was allowed to continue until the closing months of the war. Saigon saw almost no fighting during World War II, but nearly three decades followed during which the city was attacked, threatened, and eventually overrun.

A NEW IDENTITY

Although the victorious North Vietnamese renamed Saigon Ho Chi Minh City, the new name is largely confined to official use. The overwhelming majority of the city's residents still refer to their city as Saigon, and the name officially persists as that of the downtown area, which is also known as District One. The city comprises 22 districts, most of which are numbered rather than named. Cholon district (District Five) has a large ethnic Chinese population.

Ho Chi Minh City attracts foreign visitors once more. Sidewalk cafés, street markets, and kiosks bustle, and the city is busy with traffic. Industries have revived. However, much of the city appears rundown and the former public buildings have lost their function. South Vietnam's former legislative building is a theater, while the grandiose 1960s former government building stands empty except for displays depicting the capture of Saigon by the North Vietnamese. Now called the Reunification Palace, the huge complex is a reminder of the city's former capital status. The War Remnants Museum houses photographs, military equipment, and vehicles, and other displays that tell Communist Vietnam's version of events from the first uprising against French rule through the fall of Saigon in 1975.

The city has relatively few ancient monuments. One of the few surviving buildings from Saigon's early history is the Giac Lac pagoda, which dates from the 1740s. The pagoda, which is still a functioning monastery, was largely untouched by war and retains its original appearance and decoration. It houses ornate tombs and a large statue of the goddess of mercy.

Notre Dame Square still maintains the appearance of a French colonial plaza. The Roman Catholic cathedral on the square resembles a late nineteenth-century European church. Ho Chi Minh Square is dominated by a vast statue of Ho Chi Minh. The nearby City Hall, which is the headquarters of the city's Communist Party rather than being the seat of the city's administration, combines arches, towers, and balconies in an ornate style of decoration that echoes large French city halls. Saigon was once known as the "Paris of Asia," and Ho Chi Minh City still has many French-style eating places and food markets.

The city hall (the People's Palace) in Ho Chi Minh City was built by the French to resemble the city hall of Paris, France. In modern times, a statue of Ho Chi Minh stands in the grounds.

C. CARPENTER

Hué

Hué is a relatively small city: provisional returns from the 1999 census record that the metropolitan area was home to 265,000 people, while 210,000 residents lived within the city limits. Despite its compact size, Hué is one of the most historic cities in Vietnam; it was the Vietnamese royal capital until 1945.

From the middle of the sixteenth century through the end of World War II (1939–1945), Vietnamese emperors ruled central and southern Vietnam (the empire of Annam) from Hué. After 1883, the monarchs were subject to French colonial rule.

A STRATEGIC SITE

Hué is in central Vietnam, strategically placed between the fertile Red River Valley in the north and the Mekong Delta in the south, although the Mekong Delta region did not become Vietnamese until the seventeenth century, when the power of the Khmer Empire to the west waned. The city lies on a plain that is constricted between the foothills of the Annamese Cordillera to the west and the South China Sea to the east. Routes from north to south funnel through the city, which is a crossing point of the Huong (or Perfume) River, about 5 miles (8 km) from the coast. At this strategic location, the Annamese rulers built a great defensive citadel on the left bank of the Huong River.

The mausoleum of Emperor Khai Dinh was built between 1920 and 1931. French influences can be seen in both the design of the complex and the materials used.

AN IMPERIAL CAPITAL

A 7-mile (11 km) wall surrounds the citadel. The walls are up to 69 feet (21 m) thick and pierced by ten land gates and two water gates. The complex owes its design to three cultures: the imperial city is a Chinese idea, the buildings within its walls are Vietnamese, but the defensive nature of the citadel owes something to the French military engineer Sébastien Vauban (1633–1707). A second set of walls delineates the imperial enclosure (Da Noi) within the outer fortifications. Da Noi is entered by four gates, one of which—Ngo Non (the Moon Gate)—could be used only by the monarch. A third walled enclosure within Da Noi protects the Forbidden Purple City, the private domain of the imperial family. Within the forbidden city, the Thai Hoa Palace (the Palace of Supreme Peace), the imperial audience chamber, is approached across the Golden Water Bridge. Six miles (10 km) outside Hué is the mausoleum of Emperor Khai Dinh (reigned 1916–1925). The buildings combine elements of Western and Eastern architecture and design.

A MODERN CITY

A commercial quarter to serve the court and its employees rose immediately east of the fort. The French built a colonial city across the Huong River, facing the fort. From 1802, emperors of the Nguyen dynasty embellished the fort, embarking on the greatest period of building in the Forbidden City. The Japanese invaded Vietnam in 1940 and occupied Hué until 1945. The last Annamese emperor Bao Dai (1913–1997) reigned in Hué as a figurehead under the French, and the city ceased to be a capital in 1949 when Saigon became capital of what later became South Vietnam.

Few cities in Vietnam suffered more damage than Hué during the Vietnam War in the 1960s and 1970s. In 1968, in the so-called Tet Offensive, Communist forces severely damaged many of the historic buildings within Da Noi. Many buildings were later repaired or rebuilt, and in 1993 the citadel was proclaimed a UNESCO World Heritage site. Hué attracts tourists and is a commercial and educational center, with a university. Its industries include decorative arts and food processing.

C. CARPENTER

ECONOMY

With a population officially estimated at more than 82 million people in 2004, Vietnam is a densely populated nation with a developing economy. Since the 1980s, Vietnam has taken steps to liberalize its economy with some degree of success.

Vietnam has one of the highest economic growth rates of Asia's emerging economies. This rate of growth is not likely to diminish, and Vietnam gained membership of the World Trade Organization (WTO) in 2005.

The economic modernization of Vietnam followed a troubled period of its history that included occupation by Japanese forces during World War II (1939–1945), a war of independence against a colonial power (France) that ended in 1954, partition into the warring states of North and South Vietnam, and the Vietnam War, in which United States forces fought alongside Southern Vietnamese troops against the North Vietnamese and local Communist insurgents until 1975. Decades of war did much to damage Vietnam's infrastructure and delay development. In 1976, Vietnam reunited, but the economic integration of the two different economies created many problems.

A decade (1976–1986) of economic stagnation because of conservative Communist rule followed reunification. In 1986, under more liberal political leaders, Vietnam opted for economic modernization with the introduction of an economic policy platform termed Doi Moi, or "reconstruction." Doi Moi policies encouraged decentralization of economic management, orientation to free monetary markets, internationalization of external economic relations, and a reliance on the private sector for growth, along with many other minor adjustments within the framework of Communist ideology.

Vietnam's political and economic development strategy is underpinned by the philosophical ideals of socialism: the government proclaims that all the peoples of Vietnam should benefit from policies aimed at reducing poverty and ensuring social justice while achieving growth. This overarching goal informs the policies and recommendations found in the Comprehensive Poverty Reduction and Growth Strategy (CPRGS) of 2003, which outlines the aims and policy of all government ministries.

ECONOMIC CHALLENGES

Economic reconstruction in Vietnam has been rapid, producing growth rates in GDP (gross domestic product; the total value of all the goods and services produced in a country in a set period of time, usually one year) of around 7.2 percent. However, the benefits are largely restricted to the major centers of Hanoi and Haiphong in the north and Ho Chi Minh City (formerly Saigon) in the south. Spreading the effects of growth across the nation is a major challenge. Poverty remains widespread in rural areas, with 19.5 percent of the total population below the poverty line in 2004. Accession to the WTO, with its demands for structural adjustments of the economy, should bring depth to economic development, with more benefits for the Vietnamese people.

Since the mid-1990s, Vietnam has achieved remarkable success in its transition to a market economy. The reform process begun under the policy of Doi Moi continues relatively unimpeded, further enhancing Vietnam's integration into the world economy. Economic growth in the early years of the twenty-first century has averaged more than 7 percent per year, with GDP totaling over $232.2 billion (2005), adjusted for purchasing power parity (PPP), a formula that allows comparison between living standards in different countries. Nevertheless, Vietnam remains a less developed country, and a number of serious challenges to its economic progress lie ahead.

The government's yearly economic growth rate target is 8.5 percent, but this is not easily reached owing to both internal and external factors. Sharp increases in world crude oil prices hit the economy, which relies upon imported oil. Increased oil prices put pressure on the high inflation rate. The consumer price index (CPI) rose 9.5 percent in 2004, a significant rise from 2003 and the highest recorded increase since 1990.

The effects of the avian (bird) flu epidemic also impacted growth as resources were diverted to cope with the problem. Avian flu claimed hundreds of lives since its outbreak in

Standard of Living

Vietnam has a low standard of living compared with its more developed neighbors Thailand and Malaysia, with 19.5 percent of the population living below the official poverty line. However, Vietnam has a higher standard of living than its immediate neighbors Cambodia and Laos. There is growing inequality, with widening differences in the standard of living in the cities and the countryside. The per capita GDP was $2,800 in 2005; this figure is adjusted for purchasing power parity (PPP), a formula that allows comparison between living standards in different countries.

Vietnamese work in the state-owned Hiep Hung shoe factory in Ho Chi Minh City making sports shoes for the Reebok company.

2003 and forced local farmers to kill around 50 million fowl, causing a gross loss of almost $90 million. The epidemic could have serious long-term consequences for both agriculture and tourism.

One of the most encouraging aspects of the economy has been its ability to attract both foreign direct investment and official development assistance (ODA). Vietnam anticipates attracting between $5 billion and $6 billion a year of foreign direct investment capital as a result of legal reforms and incentives implemented to improve the nation's investment climate. Vietnam also hopes to receive close to $11 billion in ODA during the period 2005 through 2010 in order to reach the targeted economic growth rates. While it is estimated that Vietnam needs around $1.8 billion of ODA capital per year to maintain a sustainable annual economic growth rate of around 7 percent, remittances (money sent home) from Vietnamese living abroad remain the major source of foreign exchange.

The government continues to play a major role in the economy despite a change in ownership of nearly 2,300 state-owned enterprises since 1992. The state-owned sector has not been privatized but is subject to a process known as equitization, under which ownership is diversified but the state retains a share in the enterprise. In theory, enterprises were to become public-private partnerships, but an increasing number are privately owned and run. Reform of state-owned enterprises (SOEs) has been slower than planned, and the state remains involved in finance, telecommunications, energy, and manufacturing. Vietnamese industry faces many problems, including outdated technology, nontransparent information, ineffective supervision, complicated conflict resolution, and a lack of provisions to protect Vietnamese investors and minority shareholders. The current state policy has not created a competitive environment for enterprises in all economic sectors. The business environment still lacks proper structure in terms of the legal framework and institutions, market structure, and competing capacity. Increasing the effectiveness and competitiveness of SOEs is a necessary condition if Vietnam hopes to fully benefit from membership in the WTO.

Vietnam has continued to improve the quality of life of its citizens. Literacy rates are over 90 percent, and life expectancy is nearly 74 years for women and 68 years for men. While the number of people living in poverty declined substantially toward the end of the twentieth century, many social challenges remain. The disparity of living standards between regions and social groups is rising, and one-third of children under age five are underweight. Economic growth has also come at the expense of deteriorating air and water quality, threatening health and economic sustainability.

Sustainable economic development in Vietnam will also require improving the quality of the labor force. There is a serious shortage of skilled workers in many fields, and it will be necessary for Vietnam to obtain assistance in education and training from other counties. The Vietnamese educational system is inferior in training and in vocational and management skills, and the economy will need greater numbers of highly skilled new entrants to the labor market in the coming years.

RESOURCES

Vietnam is rich in natural resources. Most of the nation's mineral deposits are located in the north, where there are estimated coal reserves of approximately 20 billion tons (18.1 billion metric tons). Other mineral resources currently mined include deposits of phosphates, manganese, bauxite, chromate, and other metal ores. Sustainable exploitation of these resources is a key policy in the development strategies of the Vietnamese government. Offshore oil and gas deposits are sufficient to meet domestic needs of crude oil and provide a modest export income; however, imports of refined oil are still required. Revenue from exploiting large submarine oil reserves in the region of the disputed Spratly Islands in the South China Sea would be a valuable addition to Vietnam's income if production could be assured.

Rich red alluvial soil in the Mekong Delta in the south and the Red River Delta in the north makes a strong agricultural base possible. Forests are modest in Vietnam, covering under 30 percent of land area (the result of long-term deforestation and defoliation), and unlike the rich timber resources of some Southeast Asian nations, Vietnam's forests have not contributed significantly to the development of the nation. However, forestry is becoming important, and there is an increasing demand for timber products from Vietnam.

Traditional resource development and resource protection are in conflict in Vietnam because of the immediate desire for rapid growth. The authorities wish to develop the Vietnamese economy quickly while ensuring the protection of the environment and a comprehensive reduction in poverty. These aims are not always complementary.

EMPLOYMENT IN VIETNAM

Sector	Percentage of labor force
Agriculture	57
Industry	37
Services	6

Source: Government of Vietnam, 2005

There has been steady growth in the service sector since 2000, and some sources suggest that up to 25 percent of the labor force is now employed in the sector. In 2005, government figures showed that 6 percent of the labor force was unemployed. This figure is widely considered to be an underestimate, with the real total much higher.

Large container ships import and export goods to and from Vietnam via Ho Chi Minh City's docks along the Mekong River.

Vietnam has other important resources. The natural beauty of the landscape of Vietnam pays dividends with an expanding tourism industry. Tourists aid local and national economic development by spending money while enjoying the landscape and culture of Vietnam. In addition, the people of Vietnam are a major resource as they work industriously to advance both the nation's economic development and their personal fortunes in all sectors of the economy.

AGRICULTURE

Development of the agricultural sector is a fundamental part of government economic policy to ensure sustainable growth and reduce poverty. Agriculture contributes just over 20 percent of Vietnam's GDP. Vietnam earned $4 billion from the export of agricultural products in 2004, and the government expects to increase agricultural exports by $500 million. Agricultural holdings occupy approximately 26 percent of the land, and over 40 percent of the arable land is irrigated. Farming conditions vary widely from tropical in the south to monsoon conditions in the northern regions, with hot rainy summer seasons and dry winter periods. Approximately 57 percent of the labor force is engaged in farming and about 38 percent of Vietnam's poor are engaged in agricultural activity.

The main agricultural products are rice, coffee, tea, corn, potatoes, rubber, soybeans, bananas, sugar, poultry, and hogs. Rice is the major agricultural export, and Vietnam has moved from being a rice importer to a rice exporter. Vietnam is currently the second-largest exporter of Robusta coffee, one of the most commercially important types of coffee. Robusta coffee accounts for around 40 percent of world production and is more resistant to disease than Arabica coffee, the most widely grown type of coffee. Further expansion in coffee growing is encouraged.

Raising livestock is important, but poultry raising has been hit by the avian influenza epidemic. The epidemic hindered poultry farming for both domestic consumption and export. Vietnam placed an internal ban on duck and goose farming in an attempt to stem the disease, and there was a mass cull of poultry.

Seafood is emerging as a profitable industry. A major development in shrimp farming has brought employment to many poor people, and an estimated 2 million people are now involved in Vietnam's shrimp industry, many of them farmers who live on the margins of poverty. Shrimp exports rank among Vietnam's top five foreign exchange earners.

INDUSTRY

While Vietnam remains a predominantly agrarian economy, the industrial sector has played a more important role over time and is the backbone of efforts to advance the nation's welfare. Industry and construction make up more than 40 percent of the country's GDP, and the value of industrial production has risen by over 12 percent on an annual basis since the mid-1990s. Nevertheless, the government's goal of becoming an industrial economy by the year 2020 is not likely to be met due to inadequacies in the infrastructure and a shortage of trained skilled labor.

The major industrial products are food processing, garments, shoes, light machinery, mining, cement, chemical fertilizer, and oil and gas. Industrial production has grown annually and industrial products account for almost three-quarters of Vietnam's total exports by value. Industry is concentrated in the three main metropolitan areas: Ho Chi Minh City (formerly Saigon), Hanoi, and Haiphong.

Industrial production by the nonstate enterprise sector has recorded significantly higher growth rates than state sector enterprises. Corporations in which foreign organizations have invested achieved the highest growth rates. The Law on Enterprise implemented in 2000 had a significant positive impact on the number of private enterprises, and a revision of the law implemented in 2005 is expected to further remove obstacles for foreign businesses.

SERVICES

The services sector in Vietnam remains largely underdeveloped but is expanding rapidly, with annual growth rates of around 7.7 percent. The government of Vietnam views the services sector as an engine for growth and poverty reduction and plans to increase the contribution of the services sector to the GDP to 45 percent by 2010. The attention paid to the services sector is spurred by the nation's need to liberalize services in order to meet the WTO accession requirements. Opening up the services sector is a challenge because of the low competitiveness of the domestic service providers and the

Rice farmers in the north of Vietnam rely on rainfall to irrigate their small terraced plots of land.

**VIETNAM
Industry and Resources**

— Principal oil pipelines
— Principal gas pipelines
⬭ Principal oil fields
⬭ Principal gas fields
🏍 Agricultural industry
☾ Building materials/Cement
⬚ Chemicals
⬚ Consumer goods
♛ Decorative arts
✿ Engineering
🐟 Fishing
🮠 Food processing
🍾 Glassware
⚒ Metalworking
$ Services/Commerce
⛴ Shipbuilding
▦ Textiles
🌲 Timber
🧳 Tourism

Mineral deposits

Ⓒ Coal
Ⓕ Iron Ore
Ⓣ Tin
Ⓒ Copper

Transportation

— Major roads
— Major railroads
✈ Major airports
⊗ Major ports

Gulf of Tonkin

Gulf of Thailand

South China Sea

N

0   100   200 miles
0   160   320 km

VIETNAM'S GDP

The Vietnamese gross domestic product (GDP) was $232.2 billion in 2005. The figure is adjusted for purchasing power parity (PPP), an exchange rate at which goods in one country cost the same as goods in another. PPP allows a comparison between the living standards in different nations.

MAIN CONTRIBUTORS TO VIETNAM'S GDP

Agriculture	20.9 percent
Industry	41.0 percent
Services	38.1 percent

Source: CIA, 2005

sector itself. Consequently, increased competition by foreign services providers will place local providers, especially those with no comparative advantage or those who are highly protected, under pressure. The adjustments in this area are underway; 70 percent of new foreign direct investment in Vietnam is in the services sector.

Diversification of services is important. Current key services areas include banking and finance, tourism, telecommunications, education, health care, and public services. Tourism, in particular, contributes to the rapid expansion of the services sector, with an increase of 8.5 percent in 2004 (despite the downturn in visitor numbers following the outbreak of avian flu). The tourist sector predicts an overall growth rate of 7.7 percent from 2006 through 2015. The Vietnamese government has actively supported tourism, with attempts to improve and increase the tourist infrastructure by a direct investment of $35 million in 2005, following an investment of $32 million in 2004. While the major cities and the former imperial city of Hué, a UNESCO World Heritage site since 1993, receive the greatest number of foreign visitors, government investment in the rural forest and mountain regions is also significant. The authorities believe that increased tourism in rural areas is important for their development.

The services sector provides about a half million new jobs each year. Consequently, government policies target the sector in the development plans for 2006 through 2010. The program envisions intense investment in tourism, aviation insurance, construction, and other services that are considered to have great potential for the development of Vietnam. Many service jobs are currently in the retail and small enterprise sector, but Vietnam is viewed increasingly as the next international center for the development of computer software. Vietnam has a youthful labor force that is increasingly aware of information technology; the authorities estimate that the Vietnamese will be able to produce computer software around 90 percent more cheaply than the United States and between 33 percent and 70 percent more cheaply than India, thus giving it a very competitive edge to exploit the market.

TRADE

Vietnamese exports have been steadily rising but, at the same time, the rapid economic growth has fueled a rising demand for imported consumer goods. While trade surpluses are maintained with the United States and European countries, trade deficits with Asian neighbors have been the norm. In 2005, Vietnam's total trade deficit reached $4.7 billion: exports stood at an estimated $32.2 billion and imports at $36.9 billion. The trade gap is expected to widen as Vietnam further integrates into the world's economy. Trade commitments negotiated as part of the ASEAN Free Trade Area (AFTA, the Southeast Asia economic trading organization) will require a reduction in tariffs on a number of commodities and is expected to negatively affect Vietnamese exports in those industries.

In 2004, Vietnam's exports grew by almost 30 percent. The largest component of export revenues is crude oil. Other major exports are textiles, garments and footwear, seafood, timber products, rice, coffee, cashew nuts, pepper and coal. The largest markets for Vietnamese goods are the United States (which took 21 percent of Vietnam's exports in 2005), Japan (13 percent), Australia (8 percent), China including Hong Kong (8 percent), Singapore (5 percent), and Germany.

Exports of textiles and garments began to falter in the face of tough competition from China as a result of the end of the WTO quota system. In addition, the high cost of imported materials for the textile industry, as well as shortages in skilled labor, impacted the profitability of Vietnam's textile and clothing industry.

Imports into Vietnam grew by over 25 percent in 2004 and are expected to grow owing to consumer demand and an expanding private sector. Vietnam's major imports are refined petroleum products, fertilizer, steel ingots, pharmaceuticals, machinery and spare parts, textile and garment materials, plastics, and chemicals. Imports into Vietnam are mainly from China including Hong Kong (providing 16 percent

Employees work at a Pepsi Cola bottling plant in Ho Chi Minh City. Multinational companies are investing in Vietnam.

of imports in 2005), Singapore (12 percent), Taiwan (11 percent), South Korea (11 percent), Japan (10 percent), and Thailand. Trade with neighboring Cambodia and Laos is not significant.

The Bilateral Trade Agreement signed with the United States in November 2001 significantly increased Vietnamese exports to that country, and Vietnam has become an important market for American civil aircraft. Trade tensions between the two countries, however, were heightened due to duties imposed by the United States on Vietnamese catfish and shrimp producers as a result of dumping allegations filed by U.S. fishers.

TRANSPORTATION AND COMMUNICATION

The Vietnamese government has targeted the development of transportation, especially roads, as a national priority. Road transportation dominates in the movement of peoples and goods in both urban and rural areas. Vietnam has 5138.085 miles (222,179 km) of roads, and there was a rapid development of the highway network in the two decades after 1986. However, less than one-half of roads, are paved. Ho Chi Minh Highway is a major symbol of the physical and economic reunification of North and South Vietnam. The highway, which is over 1,367 miles (2,200 km) long, runs from the Chinese border in the north to the far south of the nation. Vietnam's road system is under increasing stress in urban areas as modernization and rising domestic incomes have encouraged private ownership of motorcycles and cars. However, road planning is difficult as the government has no accurate count of the number of vehicles on the road. Automobile ownership is an outward sign of growing urban wealth, and the rapid increase in motorized transportation has become an urban planning issue and an environmental concern. Road usage in rural areas is less critical, but programs to upgrade and pave roads in the countryside to encourage rural economic development are dependent on contributions and labor from local communities.

The railroad system remains an entirely state-owned enterprise and links the county's major cities with 1,616 miles (2,600 km) of track. The rail system undergoes constant renovation, and while the rail authorities can use their limited income from freight and passengers to purchase modern rolling stock and manage operations, the rail infrastructure remains dependent on government subsidies. Marine transportation plies the eastern coastline and relies on six key ports with a 194-ship national commercial fleet. Air transportation in Vietnam is steadily gaining in importance, but the industry remains largely underdeveloped in comparison to other regional competitors. Vietnam Airlines, the national carrier, is a state-owned company.

While the government is investing in the modernization of Vietnam's telephone system, telecommunications in Vietnam lag behind the systems in many neighboring countries. In 2004, there were more than 10 million telephone lines, and nearly 5 million people had a mobile cellular phone. In 2005, approximately 6 million Vietnamese had Internet access.

A. CULLEN

Further Research

WORLD GEOGRAPHY

Brown, James H., and Mark V. Lomolino. *Biogeography.* Sunderland, MA: Sinauer Associates Publishers, 1998.

Butzer, Karl W. *Geomorphology from the Earth.* Reading, MA: Addison-Wesley Educational Publishers, 1976.

Clark, Audrey N. *Longman Dictionary of Geography: Human and Physical.* New York: Longman, 1985.

Lydolph, Paul E. *Weather and Climate.* Lanham, MD: Rowman and Littlefield, 1985.

National Geographic Family Reference Atlas. Washington, DC: National Geographic Society, 2004.

Oliver, John E., and Rhodes W. Fairbridge, eds. *The Encyclopedia of Climatology.* Van Nostrand Reinhold, New York: 1987.

The Statesman's Yearbook 2004: The Politics, Cultures, and Economies of the World. New York: St. Martin's Press, 2004

Strahler, Arthur N., and Alan H. Strahler. *Modern Physical Geography.* 3rd ed. Hoboken, NJ: John Wiley and Sons, 1987.

Times Atlas of the World: Comprehensive Edition. New York: Crown Publishers, 1999.

Trewartha, Glenn T., and Lyle H. Horn. *An Introduction to Climate.* 5th ed. New York: McGraw-Hill, 1980.

REGIONAL GEOGRAPHY, HISTORY, AND CULTURAL EXPRESSION

Acharya, Amitav. *Constructing a Security Community in Southeast Asia: ASEAN and the Problem of Regional Order.* New York:, Routledge , 2001.

Allen, Douglas, and Ngô Vinh Long, eds. *Coming to Terms: Indochina, the United States, and the War.* Boulder, CO: Westview Press, 1991.

Briggs, Lawrence Palmer. *The Ancient Khmer Empire.* Philadelphia: American Philosophical Society, 1951.

Caldarola, Carlo, ed. *Religions and Societies, Asia and the Middle East.* New York: Mouton, 1982.

Chandler, David P., and David Joel Steinberg, ed. *In Search of Southeast Asia: A Modern History.* Honolulu: University of Hawaii Press, 1987.

Chawla, Sudershan, Melvin Gurtov, and Alain-Gerard Marsot. *Southeast Asia under the New Balance of Power.* New York: Praeger, 1974.

Chomsky, Noam, and Edward S. Herman. *After the Cataclysm, Postwar Indochina and the Reconstruction of Imperial Ideology.* Boston, MA: South End Press, 1979.

Coe, Michael D. *Angkor and the Khmer Civilization.* New York: Thames and Hudson, 2003.

Duiker, William J. *U.S. Containment Policy and the Conflict in Indochina.* Stanford, CA: Stanford University Press, 1994.

Forman, Werner. *Indian Sculpture: Masterpieces of Indian, Khmer and Cham Art.* New York: Hamlyn, 1970.

Haley, P. Edward. *Congress and the Fall of South Vietnam and Cambodia,* Rutherford, NJ: Fairleigh Dickinson University Press, 1982.

Hammer, Ellen J. *The Struggle for Indochina.* Stanford, CA: Stanford University Press, 1954.

Heine-Geldern, Robert. *Conceptions of State and Kingship in Southeast Asia.* Ithaca, NY: Southeast Asia Program, Dept. of Far Eastern Studies, Cornell University, 1956.

Hood, Steven J. *Dragons Entangled: Indochina and the China-Vietnam War.* Armonk, NY: M. E. Sharpe, 1992.

Keyes, Charles F. *The Golden Peninsula: Culture and Adaptation in Mainland Southeast Asia.* Honolulu: University of Hawaii Press, 1995.

Livo, Norma J., and Dia Cha, eds. *Folk Stories of the Hmong: Peoples of Laos, Thailand, and Vietnam.* Englewood, CO: Libraries Unlimited, 1991.

Lomperis, Timothy J. *From People's War to People's Rule: Insurgency, Intervention, and the Lessons of Vietnam.* Chapel Hill: University of North Carolina Press, 1996.

McMahon, Robert J. *The Limits of Empire: The United States and Southeast Asia since World War II.* New York: Columbia University Press, 1999.

Neher, Clark D., and Ross Marlay. *Democracy and Development in Southeast Asia: The Winds of Change.* Boulder, CO: Westview Press, 1995.

Norman, Owen G., ed. *The Emergence of Modern Southeast Asia.* Honolulu: University of Hawaii Press, 2005.

Osborne, Milton E. *The French Presence in Cochinchina and Cambodia: Rule and Response (1859–1905).* Ithaca, NY: Cornell University Press, 1969.

Osborne, Milton E. *The Mekong: Turbulent Past, Uncertain Future.* New York: Atlantic Monthly Press, 2000.

Rawson, Philip S. *The Art of Southeast Asia: Cambodia, Vietnam, Thailand, Laos, Burma, Java, Bali.* New York: Thames and Hudson, 1990.

Scalapino, Robert A., ed. *The Communist Revolution in Asia: Tactics, Goals, and Achievements.* Englewood Cliffs, NJ: Prentice-Hall, 1969.

Stuart-Fox, Martin. *A Short History of China and Southeast Asia: Tribute, Trade, and Influence.* Crows Nest, Australia: Allen and Unwin, 2003.

Swearer, Donald. *The Buddhist World of Southeast Asia.* Albany: State University of New York Press, 2005.

TRAVEL LITERATURE

Colet, John, and Joshua Eliot. *Vietnam Handbook*. Lincolnwood, IL: Passport Books, 1997.

Colet, John, Joshua Eliot, and Jane Bickersteth. *Cambodia Handbook*. Lincolnwood, IL: Passport Books, 1997.

Eliot, Joshua, and Jane Bickersteth. *Laos Handbook*. Lincolnwood, IL: Passport Books, 1997.

Let's Go Southeast Asia. New York: St. Martin's Press, 2004.

Lewis, Norman. *A Dragon Apparent: Travels in Cambodia, Laos, and Vietnam*. London: Eland, 2003.

Rooney, Dawn. *Angkor Observed*. Bangkok, Thailand: Orchid Press, 2003.

CAMBODIA

Bhandari, C. M. *Saving Angkor*. Bangkok, Thailand: Orchid Press, 2002.

Chandler, David P. *A History of Cambodia*. Boulder, CO: Westview Press, 2000.

Chandler, David P. *The Land and People of Cambodia*. 1st ed. Philadelphia: Lippincott, 1972.

Chandler, David P. *The Tragedy of Cambodian History: Politics, War, and Revolution since 1945*. New Haven, CT: Yale University Press, 1991.

Coates, Karen J. *Cambodia Now: Life in the Wake of War*. Jefferson, NC: McFarland, 2005.

Coe, Michael D. *Angkor and the Khmer Civilization*. New York: Thames and Hudson, 2003.

Cook, Susan E., ed. *Genocide in Cambodia and Rwanda: New Perspectives*. New Brunswick, NJ: Transaction Publishers, 2005.

Curtis, Grant. *Cambodia Reborn?: The Transition to Democracy and Development*. Washington, DC: Brookings Institution, 1998.

Edmonds, I. G. *The Khmers of Cambodia: The Story of a Mysterious People*. 1st ed. Indianapolis, IN: Bobbs-Merrill, 1970.

Finot, Louis. *Ruins of Angkor, Cambodia, in 1909*. Bangkok, Thailand: River Books, 2001.

Gilboa, Amit. *Off the Rails in Phnom Penh*. Bangkok, Thailand: Asia Books, 1998.

Green, Robert. *Cambodia*. San Diego, CA: Lucent Books, 2003.

Haas, Michael. *Cambodia, Pol Pot, and the United States: The Faustian Pact*. New York: Praeger, 1991.

Jackson, Karl D., ed. *Cambodia, 1975–1978: Rendezvous with Death*. Princeton, NJ: Princeton University Press, 1989.

Jacques, Claude. *Ancient Angkor*. Bangkok, Thailand: River Books, 2006.

Jacques, Claude, and Michael Freeman. *Angkor: Cities and Temples*. Bangkok, Thailand: River Books, 1999.

Jeldres, Julio, and Somkid Chaijitvanij. *The Royal Palace of Phnom Penh and Cambodian Royal Life*. Bangkok, Thailand: Bangkok Post, 1999.

Jessup, Helen Ibbitson. *Art and Architecture of Cambodia*. New York: Thames and Hudson, 2004.

Kiernan, Ben, and Chanthou Boua, eds. *Peasants and Politics in Kampuchea, 1942–1981*. Armonk, NY: M. E. Sharpe, 1982.

Marston, John, and Elizabeth Guthrie. *History, Buddhism, and New Religious Movements in Cambodia*. Honolulu: University of Hawaii Press, 2004.

Poncar, Jaro. *Angkor Revisited*. Bangkok, Thailand: River Books, 2000.

Riddle, Tom. *Cambodian Interlude: Inside the 1993 United Nations' Election*. Bangkok, Thailand: Orchid Press, 1997.

Roveda, Vittorio. *Khmer Mythology: Secrets of Angkor Wat*. Trumbull, CT: Weatherhill, 1997.

Shawcross, William. *Sideshow: Kissinger, Nixon, and the Destruction of Cambodia*. New York: Simon and Schuster, 1987.

Snellgrove, David. *Khmer Civilization and Angkor*. Bangkok, Thailand: Orchid Press, 2001.

Steinberg, David J., and Chester A. Bain, et al. *Cambodia: Its People, Its Society, Its Culture*. New Haven, CT: HRAF Press, 1957.

Stuart-Fox, Martin. *The Murderous Revolution*. Bangkok, Thailand: Orchid Press, 1998.

Vickery, Michael. *Cambodia, 1975–1982*. Boston: South End Press, 1984.

Vickery, Michael. *Kampuchea: Politics, Economics, and Society*. Boulder, CO: L. Rienner Publishers, 1986.

Yagama Reddy, Y. *Cambodia: Its People and Economy*. Tirupati, India: Centre for Studies on Indochina, Sri Venkateswara University, 1995.

LAOS

Asmusson, Fleur Brofos. *Lao Roots*. Bangkok, Thailand: Orchid Press, 1997.

Asselin, Pierre. *A Bitter Peace: Washington, Hanoi, and the Making of the Paris Agreement*. Chapel Hill: University of North Carolina Press, 2002.

Bountavy Sisouphanthong, and Christian Taillard. *Atlas of Laos: The Spatial Structures of Economic and Social Development of the Lao People's Democratic Republic*. Copenhagen, Denmark: NIAS, 2000.

Bouphanouvong, Nakhonkham. *Sixteen Years in the Land of Death*. Bangkok, Thailand: White Lotus, 2003.

Brown, MacAlister, and Joseph J. Zasloff. *Apprentice Revolutionaries: The Communist Movement in Laos, 1930–1985*. Stanford, CA: Hoover Institution Press, 1986.

Dommen, Arthur J. *Laos: Keystone of Indochina*. Boulder, CO: Westview Press, 1985.

Evans, Grant. *Lao Peasants under Socialism*. New Haven, CT: Yale University Press, 1990.

Evans, Grant. *A Short History of Laos: The Land in Between*. Crows Nest, Australia: Allen and Unwin, 2002.

Gunn, Geoffrey C. *Rebellion in Laos: Peasant and Politics in a Colonial Backwater*. Bangkok, Thailand: White Lotus Press, 2003.

Hamilton-Merritt, Jane. *Tragic Mountains: The Hmong, the Americans, and the Secret Wars for Laos, 1942–1992.* Bloomington: Indiana University Press, 1993.

Kremmer, Christopher. *Bamboo Palace.* Chiang Mai, Thailand: Silkworm Books, 2003.

Kremmer, Christopher. *Stalking the Elephant Kings: In Search of Laos.* Chiang Mai, Thailand: Silkworm Books, 1997.

Mansfield, Stephen. *Lao Hill Tribes: Traditions and Patterns of Existence.* New York: Oxford University Press, 2000.

Marini, Gio Filippo de, Walter E. J. Tips, and Claudio Bertuccio. *A New and Interesting Description of the Lao Kingdom (1642–1648).* Bangkok, Thailand: White Lotus Press, 1998.

Ngaosrivathana, Mayoury and Kennon Breazeale, eds. *Breaking New Ground in Lao History: Essays on the Seventh to Twentieth Centuries.* Chiang Mai, Thailand: Silkworm Books, 2002.

Rigg, Jonathan. *Living with Transition in Laos: Living with Change in Southeast Asia.* New York: Routledge Curzon, 2005.

Savada, Andrea Matles, ed. *Laos: A Country Study.* Washington, DC: Federal Research Division, Library of Congress, 1995.

Simms, Peter, and Sanda Simms. *The Kingdoms of Laos: Six Hundred Years of History.* Richmond, Surrey, UK: Curzon, 2001.

Stuart-Fox, Martin. *The Lao Kingdom of Lan Xang: Rise and Decline.* Bangkok, Thailand: White Lotus Press, 1998.

Stuart-Fox, Martin, ed. *Contemporary Laos: Studies in the Politics and Society of the Lao People's Democratic Republic.* New York: St. Martin's Press, 1982.

Weldon, Charles. *Tragedy in Paradise.* Bangkok, Thailand: Asia Books, 1999.

Zasloff, Joseph J., and Leonard Unger, eds. *Laos: Beyond the Revolution.* New York: St. Martin's Press, 1991.

VIETNAM

Beresford, Melanie. *Vietnam: Politics, Economics, and Society,* New York: Pinter, 1988.

Brazier, Chris. *Vietnam: The Price of Peace.* Oxford, UK: Oxfam, 1992.

Brittan, Dolly. *The People of Vietnam.* 1st ed. New York: PowerKids Press, 1997.

Brown, T. Louise. *War and Aftermath in Vietnam,* New York: Routledge, 1991.

Burchett, Wilfred. *Vietnam: The Inside Story of the Guerrilla War.* New York: International, 1965.

Buttinger, Joseph. *The Smaller Dragon: A Political History of Vietnam.* New York: Praeger, 1958.

Campagna, Anthony S. *The Economic Consequences of the Vietnam War.* New York: Praeger, 1991.

Chandler, Robert W. *War of Ideas: The U.S. Propaganda Campaign in Vietnam.* Boulder, CO: Westview Press, 1981.

Chapuis, Oscar. *The Last Emperors of Vietnam: From Tu Duc to Bao Dai.* Westport, CT: Greenwood Press, 2000.

Chesneaux, Jean. *The Vietnamese Nation: Contribution to a History.* Sydney, Australia: Current Book, 1966.

Chomsky, Noam. *American Power and the New Mandarins.* New York: New Press, 2002.

Chomsky, Noam. *At War with Asia.* New York: Pantheon, 1970.

DeMatteis, Lou. *Portrait of Vietnam.* New York: Norton, 1996.

Duiker, William J. *The Communist Road to Power in Vietnam.* Boulder, CO: Westview Press, 1996.

Duiker, William J. *Vietnam since the Fall of Saigon.* Athens: Ohio University Press, 1989.

Elliot, David. *The Vietnamese War: Revolution and Social Change in the Mekong Delta.* Armonk, NY: M. E. Sharpe, 2002.

Elliott, W. P., et al. *Vietnam: Essays on History, Culture, and Society.* New York: Asia Society, 1985.

Errington, Elizabeth Jane, and B. J. C. McKercher, eds. *The Vietnam War as History.* New York: Praeger, 1990.

Fall, Bernard B. *The Two Viet-Nams: A Political and Military Analysis.* New York: Praeger, 1967.

Fall, Bernard, ed. *Ho Chi Minh on Revolution: Selected Writings, 1920–1966.* New York: Praeger, 1967.

Forde, Adam, and Stefan de Vylder. *From Plan to Market: The Economic Transition in Vietnam.* Boulder, CO: Westview Press, 1996.

Frost, Helen. *A Look at Vietnam.* Mankato, MN: Pebble Books, 2003.

Gurtov, Melvin. *The First Vietnam Crisis: Chinese Communist Strategy and United States Involvement, 1953–1954.* Westport, CT: Greenwood Press, 1985.

Halberstam, David. *Ho.* New York: Random House, 1971.

Herr, Michael. *Dispatches.* New York: Vintage, 1991.

Hickey, Gerald Cannon. *Village in Vietnam.* New Haven, CT: Yale University Press, 1964.

Kim Khánh Huynh, *Vietnamese Communism, 1925–1945.* Ithaca, NY: Published under the auspices of the Institute of Southeast Asian Studies, Singapore, by Cornell University Press, 1982.

Jamieson, Neil L. *Understanding Vietnam.* Berkeley: University of California Press, 1993.

Kalman, Bobbie. *Vietnam: The Land.* New York: Crabtree Publishers, 2002.

Karnow, Stanley, *Vietnam: A History.* New York: Viking, 1991.

Kolko, Gabriel. *Anatomy of a War: Vietnam, the United States, and the Modern Historical Experience.* New York: Pantheon, 1985.

Langer, Paul Fritz, and Joseph J. Zasloff. *North Vietnam and the Pathet Lao; Partners in the Struggle for Laos.* Cambridge, MA: Harvard University Press, 1970.

Lomperis, Timothy. *From People's War to People's Rule: Insurgency, Intervention, and the Lessons of Vietnam.* Chapel Hill: University of North Carolina, 1996.

Marr, David G. *Vietnamese Anticolonialism, 1885–1925.* Berkeley: University of California Press, 1971.

Neu, Charles E. *America's Lost War: Vietnam, 1945–1975.* Wheeling, IL: Harlan Davidson, 2005.

Nhu Tang, Truong. *A Vietcong Memoir.* New York: Vintage Books, 1986.

Pelley, Patricia M. *Postcolonial Vietnam: New Histories of the National Past.* Durham, NC: Duke University, 2002.

Post, Ken. *Revolution, Socialism, and Nationalism in Viet Nam.* Brookfield, VT: Dartmouth, 1994.

Prados, John. *The Blood Road: The Ho Chi Minh Trail and the Vietnam War.* New York: Wiley, 1999.

SarDesai, D. R. *Vietnam: The Struggle for National Identity.* Boulder, CO: Westview Press, 1992.

Schulzinger, Robert D. *A Time for War: The United States and Vietnam. 1941–1975,* New York: Oxford University Press, 1997.

Shipway, Martin. *The Road to War: France and Vietnam, 1944–1947.* Providence, RI: Berghahn Books, 1996.

Summers, Harry G., Jr. *On Strategy: A Critical Analysis of the Vietnam War.* Novato, CA: Presidio Press, 1982.

Taylor, Keith Weller. *The Birth of Vietnam.* Berkeley: University of California Press, 1983.

Terzani, Tiziano. *Saigon 1975, Three Days and Three Months.* Bangkok, Thailand: White Lotus, 1997.

Thrift, Nigel, and Dean Forbes. *The Price of War: Urbanization in Vietnam, 1954–1985.* Boston: Allen & Unwin, 1986.

Tucker, Spencer C., ed. *Encyclopedia of the Vietnam War: A Political, Social, and Military History.* New York: Oxford University Press, 2000.

Werner, Jayne, and David Hunt, eds. *The American War in Vietnam.* Ithaca, NY: Cornell University Press, 1993.

A Winding River: The Journey of Contemporary Art in Vietnam. Washington, DC: Meridian International Center, 1997.

Windrow, Martin. *The Last Valley: Dien Bien Phu and the French Defeat in Vietnam.* Cambridge, MA: Da Capo Press, 2005.

Woodside, Alexander. *Community and Revolution in Modern Vietnam.* Boston: Houghton Mifflin, 1976.

PERIODICALS AND OTHER MEDIA

Allen, Douglas. "Antiwar Asian Scholars and the Vietnam/Indochina War." *Bulletin of Concerned Asian Scholars* 21 (1989): 112–134.

Anderson, David. "Eisenhower, Dienbienphu, and the Origins of U.S. Military Intervention in the Vietnam." *Mid-America* 71 (1989).

Chandler, David. "Cambodia after the Khmer Rouge: Inside the Politics of Nation Building." *Pacific Affairs.* 77 (2004): 270-271.

Chomsky, Noam. "Intervention in Vietnam and Central America: Parallels and differences." *Monthly Review* 37 (1982): 1–29.

Fall, Bernard. "Local Administration under the Viet Minh." *Pacific Affairs* 27 (1954): 50–57.

Fall, Bernard. "The Political-Religious Sects of Vietnam." *Pacific Affairs* 28 (1955): 235–253.

Finkelstein, David M. "Vietnam: A Revolution in Crisis." *Indochina Issues* 78 (1988): 973-990.

Galambos, Louis. "Paying Up: The Price of the Vietnam War." *Journal of Policy History* 8 (1996).

Ganesan, N. "ASEAN's Relations with Major External Powers." *Contemporary Southeast Asia* 22 (2000): 258–278.

Gordon, Alec. "The Role of Class Struggle in North Vietnam." *Monthly Review* 29 (1978).

Hickey, Gerald Cannon. "The Vietnamese Village through Time and War." *Vietnam Forum* 10 (1987).

Hunt, David. "Village Culture and the Vietnamese Revolution." *Past & Present* 94 (1982): 131–157.

Ireson, W. Randall, and Carol J. Ireson. "Laos: Marxism in a Subsistence Rural Economy." *Bulletin of Concerned Asian Scholars* 21 (1989): 59–75.

Jackson, Larry R. "The Vietnamese Revolution and the Montagnards." *Asian Survey* 9 (1969): 313–330.

McLeod, Mark W. "Indigenous Peoples and the Vietnamese Revolution, 1930–1975." *Journal of World History* 10 (1999): 353–389.

Pluvier, Jan. "The Vietnam War of Independence (1945–54) and Historical Objectivity." *Journal of Contemporary Asia* 3, no. 3 (1973).

Vlastos, Stephen. "Losing the Vietnam War." *Radical History* 55 (1993).

Wiesner, Louis A. "Vietnamese Exodus from the North and Movement to the North, 1954–55." *Vietnam Forum* 11 (1988): 214–243.

ELECTRONIC RESOURCES

Country Studies, Cambodia, Federal Research Division, Library of Congress.
http://countrystudies.us/cambodia

Country Studies, Laos, Federal Research Division, Library of Congress.
http://countrystudies.us/laos

Country Studies, Vietnam, Federal Research Division, Library of Congress.
http://countrystudies.us/vietnam

Critical Asian Studies.
www.bcasnet.org

Southeast Asia News.
www.southeastasianews.net

The World Factbook. CIA.
www.odci.gov/cia/publications/factbook/index.html
(for facts about Cambodia, Laos, and Vietnam).

Index

WORLD AND ITS PEOPLES

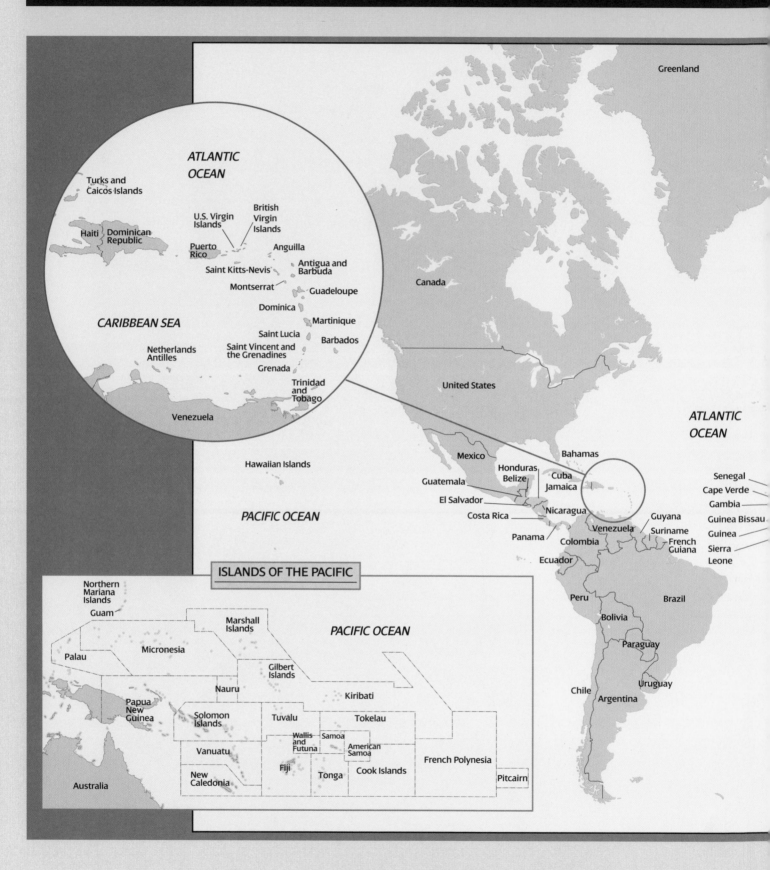

ATLANTIC OCEAN

Turks and Caicos Islands

Haiti
Dominican Republic

U.S. Virgin Islands
British Virgin Islands

Puerto Rico
Anguilla

Saint Kitts-Nevis
Antigua and Barbuda

Montserrat
Guadeloupe

Dominica
Martinique

CARIBBEAN SEA

Saint Lucia
Barbados

Netherlands Antilles
Saint Vincent and the Grenadines

Grenada

Trinidad and Tobago

Venezuela

Greenland

Canada

United States

ATLANTIC OCEAN

Hawaiian Islands

Mexico
Bahamas

Honduras
Belize
Cuba
Jamaica
Senegal
Cape Verde

Guatemala
Gambia

El Salvador
Nicaragua
Guinea Bissau

PACIFIC OCEAN

Costa Rica
Guyana
Guinea

Panama
Suriname
French Guiana
Sierra Leone

Colombia

Venezuela

Ecuador

Peru
Brazil

Bolivia

Paraguay

Chile
Uruguay

Argentina

ISLANDS OF THE PACIFIC

Northern Mariana Islands

Guam

Marshall Islands

PACIFIC OCEAN

Micronesia

Palau

Gilbert Islands

Nauru

Kiribati

Papua New Guinea

Solomon Islands
Tuvalu
Tokelau

Wallis and Futuna
Samoa

Vanuatu
American Samoa

Fiji
French Polynesia

Tonga
Cook Islands

New Caledonia

Pitcairn

Australia